The
Rushdie
File

Contemporary Issues in the Middle East

The Rushdie File ∽

**Edited by Lisa Appignanesi
and Sara Maitland**

Syracuse University Press

FIRST NORTH AMERICAN EDITION 1990
99   98   97   96   95   94   93   92   91   90   6   5   4   3   2   1

In association with the Institute of Contemporary Arts, London. The ICA is an educational charity which encourages experimentation and innovation in all art forms and provides a proving ground for new work and ideas.

Permission to quote from materials listed below is gratefully acknowledged:

"Rushdie's Book Is an Insult," by Jimmy Carter, March 5, 1989; "Words for Salman Rushdie," March 12, 1989 (Book Review); and "Rushdie's Publisher Assails Censorship by Terrorism," by Edwin McDowell, February 19, 1989. Copyright © 1989 by The New York Times Company. Reprinted by permission.

"Lessons of the Rushdie Affair," by William Pfaff. 1989, Los Angeles Times. Reprinted with permission.

"The Rushdie Riddle," by Letty Cottin Pogrebin. © 1989 by Letty Cottin Pogrebin. Reprinted from *Ms.* magazine by permission of the author.

LIBRARY OF CONGRESS CATALOGING-IN-PUBLICATION DATA
The Rushdie file / edited by Lisa Appignanesi and Sara Maitland. —
    1st ed.
        p. cm.
    "All the material in this book has been previously printed or spoken"—Acknowledgments.
    ISBN 0-8156-2494-8 (alk. paper). — ISBN 0-8156-0248-0 (pbk. : alk. paper)
    1. Rushdie, Salman. Satanic verses. 2. Rushdie, Salman—Censorship. 3. Freedom of the press—History—20th century—Sources. 4. Censorship—History—20th century—Sources. 5. Islam and literature. I. Appignanesi, Lisa. II. Maitland, Sara, 1950–   .
PR9499.3.R8S2837   1990
823—dc20   89-48413
                CIP

Printed in the United States of America

Contents

The Editors

Lisa Appignanesi is Deputy Director of the Institute of Contemporary Arts in London and editor of the ICA Documents Series. Her latest book is a biographical portrait of Simone de Beauvoir.

Sara Maitland is a writer and theologian, whose most recent fiction, *A Book of Spells,* is now available in paperback from Methuen.

Preface to the
North American Edition

On 26 September 1988, *The Satanic Verses* by Salman Rushdie was published in the United Kingdom by Viking Penguin. The book was eagerly awaited. Ever since he had won the most prestigious of literary awards in Britain, the Booker Prize, for his novel *Midnight's Children* (1981), Rushdie—a British resident born in India to a Muslim family—had been regarded as an important and challenging contemporary novelist. More than that, his fictions stirred controversy. *Midnight's Children* had angered the Gandhi family and provoked a debate on censorship in India, and his next novel, *Shame* (1983), had been promptly banned in Pakistan.

In a 1984 essay, "Outside the Whale," published in the magazine *Granta*, Rushdie had argued that writers today could not live inside the whale, insulated from history and politics. "The modern world," Rushdie wrote, "lacks not only hiding places, but certainties." He continued: "If writers leave the business of making pictures of the world to politicians, it will be one of history's great and most abject abdications."

Rushdie's words now seem to bear an ominous quality. *The Satanic Verses* has placed him definitively outside the whale in "the unceasing story, the quarrel, the dialectic of history." Early critical acclaim for the novel was soon met by readings of a radically different kind from various Muslim communities around the world. These readings saw the book as a deliberate and aggressive blasphemy against Islam. By the fifth of October, the new book was banned in India; and there, as in the rest of the world, protests against it escalated with remarkable rapidity.

In February 1989, the month the book was officially published in the United States, it was publicly burned in Britain. Demonstrations against it in India and Pakistan developed into riots. Early in that month, five people were killed in Pakistan, and another lost his life in Kashmir. Then, on 14 February, Iran's Ayatollah Khomeini issued a legal ruling (*fatwa*) that imposed a death sentence against the author and his publishers throughout the world. Subsequently, a reward amounting to a million and a half dollars was offered to Rushdie's "executioner." These developments resulted in a storm of international protest.

Rushdie was forced into hiding and given police protection. Some bookstores took *The Satanic Verses* off their shelves in the face of threatened and actual bombings; some publishers who had signed deals for foreign language editions withdrew. For many in the West, this cycle of intimidation raised crucial questions about freedom of expression, censorship, and international law.

For the Islamic world and some other observers, the issues were more about cultural identity and religious integrity. These actions and reactions seemed to emphasize fundamentally conflicting freedoms and basic differences in values between the Islamic and Western traditions.

We believe these perceived differences need to be better understood. They have a resonance beyond the Rushdie affair itself, beyond a single book and its individual author. The need for deeper comprehension and open debate on these issues is the major impetus for *The Rushdie File*. The book, with its diverse collection of views and opinions, is designed to promote understanding and further reflection.

The Rushdie File began with a conference held at the Institute of Contemporary Arts in London on 19 March 1989. There was a strong feeling among the participants that more discussion of the issues raised by the publication of *The Satanic Verses* was crucial and that an easily accessible document, chronicling events from the start of the affair, was necessary. This book responds to both those needs.

The Rushdie File is organized into five sections. The first, called "The Author and the Book," is composed mainly of a sampling of initial reviews, interviews, and stories about the author that appeared in the West at the time of *The Satanic Verses*'s publication. Part II, "The Mounting Protest," documents the growing outrage that the book's publication provoked in Muslim communities, first in India, then in the United Kingdom and elsewhere. Next, "The Khomeini Fatwa" provides the essential statements on Rushdie and his novel that emanated from Iran in mid-February 1989. "The International Response" collects the diverse comments, news stories, editorials, and resolutions offered in reaction to the *fatwa* in countries around the world. The last section, "Reflections," presents fuller essays and statements that take a broader view on the issues raised by this affair. A chronology of important events precedes the collected text.

Millions of words have been written and spoken about *The Satanic Verses* and the events sparked by it around the world. From those voluminous sources, we have tried to select the best and most representative materials that fairly and fully reflect all points of view. In this edition, additional selections from the American and Canadian media have been included.

Throughout the period we worked on *The Rushdie File*, we were continually haunted by the tragic aspects of the affair—the perceived threats and insults to communities; the actual threats to lives; the lives actually lost. We hope that this book will help everyone to think through the vexed issues raised by the affair and that somehow we will all learn to acknowledge and respect our differences in a spirit of mutual toleration.

London   Lisa Appignanesi
September 1989   Sara Maitland

Acknowledgments

All the material in this book has been previously printed or spoken. We gratefully acknowledge the permission to reprint granted to us by individual writers and journalists, as well as by the BBC and the *BBC Survey of World Broadcasts, The Baltimore Sun, The Bradford Telegraph & Argus, The Casper Star-Tribune, The Christian Science Monitor, The Chronicle of Higher Education, The Daily Telegraph, The Detroit News, Die Zeit, The Economist, Economic and Political Weekly, Evening Standard, The Financial Times, The Guardian, Impact International, The Independent, India Today, The Indian Post*, Islamic Society of North America, *Jewish Chronicle, Los Angeles Times, Ms. Magazine, Le Monde, New Statesman and Society, New York Review of Books, The New York Times, The Observer*, Pen International, *Publishers Weekly, Sunday, The Sunday Times (London), Der Spiegel, The Tablet, The Telegraph, 30 Days, The Times* (London), *The Times of India, The Toronto Globe & Mail*, and *U.S. News & World Report*.

In preparing this edition, we have had invaluable help from many people and many institutions. We wish to extend our thanks to the organization Article 19, which acts as a headquarters for the International Salman Rushdie Committee, to Arnold Wesker, John Forrester, Malise Ruthven, Matthew Hoffman, Alan Yentob, Dona Soto-Morettini, Ursula Owen, Hilary Rubinstein, Victoria Barnsley, and Jane Charteris. For assistance in expanding and editing the material from the United States and Canada, we are grateful to Ronald Chrisman, Charles Backus, Roger Allen, John Esposito, Yvonne Haddad, Tareq Ismael, Kenneth Stein, and John Voll.

Chronology

26 September 1988	*The Satanic Verses*, by Salman Rushdie, published in UK by Viking Penguin
5 October 1988	Book banned in India
8 November 1988	Book wins the Whitbread "best novel" award in England
24 November 1988	Book banned in South Africa
14 January 1989	Book burned in Bradford, England
27 January 1989	Demonstrations in Hyde Park and petition to Penguin to cease publication
1 February 1989	Home Secretary Douglas Hurd announces that the British government has no plans to change blasphemy laws in response to Muslim demands
12 February 1989	Five killed in rioting in Islamabad, Pakistan
13 February 1989	One killed and over one hundred injured in riot in Kashmir, India
14 February 1989	Ayatollah Khomeini of Iran issues *fatwa* against Rushdie and his publishers
15 February 1989	National day of mourning in Iran Demonstration outside the British Embassy in Tehran All Viking Penguin books banned from Iran Million-and-a-half-dollar price placed on Rushdie's life Harold Pinter leads writers' delegation in support of Rushdie to 10 Downing Street
16 February 1989	Rushdie and wife, Marianne Wiggins, go into hiding
17 February 1989	Iranian president suggests that Rushdie apologize Canada bans import of the book Several US bookstore chains pull the book from their shelves
18 February 1989	Rushdie expresses regret
19 February 1989	Rushdie's apology is rejected and the death sentence is reconfirmed

20 February 1989 — Britain gets strong support from foreign ministers of the European Community
All EC countries withdraw their ambassadors from Iran

22 February 1989 — Book officially published in USA
The organization US PEN calls writers' meeting in New York

24 February 1989 — Rioting in Bombay

26 February 1989 — Thousands of Muslims demonstrate against Rushdie in New York City

28 February 1989 — Two bookstores in Berkeley, California, firebombed

2 March 1989 — World Writers' Statement issued in defence of Rushdie and free speech

7 March 1989 — Iran breaks off diplomatic relations with Britain

15 March 1989 — Nobel Prize committee split over including the book in its considerations

16 March 1989 — Islamic Conference Organization, while critical of the book, refuses to support Iran over death threat

29 March 1989 — Two moderate Muslim religious leaders, after expressing opposition to censorship, are killed in Brussels

27 May 1989 — 50,000 Muslims demonstrate against the book in central London

4 June 1989 — Khomeini dies, but *fatwa* against Rushdie remains unchanged

3 August 1989 — Bomb blast in London which kills terrorist is said to be part of "a bold operation" against Rushdie

17 August 1989 — Western newspapers report that Rushdie remains in hiding and frequently on the move to avoid death threat
To date, more than 1.1 million hardcover copies of the book have been sold

Notes on the Text

Throughout this book, transitional passages by the editors are printed in italics. Specific source citations usually appear at the end of each document. The name of the source on its own indicates that the full text of an article has been quoted; the word *from* designates an extract. Occasionally, substantial chunks of text within an article have been omitted, to avoid repetition, as indicated by ellipses. In this North American edition, no attempt has been made to standardize spelling, punctuation, or style, all of which have been left as they appeared in the original sources.

The
Rushdie
File

I

The Author and
the Book ⌒

The marked man: a writer driven by life to dissent

'Saleem Sinai was born at midnight, the midnight of India's independence, and found himself mysteriously "handcuffed to history" by the coincidence.'

So began the dustjacket blurb on *Midnight's Children*, the novel which brought world fame to Salman Rushdie, who now finds himself wretchedly handcuffed to history with a price on his head.

It is a strange turnabout that he is the centre of universal sympathy and goodwill. 'Poor Salman,' as he now is, was only a short time ago the focus of quite different feelings in the literary world. His offence then was to have abandoned both his publisher (Liz Calder, who expected to launch her imprint, Bloomsbury, with her star author) and his agent (Deborah Rogers), and signed on with Viking for the sum of $850,000. Envy being what it is, the amount did not altogether endear him to fellow scribes.

Defections are nothing new in the book world, but this was unusually acrimonious. Feelings were wounded, the breach remained unhealed and Rushdie seemed to feel there was a vendetta against him. But whatever the feelings of others, one thing was plain: his overriding ambition on behalf of his own work. His next book, he knew, would be *the* book, though he could not have foreseen in what manner *The Satanic Verses* would etch his name on history.

Rushdie was born in Bombay in June 1947, two months before the hero of *Midnight's Children*, to a Muslim family who spoke both English and Urdu at home, and who later moved to Karachi. It was not a particularly literary background; his chief literary influence in childhood, he says, was *The Arabian Nights*.

He went to an English mission school and in 1961 was sent to

Rugby, where he first encountered the 'wog-baiting' of English public schoolboys. He has ever since been an angry scourge of British racialism, which he believes is endemic, though he will acknowledge that he has been shielded from its uglier manifestations by being so pale-skinned and so well-educated, with his impeccable English voice, more Rugby than Raj.

His relationship with his father, a wealthy businessman who died in 1987, was often stormy. But the family accepted Rushdie's loss of his faith (which left him with 'a God-shaped hole inside'), and his marriages, first to an Englishwoman, Clarissa, mother of his son, and latterly to Marianne Wiggins, the American author, who is more than a match for his writing talent.

After Rugby he followed his father to King's College, Cambridge, where he read history. It was, he believes, his good fortune not to read English literature; it meant he could select books at random, so he read *Tristram Shandy* 'with a sense of discovery, as if it had been written yesterday'. He did not write for the undergraduate organs, *Varsity* and *Granta*, nor did he speak in union debates; instead he was involved in theatre, in the era of Clive James, Germaine Greer and David Hare, and after coming down worked for a time in fringe theatre at the Oval House, Kennington, in the musical *Viet Rock*.

But he was already determined to succeed as a writer. He worked as an advertising copywriter on slogans for Aero and the Milk Marketing Board, who later adopted the 'Naughty but Nice' tag for cream cakes, which it first rejected. (It was never Rushdie's claim to have actually coined the phrase; he is not *that* arrogant.)

While away from the drawing-board he was beavering away at a novel which he shelved. His first published work, *Grimus*, was written expressly for Gollancz's Science Fiction prize, which it did not win. But his belief in his great destiny was unshaken and he gave up his advertising job to write full-time well before the success of *Midnight's Children* was assured by its winning the Booker Prize.

At once his fame and importance outweighed the attention given to most young novelists. He excited the wrath of the Gandhi family, to whom he had to apologise. His appearance took on a glowering, saturnine quality as his beard grew, his hair receded and his eyes glared under hooded lids. In interviews and profiles he emerged as someone who was driven, obsessive.

It would be unthinkable for Rushdie to point out how ludicrously out of proportion the *Satanic Verses* situation has become. It is not in his nature to say 'Oh come on, it's just a book.' He would perhaps have liked its literary importance to be its claim to attention; but significance of some sort it must have. He does not respond with grace even to the mildest criticism; his temper is apt to flare, his opinions are entrenched and passionate.

To sum up the intransigence Rushdie faces, consider the open letter to him from Syed Shahabuddin, the MP who first raised the whole affair and published in *The Times of India*: 'You are aggrieved that some of us have condemned you without a hearing, and asked for a ban without reading your book. I have not read it, nor do I intend to. I do not have to wade through a filthy drain to know what filth is.'

Even before the Ayatollah's promise of martyrdom for an assassin, when the book was merely being burned in Bradford (which in retrospect looks a relatively harmless gesture, however deplorable) Rushdie took the Islamic threats seriously. He was struck by the extent and efficiency of their organisation, and taken aback by the hatred and loathing in their vilification. In print he was accused of being a deracinated Indian who denied his own background, of being published by a Jew and of wishing to be known by an English name to his English friends: a complete myth.

He knew his book would be regarded as blasphemy. But, as he has explained, he worked from primary sources; he long ago made a study of Muhammad (he wrote a paper on Muhammad, Islam and the Rise of the Caliph for Part II of his history tripos) and the books he read are banned in the fundamentalist Islamic world. 'But a writer must suppress the knowledge of what effect his words will have, in order to do the writing. If I thought this whirlwind was going to be unleashed, I could not have written.'

'This is the saddest irony of all,' he wrote. 'That after working for five years to give voice and fictional flesh to the immigrant culture of which I am myself a member, I should see my book burned, largely unread, by the people it's about. The zealot protests serve to confirm, in the Western mind, all the worst stereotypes of the Muslim world.'

Until his house was boarded up and put under police guard, Rushdie lived in no great style in a Victorian terrace in Islington. He was one of the original invitees to the 20th June Group of anti-Thatcher writers who meet at Antonia Fraser and Harold Pinter's house in Campden Hill Square, and is a Charter 88 signatory.

He was looking forward to the now-cancelled trip to America to publicise the book, which no whistle-stop tour or talk-show appearances could ever more fully publicise, thanks to the mullahs. It had been said that he might go and live in America; but he said (just three weeks ago) that it was much more likely he would go back to India to live. 'As one reaches middle age one needs to cement the connection. It's a country I still feel very close to.'

That, of course, can no longer be the case. He was grateful to Britain: 'If I were in Pakistan now I'd be dead.' But what kind of existence, in hiding from the fanatics, he can look forward to now (even after yesterday's apology) is almost impossible to contemplate.

(*Sunday Times*, London, 19 Feb. 1989)

Salman Rushdie: hiding from himself

JOHN GRAY

Somewhere in Britain, Salman Rushdie is hiding from pursuers, hiding from people for whom his death would be a divine mission and a bonus of two or three million dollars.

The experience is not entirely new. For most of his 41 years, some might say, Mr. Rushdie has been in hiding—hiding from himself and pursuing himself at the same time.

As the author himself would put it, he is and he is not.

Seldom has a book inspired such a drumroll of protest as has been inspired by Mr. Rushdie's still largely unknown novel *The Satanic Verses*.

On the streets of Britain, Pakistan and India, thousands protest and a half-dozen die. The book is banned in Islamic countries. It is deemed blasphemous, an egregious insult to Allah and Mohammed and all of Islam.

The spiritual leader of Iran, Ayatollah Ruhollah Khomaini, whose influence extends throughout the Islamic world, sentences Mr. Rushdie to death. Another cleric puts a price on the head of "this mercenary of colonialism."

Perhaps only the soaring imagination of Salman Rushdie himself could conceive of events on such a scale.

He was born in India at the cusp of the British empire. Seven weeks later the colony that was the jewel in the crown of empire had become two independent nations, embroiled in a terrible internecine war.

Mr. Rushdie's parents were Moslems, originally from Kashmir, but they were prospering in Bombay so they decided to stay in India rather than move to the Moslem state of Pakistan.

When he was 13, following the custom of wealthy upper-middle-class Indians, his parents sent him to school in Britain. He would have an education and he would be a gentleman.

In *The Satanic Verses* there is a scene in which one of the principal characters, as a young Indian at an English school, spends 90 minutes trying to sort his way through the bones of a kipper at breakfast. Nobody helps him. The incident is autobiographical. Mr. Rushdie has not eaten a kipper since.

Years later he would look back on his school days as the time he discovered that, despite his efforts, he would never be a part of these people with whom he had gone to live. And it was not just that he was an Indian in a white country.

"I think the central mistake was not being foreign, but being bad at games, which are the heart of the public school ethic. I would have been accepted by my peers, been captain of the eleven and grown up a kind of ultra-rightist Indian businessman."

In time he would also discover that he was no longer entirely of the subcontinent from which he had come.

By the time he finished his years at Rugby, his parents had moved to Pakistan. He went to see them, just in time for the 1965 Indo-Pakistan war.

"I didn't particularly feel India was my enemy, because we'd only very recently come to Pakistan. And yet if somebody's dropping bombs on you, there is really only one reaction that you can have toward them, which is not friendly.

"So I was very deranged by it, and in the end my parents more or less forcibly threw me on a plane to England, where I was about to start university."

It was at Cambridge that he started down one of the paths that led to *The Satanic Verses*. He was studying history and he read deeply about Islam.

After Cambridge, he returned to Karachi, where he ran headlong into militant Islam. He was involved in a television production of a play that mentioned pork. Even though the reference was derogatory, the play was censored.

After another incident of censorship, he moved back to England to join the growing community of Asians that now numbers nearly two million, that is Asian but not Asian, English but not English.

The Moslem community especially has clung to its faith as a bulwark against the surrounding society. The children speak with English accents and listen to rock, but the cultural imperatives of Islam endure.

As a first-generation immigrant, Mr. Rushdie is at the core of that conflict: "I know how you can be here, and, in a way, still there." When he returns for a visit to India or Pakistan, he dreams in Urdu.

Indeed, he has written that *The Satanic Verses* is "an attempt to write about migration, its stresses and transformations, from the point of view of migrants from the Indian subcontinent."

Although he has recently found the tensions of the immigrant community working against him and his novel, there is also a dynamic of growth. Countries like Canada have been built on the creative tensions of immigration; in countries like Britain, Mr. Rushdie's is a new and sometimes unwelcome thesis.

In addition to the wrenching of the soul, he writes, "the migrant is not simply transformed by his act; he also transforms the new world. Migrants may well become mutants, but it is out of such hybridization that newness can emerge."

(*Globe & Mail*, Toronto, 18 Feb. 1989)

SEAN FRENCH
Talks to Salman Rushdie

I once heard you suggest that novels should be given tariffs like dives. Is this a high tariff novel?

Like the Olympics? I like the idea of the level of difficulty. I've always thought the glorious failure preferable to the quiet success. And this new novel is about as risky as I could get.

In what way?

The Satanic Verses is very big. There are certain kinds of architecture that are dispensed with. *Midnight's Children* had history as a scaffolding on which to hang the book; this one doesn't. And since it's so much about transformation I wanted to write it in such a way that the book itself was metamorphosing all the time. Obviously the danger is that the book falls apart.

The two main characters represent an opposition between good and evil. How did this come about?

I had thought that the devil-angel relationship would be straightforward. What I found was that my view of them changed radically. And it was when I came to see how the emotional lives of these two characters connected that I began to know how to write the book. But it took ages.

You've described their fall into England from a plane as a 'drastic act of immigration.' Is this *A Passage to India* in reverse? A Passage to England?

It wasn't conscious. It's more to do with autobiography. (Not that Chamcha is me.) I wanted to write about a thing I find difficult to admit even to myself, which is the fact that I left home. And my relationship with India, although it remains quite close, is with a country I know I'm not going to live in. I wanted to write about someone who does, maybe provisionally, find his way back.

It's also a fable about Islam. How do the two themes fit together?

The real answer is almost non-verbal. It has to do with having a kind of shape in your mind. One of the themes has to do with religious faith, from the point of view of someone who would no longer describe himself as religious. I don't believe that angels appear and talk to people. On the other hand, revelation seems to me to be genuine.

One of the things I also wanted to do was to write about imported cultures. The history of the London we live in is a composite history of all the peoples who are nowhere: Islamic history, Polish history, Caribbean history.

Isn't there a risk that your readers won't know about Islam?

Well, of course, many of the book's readers *will* know about Islam—they may not be white. To my mind, that varied reading of my books has been true of everything I've written. To simplify: in England people read *Midnight's Children* as a fantasy, in India people read it as a history book. But if you know nothing of Islam the novel still ought to work at the level of pure story. It's about the beginning of a religion the question of temptation, of compromise.

In the book London is an imaginary city as well as Jahilia.

I suppose I was writing about a sense of the city as an artificial, invented space which is constantly metamorphosing. It doesn't have roots, it has foundations. There are things that seem not to belong together, except that it is part of the metropolitan experience that such things do not belong together and do live side by side—that you can live upstairs from Khomeini. What I've tried to do is to set alongside each other in odd, sometimes raw juxtapositions all sorts of different bodies of experience to show what frictions and sparks they make.

Why do the characters change so much?

That really is at the heart of the novel. Do we change our natures or do we in some essential way remain the same under all the pressures, whether we actually grow horns or not? I'm not sure myself. I feel different things on different days—that's one of the problems of having a multiple nature. But certainly the sense of a homogeneous, self-contained character is something I can't accept any more. The way I look at a person now is composed of all sorts of irreconcilable elements, and I'm getting more and more interested in writing about them.

So it's not now possible to write in a traditional way?

Well it's not possible for me. Because I have undergone very radical alterations. I'm not who I was supposed to be. If you look at where I was born and the family in which I grew up and the kind of life that normally happens to people who grow up in such worlds, I stepped out of that world, rather like Gibreel. I have had the sense of having frequently to reconstruct my life. So that thing about shifting yourself and wondering if there's anything left of the original person or not is something that's very internal to me. It gives me the sense of character as being mutable . . .

(from *Observer*, London, 25 Sept. 1988)

Magnificent puzzle
NISHA PURI
Review

The Satanic Verses is a magnificent puzzle. Like the proverbial hall of mirrors, reflection after glittering reflection creates an effect of dazzling bedevilment. As we surge forward on an irresistible tide of delighted bafflement, one thing is certain—Rushdie has written the giant novel of his maturity. This is not only his most ambitious fictional endeavour, it is also a work of truly daring creativity which recognises few frontiers beyond which the imagination must not float. It would hardly be rash to insist that *Midnight's Children* merely foretold the gusting, profound inventiveness of *The Satanic Verses*. The blood-beat of Rushdie's inimitable linguistic adventures has never been more thrilling nor, strangely, more deliberately reserved.

The Satanic Verses is not an easy read in most of its densely written parts. But then, neither is James Joyce's *Ulysses*. Yet, there is little of the Irish master's grave withdrawal. Much more than Joyce, Rushdie remains buoyantly accessible to anyone who responds to all that is good and living in the supreme fictions offered by literary genius. After 547 pages, all manner of things become clear as order is brought into the chaos with a sharp, clean tying up of sundry strands. The promised revelation bursts forth at exactly the right moment in time and space. . . .

Like an outsize Brazilian butterfly, *The Satanic Verses* soars through its many worlds on wings of pure fire as panoramic vistas stretch before and behind us linked by a series of epiphanies. There is a sideways brush with the Word in the Desert or the coming of Islam in the fabled city of Jahilia where the writers and whores are summarily executed by the proselytising Messenger Mahound. Poets, Rushdie tells us, must exist in peripheral fright both in Plato's Republic and amidst the holy terror unleashed by the prophet. Apart from this, there is the miracle that fails as the butterfly-consuming seeress, Ayesha, leads an Indian village into the Arabian Sea without once looking back at land—drowning with a blissful smoothness in a mirage of absolute belief. In the end, it is the disbeliever, the landlord of ancient lineage, Mirza Saeed Akhtar, who realises the dream in the implacable moment before dying. 'His body split apart from his Adam's apple to his groin, so that she could reach deep within him, and now she was open, they all were, and at the moment of their opening the waters parted and they walked to Mecca across the bed of the Arabian Sea.'

The Satanic Verses, quite simply, sweeps everything before it in an imaginative avalanche which is both wondrous and uplifting.

Rushdie's new novel is a perfectly self-conscious work of art caught
in a moment of vision. It possesses the consuming beauty which in
life as in art speaks of imperishable truths.

(from *Indian Post*, Bombay, 2 Oct. 1988)

So, and not so

D. J. ENRIGHT
Review

Let us begin (although Salman Rushdie doesn't) with the affair
of the Satanic Verses, revealed in the second part of his new novel,
The Satanic Verses. This second part is entitled 'Mahound,' a dis-
respectful name for Mohammad, found for example in Spenser to
signify a heathen idol by whom wicked characters swear, and likewise, though perhaps also as a metrically convenient alternative to
'Makomete,' in Chaucer. *The Satanic Verses* has been banned in
India on the grounds that it is offensive to Muslims, but in fact
nobody in it is treated with very much respect; gods, angels, demons,
prophets, they are all of them all too human, and most of the time
unable to distinguish between good and evil. If they can't, how can
we ordinary mortals be expected to?

The magical city of Jahilia is composed wholly of sand, together
with its derivatives, glass and silicon, and the great enemy is consequently water. Mahound, 'businessman-turned-prophet,' is engaged in founding one of the world's greatest religions, in the face
of the city's swarming gods, all 360 of them. He and his three followers are clearly troublemakers, if only because they are forever
washing themselves with water. However, the Grandee of Jahilia,
the head of the ruling council, offers Mahound a deal: if Mahound's
Allah will receive a mere three of the local gods into his mono-
pantheon, then the new religion will be recognized and Mahound
given a seat on the council. The gods in question can be given the
rank of archangels, since there are already two of these: Gibreel, the
voice of Allah, and Shaitan, the latter described in the Koran as a
disobedient jinni who refused to bow down before Adam. Or better,
since the gods happen to be goddesses, they can be styled the Daughters of Allah.

Mahound's followers protest that this cannot be, for the essence
of their faith is that there is no god but Allah; but Mahound sees

the arrangements as a useful maneuver, a small concession that will bring in large numbers of converts, and he climbs Cone Mountain to consult the archangel Gibreel, Angel of the Recitation. Seemingly Gibreel speaks, and Mahound returns to Jahilia and announces the verses given to him by the angel: 'Have you thought upon Lat and Uzza, and Manat, the third, the other? They are exalted birds, and their intercession is desired indeed.'

The grandee's name is Abu Simbel. Is he, one wonders, a historical or legendary figure? Or can it be that Rushdie, having invented him, has named him after a village in Egypt that was flooded when the Aswan High Dam was created in the 1960s and its temples removed to higher ground? For we hear that the sea and maritime developments are robbing sand-based Jahilia with its camel-train economy of the city's old ascendancy. Questions of this kind raise their heads everywhere, and if the reader stops to puzzle out the answers he will never finish the book.

In accordance with Islamic tradition, Mahound later returns to Mount Cone and is given to understand the supposedly divine message came from Shaitan, the Devil, posing as Gibreel, whereupon he revokes the 'Satanic' verses and promulgates the true ones, which supplant the earlier set in the Koran. In N. J. Dawood's translation of the Koran we read:

Have you thought on Al-Lat and Al-Uzzah, and thirdly, on Manat? This is indeed an unfair distinction! They are but names which you and your fathers have invented: Allah has vested no authority in them. The unbelievers follow vain conjectures and the whims of their own souls, although the guidance of their Lord has come to them.

The 'unfair distinction' relates to earlier reiterated and indignant denials in connection with Jesus, that Allah has a son: 'When He decrees a thing He need only say: "Be" and it is . . . That they should ascribe a son to the Merciful, when it does not become Him to beget one!' To make out that he has daughters is to add insult to injury.

In the subsequent turmoil Mahound and his followers leave Jahilia for the friendly oasis of Yathrib, thus paralleling the official account of the hegira, Muhammad's flight from Mecca to Medina, which was known at that time as Yathrib. But Gibreel—whom we suspect is no archangel but more like a battered Indian ex-actor whose vocal chords are taken over by an extraneous power—reveals in an intriguing and (you could say) prophetic coda that both messages came out of his mouth: *'it was me both times, baba, me first and second also me* . . . both the statement and the repudiation, verses and converses, universes and reverses, the whole thing, and we all know how my mouth got worked.' Actually we don't all know, but it appears we are to infer that God is Satan, Satan is God. Which adds up to one form of monotheism.

The novel itself begins in modern times and with a fall from the heavens, similar to other such falls, most recently the one with which Stefan Heym began his novel *The Wandering Jew*, but dissimilar in the outcome. A hijacked Air India jet is blown up over the English Channel and, 'without benefit of parachutes or wings,' two passengers tumble unharmed to earth. One is Gibreel Farishta, the other Saladin Chamcha, two real living men, we are told, though their downward progress is termed an 'angelicdevilish fall'.

Gibreel is a famous and flamboyant Bombay superstar who has specialized in 'God stuff,' portraying impartially such diverse deities of the Indian subcontinent as Krishna, Gautama Buddha, and Hanuman, in the popular genre known to the movie world as 'theologicals.' He is traveling to England in pursuit of the beautiful 'ice queen,' Alleluia Cone, climber of Everest. Saladin is returning, after an unhappy visit with his father, to London, where he lives, a self-made 'goodandproper Englishman,' in love with 'Bigben Nelsonscolumn Lordstavern Bloodytower Queen,' with his English dreamland of equilibrium and moderation. He is an actor too, of the invisible kind, a voice, a thousand voices, much in demand on radio and in television commercials. He knows how a ketchup bottle should talk, or a packet of garlic-flavored potato crisps: 'once, in a radio play for thirty-seven voices, he interpreted every single part under a variety of pseudonyms and nobody ever worked it out.'

If, as seems likely at this stage, the angelicdevilish conglomeration is to be sorted out and divided between the two of them, then Gibreel, a violent character and unconscionable womanizer, is in the running for the role of devil, and Saladin, mild and worrying, for that of angel. Yet when they land on an English beach Saladin finds he has grown horns, cloven hooves, and a monstrous phallus, whereas Gibreel is now wearing a halo. Despite his bowler hat, Saladin is arrested as an illegal immigrant—which one might interpret as a sign of injured innocence—while Gibreel bedazzles the police, treacherously disowns his compatriot, and goes free. Messages must have got mixed up once again. Rather than cudgel one's brain over their theological status, it is wiser to think of Gibreel and Saladin as the bookends between which a series of hectic and mysteriously linked narratives is to be uneasily held.

Particularly striking is the two-fold story called 'Ayesha,' whose first and fearsome half concerns a 'bearded and turbaned Imam' in exile from his homeland, called Desh, biding his time in infidel London, or Sodom, as he sees it. He is 'a massive stillness, an immobility. He is living stone.' When the revolution begins in Desh, the overthrowing of the Westernized and hence corrupt Empress, Ayesha (that this was the name of Muhammed's favorite wife must be beside the point), the Imam flies there on Gibreel's back—the so-called archangel is, as ever, bemused, reluctant, put-upon, no matter that he may be dreaming it all—and we see the people being slaughtered as they march on the palace gates.

The revolution prevails, Ayesha turns into Al-Lat, one of the false daughters of Allah, and is destroyed in a combat involving thunderbolts and comets, and we see the people marching into the mouth of the Imam, grown monstrous, and being swallowed whole, just as earlier they had marched into the Empress's guns, martyrs still. The Imam's pronouncement becomes fact:

'After the revolution there will be no clocks; we'll smash the lot. The word *clock* will be expunged from our dictionaries. After the revolution there will be no birthdays. We shall all be born again, all of us the same unchanging age in the eye of Almighty God.'

Gibreel has earlier mused on the curious circumstance that people who believe in God should be possessed by demons. Yet later an Indian intellectual contends that we cannot 'deny the ubiquity of faith' nor should we mock at the masses for what we see as their deludedness. Rushdie's book is copious in thesis and antithesis, but, not too surprisingly, synthesis hovers beyond it.

The second half begins charmingly, in a village where butterflies abound, and the landowner Mirza Saeed is devoted to his wife, Mishal. A young peasant girl appears, an epileptic, an eater of amenable butterflies, and to his horror he lusts after her. Mishal is found to have inoperable breast cancer, and Ayesha—for that is the peasant girl's name—declares that she is married to Gibreel and the archangel has told her that the village must go on a pilgrimage to Mecca, on foot, for the Arabian Sea will open to let them through. As did the Red Sea for Moses and the children of Israel in the Koran as well as the Bible. 'Everything is required of us, and everything will be given.' The sequel, recounted in a later chapter, is protracted, disjointed and ambiguous; perhaps the pilgrims crossed the sea, perhaps the pilgrims drowned in the sea. In the ritual opening words of Arab storytellers, deployed repeatedly here, 'It was so, it was not so.'

'Ellowen Deeowen': as Mahound is to Muhammad, so is Babylon to Britain, whose capital city is Babylondon. The London scenes are both strong and weak, brilliant and muzzy, banal and inventive. Picked up as an illegal immigrant, though actually a British citizen (even a member of the Garrick Club), Saladin is beaten up nastily in the police van. While this looks like another instance of police brutality toward what are termed 'ethnics,' the fact that he sports horns, cloven hooves, and an immense erection, and moreover litters the van with soft pellets of excrement, hardly augurs well for an easy ride. The policemen gloat over the effects of feeding their horses richly on the eve of the expected trouble: getting showered with shit provokes the demonstrators into violence, *'an' then we can really get amongst them, can't we just.'*

This could be an attack on police methods; it could be a sendup of right-minded attacks on police methods. Blacks and browns, it begins to seem, are lovable rogues or displaced metaphysicians, and whites are racist yahoos or middle-class bigots, until they all dissolve into ultra-Dickensian phantasmagoria. The scene in the 'ethnic' Club Hot Wax, where effigies of Enoch Powell and Margaret Thatcher ('Mrs Torture') are melted down to cries of *'burn-burn-burn'* and 'the fire this time,' doesn't contribute to racial harmony; and yet it might be thought that the engagingly wild, Westernized daughters of Muhammad Sufyan, proprietor of the Shaandaar Café, hold out some hope for a racially integrated future, more or less, after all. Saladin rhapsodizes over London's record as an asylum,

'a role it maintained in spite of the recalcitrant ingratitude of the refugees' children; and without any of the self-congratulatory huddled-masses rhetoric of the 'nation of immigrants' across the ocean, itself far from perfectly open-armed. Would the United States, with its are-you-now-have-you-ever-beens, have permitted Ho Chi Minh to cook in its hotel kitchens? What would its McCarran-Walter Act have to say about a latter-day Karl Marx, standing bushy-bearded at its gates, waiting to cross its yellow lines?'

But Saladin is reckoned by some to be a 'Brown Uncle Tom, more English than the British. Rushdie is having it both ways again—'What one hates in whites one must also hate when it turns up, inverted, in black'—and it won't do to make heavy weather of light farce or break a hornet on a wheel. 'I'm saying nothing,' is the author's own message. 'Don't ask me to clear things up one way or the other, the time of revelations is long gone.'

In his angelic avatar, or his dream, Gibreel conceives the bright idea that the 'moral fuzziness' of the English, their inability to make radical distinctions, their preference for compromise over truth, is due to their indeterminate weather, day no warmer than night, land no drier than sea. The tropicalizing of London will bring about moral precision, religious fervor, and political passion, as well as spicier food, an animated street life, and better cricketers. Dust, cholera, and cockroaches are a small price to pay for all that. It appears to be Saladin's intervention that limits Gibreel's operations to an unusually prolonged heat wave. No matter how many metamorphoses occur elsewhere, the English are not going to be turned into fundamentalists.

. . . *The Satanic Verses* is a thousand and one nights crammed into a week of evenings, a fitting successor to *Midnight's Children* and *Shame* (novels whose feasible successors it was hard to imagine), a book that nobody else in Britain (at least) would have wanted to write, or could have written. Whatever the whole may amount to, the sum of the parts is a substantial one. There isn't so much to be said in the abstract about good and evil, except to acknowledge that they, or something very like them, do exist. 'The world is incompatible, just never forget it: gaga,' says Otto Cone, ex-Cohen, a Polish émigré and Allie's father. 'Ghosts, Nazis, saints, all alive at the same time; in one spot, blissful happiness, while down the road, the inferno. You can't ask for a wilder place.' Or a more Manichaean depiction of it. . . .   (from *New York Review of Books*, 2 Mar. 1989)

A question of identity

MALISE RUTHVEN
Review

. . . If one can extrapolate a consistent theme from Rushdie's baroque elaborations of plot and character, it seems to be about the transformations of identity that affect the migrant who leaves his homeland with its familiar reference points and cultural certainties, to find himself in a game where the rules are different and all the markers have been changed. Thus the stories about the life of the Prophet Muhammad which Gibreel learns from his adoptive mother are transformed into his fantasies about the city of Jahiliya where Muhammad becomes 'Mahound' (false prophet of Crusading demonology), while the Mothers of the Believers, hallowed figures in Muslim tradition, are whores in a brothel called the Curtain (*hejab*—the word used for the veil worn by pious Muslim women). Is this really intended to be gratuitously insulting to the Prophet, as outraged Muslims insist, or is it not rather an imaginative way of charting the migrant's path from faith to scepticism, his shifting perspective of women, his attempted exorcism—consciously or otherwise—of childhood archetypes?

The appearance of doubt has a factual scholarly focus in Rushdie's use of accounts by early Muslim annalists that indicate flaws in the Qur'anic canon—in particular, the Satanic Verses of the title, where the devil is related to have inserted some verses, subsequently abrogated, in order to placate Muhammad's enemies. This and other episodes from the early history of Islam appearing in Gibreel's dreams cast doubt on the Islamic orthodoxy that the Qur'an was transmitted without any editing by Muhammad (a dogma which for any reasonable Westerner prevents an intelligent appreciation of the text).

The Satanic Verses, however, is as much about changing identities as loss of religious faith: many of its devices, such as the use of the same names by more than one character (or perhaps the same character in different guise—one cannot be sure), add emphasis to this central preoccupation. The migrant's dilemma—to change, risking loss of faith and identity, or to try to hold on to a consistent idea of selfhood—lies at the novel's heart, and provides its unexpected denouement. It is Saladin Chamcha, the 'creature of selected discontinuities, a willing re-invention of himself', who, by watching his father die (in what is a remarkably moving yet clear-eyed description), recovers his former, unassimilated selfhood as Salahuddin Chamchawala, the Bombay bourgeois; it is Gibreel, the 'untranslated man' whom the world considers 'good' for wishing to remain 'continuous', who is finally destroyed, unable to contain the eruptions of a religious megalomania which leaks into and overwhelms his waking self, 'making him that angelic Gibreel he has no desire to be'.

The rage with which this magnificent, challenging novel has been greeted by a number of Muslim organisations proves that Rushdie has touched upon some extremely raw nerves in a community experiencing the very dilemmas and transformations he portrays.

(from *Tablet*, London, 3 Dec. 1988)

The following is a translation of the review of The Satanic Verses *which appeared in the Iranian literary newspaper* Kayhan Farangi *in December, and which was subsequently republished in an edited form in* The Independent.

'Rushdie has fallen into total moral degradation'

Salman Rushdie is a writer who was born in a Muslim Indian family in 1947 in Bombay and has long been living in Britain. He has won a good number of awards in Britain and has had plenty of support from their literary circles.

Rushdie's two novels, *Midnight's Children* and *Shame*, have won him a number of important prizes, and these two novels have been translated into 20 languages, including Farsi. Furthermore, the translator of *Shame* has won the prize for translation of the best novel of the year, or perhaps more precisely, the best translation of the year. Naturally, these prizes do not mean that the translator is an accomplice in the wrongdoing of Rushdie in his later works.

Rushdie's novels are full of symbolism about contemporary political thought. *Midnight's Children* is about the contemporary history of India and *Shame* refers to the state of Pakistan. Rushdie has also written a book about Nicaragua. It is because of the similarities that he finds between subjects in his books and situations in different countries that some critics assume Rushdie's *The Satanic Verses* is a direct reference to present-day Iran. It contains certain Western-orientated hints and reactions towards the Islamic Revolution, though in essence this book, rather than addressing Iran, pays more attention to Islam.

The Satanic Verses contains a number of false interpretations about Islam and gives wrong portrayals of the Koran and the Prophet Mohamed. It also draws a caricature-like and distorted image of Islamic principles which lacks even the slightest artistic credentials.

The truth of the matter is that Rushdie's artistic and moral degradation is so immense that he even makes ridiculous comments about how Prophet Mohamed released Balal Habashi, which was a demonstration of Islam's compassionate face. *The Satanic Verses* is full of similar satanic-minded comments about Islam and our religious leaders, and this can only amount to the fact that Rushdie has fallen from the grace as a writer with a good knowledge of Islam to something like total moral degradation.

Immediately after publication of this book the awards organisations in the West rushed to brand it as one of the best literary works in recent years, and Rushdie has been nominated for the Booker Prize . . .   (*Independent*, London, 21 Feb. 1989)

Nihilistic, negative, satanic

PROF. SYED ALI ASHRAF
Review

Rushdie has written a negative satire on life. It is nihilistic. There is no positive norm. Love is presented as either sentimentality or lust. Selfishness dominates. Angels and Satan and the devils are manmade fabrications. Religious consciousness is shown only as superstition.

Rushdie then goes to the highest domain and tries to pull it down to prove that the Prophet of Islam (Peace be upon him) was not at all the perfect man history tells us of. He sides with the orientalists because that is convenient for him so that he can distort history as much as it suits him to do so. That is why he concocts a new kind of myth and turns a sexual pervert into an angel but an angel who himself does not know what message he pours into the heart of the Prophet.

It is obvious thus that Rushdie is not interested in presenting a sincere exploration into reality. He is interested in proving a theory of his own. The theory is a simple one. It is just disbelief in Proph-ethood, in the coming of 'revelations' from God and in the perfection of humanity in the life and character of Prophet Muhammad, peace and blessings of God be upon him. In order to do so, Rushdie picks up the myth of the so-called Satanic verses—which Satan is alleged to have put into the mouth of the Blessed Prophet and which he cancelled later on being informed from God. No authentic Hadith scholar has recorded this and many great Islamic scholars have re-jected it as a fabrication of the Makkan unbelievers who spread this rumour in order to cast doubt into the minds of newly converted and other people about the very authenticity of all revelations which, the Blessed Prophet claimed, to have been brought down to him by Archangel Gabriel. Rushdie has taken it as true and lost his faith in the authenticity of the revelations. Probably it is better to say that he never had any faith whatsoever, nor does he seem to be a person who has even tried to explore religious consciousness.

What is most satanic in this venture of Rushdie is that he has written this novel to satirise the Prophet and his Companions, to ridicule religious consciousness of people, to remove from the hearts of people any sense of reverence for angels, prophets, holy books, and hence any faith in God and the Hereafter. He has intentionally and deliberately distorted the history of the Blessed Prophet and his Companions though he has retained the names of the Compan-ions and chosen the name that vicious missionaries in the Middle Ages used to give to the Prophet (peace be upon him) only in order to tell people that he was not writing history.

Here we are faced with a fundamental problem. If some writer uses my name and the names of some of my friends and also selects some situations and incidents of my life and distorts them and vi-lifies them do I not have the right to charge that person for slander and defamation? Should not the Muslim community have the right to condemn this man, for blasphemy because he is using a thin veil of fiction in order to vilify the Prophet and all that they hold dear to them? As the author is not interested in presenting his own real-isation of any truth, as he is preaching an anti-Islamic theory in the guise of a novel, his liberty as a writer ends and he should be treated as anyone producing blasphemous writing is treated.

The method that he has adopted to achieve his goal is also confusing and unsuccessful from the literary point of view. How could the two characters Gibreel (Gabriel) and Saladin fall from the sky and still be alive? How could they get transformed and how could they become normal again? How could they have the normal human body and how could they at the same time move about and influence people across space and time?

Rushdie tried to learn some Sufistic terminology and some Hindu and Buddhistic terms and started playing with them in a childish way. He wanted to be realistic and fantastic at the same time. Where he failed miserably is in portraying people's feelings when they see the transformation of Saladin or Gibreel as if these are normal things. In a normal situation, these abnormal things do not happen. In a fairy tale they do. His attempt to mix normalcy and fairy tale myths created by him do not carry conviction. Had we been transported into the imaginary world completely, as C. S. Lewis does in children's tales or as is done in fairy tales, it would have been convincing. . . .

Rushdie is thus a practitioner of black magic who turns things upside down. Does he see anything great or good in human nature? Rushdie succeeds in portraying a large number of characters of which the two are the most prominent, Gibreel and Saladin. The characterisation of the Prophet, his companions and The Imam is highly twisted and incompetent. In his attempt to theorise and present a distorted version of history it was not possible for him to have any norm of behaviour which would show, as sometimes he wanted to, a conflict between good and evil. It is his incapacity to understand or respond to human greatness that makes him highly confused. Men and women may be led by superstition but Religion is not superstition. Ayesha and her followers are destroyed by their false beliefs which they sincerely held. This type of religiosity is present in human society but this should have been presented as an aberration and not genuine religious sentiment or beliefs. As against this type of pseudo-religion presented as religion, he does not present any truly religious character or even a predominantly 'good' (to use the Aristotelian concept) character in the whole novel. When the Prophet and his Companions are confused or corrupt or hypocritical like politicians where can he find a really 'good' character?

There is thus no relief in this novel. It is mentally disturbing, almost paranoic, in its love of a corrupt society. To use his own words it is 'locus classicus of incompatible realities. Lives that have no business mingling with one another sit side by side upon the omnibus' of his novel. 'One universe, on a zebra crossing, is caught for an instant, blinking like a rabbit, in the headlamps of a motor vehicle in which an entirely alien and contradictory continuum is to be found.' If that is his only intention in writing this novel, he may be said to have succeeded in presenting such contradictions in human nature. His strength as a novelist lies in his ability to portray such minds. But when we go a bit deep into his characterisation we notice that nearly all these characters are repeating the same side of human nature I shall term satanic, i.e. the world of passions and lust and selfishness not for a moment relieved by a desire to struggle with such devilish enchantments.

• *Prof. Dr Syed Ali Ashraf is Director-General, Islamic Academy, Cambridge, England, and member, Faculty of Education, University of Cambridge.*

(from *Impact International*, London, 28 Oct.–10 Nov. 1988)

The following interview with Salman Rushdie was recorded on 27 January 1989 by Bandung File and broadcast on 14 February on Channel 4.

Did you expect such a powerful reaction to this book?

I expected that the mullahs wouldn't like it. But I didn't write it for the mullahs. I've seen what the mullahs have done in Pakistan over the past 11 years—the level of oppression instituted there by islamisation. I've seen, too, how almost all the poets in Pakistan were in exile in England during that period. Only now are they beginning to think about going back.

Obviously I have a view of the world which is not theirs. I insist on my right to express it as I think fit.

It's very simple in this country. If you don't want to read a book, you don't have to read it. It's very hard to be offended by *The Satanic Verses*, it requires a long period of intense reading. It's a quarter of a million words.

The controversy, in a sense, has been about your acting on the historic text of the Koran and playing with that. How much of that was based on historical fact?

Almost entirely. Almost everything in those sections—the dream sequences—starts from an historical or quasi-historical basis, though one can't really speak with absolute certainty about that period of Mohammed's life. The records are very partial and ambiguous. But he is, after all, the only prophet who exists even partially in history. As with all the other prophets, we only have legends and stories written hundreds of years later. The interesting thing about Mohammed is that there *is* objective information about him other than the sacred text. It seemed to me, when I studied it as an historian, that that makes this whole phenomenon an historical as well as a spiritual one, and the relationship between the people involved is absolutely fascinating.

Islam is, after all, one of the greatest ideas that ever came into the world—I suppose the next idea of that size would have been Marxism—and the chance to study the birth of a great historical idea is interesting. The one thing you learn as an historian is just how fragmented and ambiguous and peculiar the historical record is. So I thought, well, let's not try and pretend to be writing a history. Let's take the themes I'm interested in and fantasise them and fabulate them and all that, so that we don't have to get into the issue: did this really happen like this or did it not?

The themes are huge. Basically, there's two questions that the book seeks to answer. When an idea comes into the world, it's faced with two big tests: when you're weak, do you compromise; when you're strong, are you tolerant? Those are the questions that those sections of the novel seek to dramatise. It shows that (and, as far as we can tell about Mohammed's life, this is also true) the answer to the first question is that, when weak, there seems [in the case of Mohammed] to have been a brief flirtation with a possible compromise—about monotheism—which was very rapidly rejected.

Now I don't think this diminishes Mohammed. All prophets face temptation. When Gibreel [the archangel] comes to Mohammed and tells him that these verses are satanic verses and should be removed—and here are the real verses—he forgave him. He said, 'Never mind, it's understandable, things like this have happened before.' I mean, it seems that Gibreel is more tolerant than some of these people attacking the book.

When Mohammed returned to Mecca in power, he was very, very tolerant. And I think, if I remember correctly, only five or six people were executed after the re-taking of Mecca. And of those five or six people, two were writers, and two were actresses who had performed in satirical texts. Now there you have an image that I thought was worth exploring: at the very beginning of Islam you find a conflict between the sacred text and the profane text, between revealed literature and imagined literature. For a writer, that conflict is fascinating and interesting to explore. So that's what I was doing, exploring.

Do you think the opposition to the book is based on people feeling weak or feeling strong?

It seems to me that nothing I can do can destroy Islam. They keep announcing that 900 million people in the world are Muslims. What can I do? How can I unmake Islam? It's not possible. So even if it were my desire, which it isn't, the idea that, somehow, a book should exist which takes a different point of view from that of the imams and be such a dangerous thing, is not convincing to me.

It seems to me completely legitimate that there should be dissent from orthodoxy, not just about Islam, but about anything—from Conservative politics, that's a kind of orthodoxy under which we all live at the moment, it's important that there should be dissent from that. If radical politics were the orthodoxy in this country I think it would be important that there should be dissent from that too.

One of the things that a writer can do is to say: Here is the way in which you're told you're supposed to look at the world, but actually there are also some other ways. Let us never believe that the way in which the people in power tell us to look at the world is the only way we can look, because if we do that, then that's a kind of appalling self-censorship.

What you've written has been called insulting to Islam and a provocation to all Muslims. Did you take delight in provocation?

It depends what you mean by provocation. Any writer wishes to provoke the imagination. You want to make people think about what you're writing. One of the reasons for writing, I believe, is to slightly increase the sum of what it's possible to think, to say 'Let's look at it a different way.' If it works, then people are provoked, and maybe they don't like it.

Almost all the people who are being so insulted and provoked and disgusted have not really read the book. But I get letters every

day from Muslims who do like the book. They write to me to say
we're not all like those people who burn books. They say they're
ashamed of what the imams are doing, about the way in which
they're bringing shame on the Muslim community in this country
by behaving in this extremely uncivilised way. So the idea that what
I'm saying is somehow outside Islam is one that I resist. I come
from a Muslim tradition, and in my family in the Indian subcontinent, there was an absolute willingness to discuss anything, there
were not these anathemas, these rules, about what you must not
talk about. I know about Islam as well, and these people's Islam is
not the only Islam.

**You've been known primarily as a world writer—perhaps
sometimes as an Indian or Pakistani writer, sometimes as a British writer—but with this book it seems that you've become a
Muslim writer.**

Anybody who reads any of my books knows how powerful the
influence of Islam has been. The fact that I would not call myself a
religious person doesn't mean that I can reject the importance of
Islam in my life. If you come from India or Pakistan, how can you
reject religion? Religion is the air everyone breathes. If you're trying
to write about that world, you can't make a simple rejection of
religion. You have to deal with it because it's the centre of the
culture.

**The heart of what they're angry about is not the specific insults,
it's to do with the whole notion of doubt.**

Doubt, it seems to me, is the central condition of a human being
in the 20th century. One of the things that has happened to us in
the 20th century as a human race is to learn how certainty crumbles
in your hand. We cannot any longer have a fixed certain view of
anything—the table that we're sitting next to, the ground beneath
our feet, the laws of science, are full of doubt now. Everything we
know is pervaded by doubt and not by certainty. And that is the
basis of the great artistic movement known as Modernism. Now
the fact that the orthodox figures in the Muslim world have declared
a jihad against Modernism is not my fault. It doesn't validate an
entire way of looking at the world which is, to my mind, the most
important new contribution of the 20th century to the way in which
the human race discusses itself. If they're trying to say that this

whole process has gone out of the window—that you can't do that, all you have is the old certainties—then, yes, I do argue.

(© Bandung File)

Words that outraged Islam

JOHN WALSH

Two brief sections from the second chapter of Salman Rushdie's *The Satanic Verses* contain all the elements that started the chain reaction which has led to death, violence and the rage of Islam.

The passages, written in a quasi-biblical rhythm, are mildly opaque, but the wrath provoked by them, and a few other paragraphs in the 547-page book, provides a salutary lesson in the power of words.

The Muslim community's sense of insult focuses on a character dreamed into existence by Gibreel Farishta, a fading and slightly demented Indian film star.

The dream-figure is a kind of angel ('halfway between Allahgod and homosap'), who is given the name of the Muslim devil-figure, Mahound (this also means 'false prophet'), and is pictured entering the fantastical city of 'Jahilia' (meaning ignorance, darkness) to found a religion.

Rushdie's constant emphasis on ambiguity should discourage readers from making hard-and-fast correspondences between his fiction and the real world (even the sand of Jahilia is 'the very stuff of inconstancy—the quintessence of unsettlement, shifting, treachery, lack-of-form'). But it is here that Muslims detect unforgivable slights.

They object to the suggestion that a shady 'businessman-turned-prophet' should be likened to the prophet Muhammad, who founded Islam in the 7th century. They resent him being shown receiving the voice of God as a whispered doubt. They hate the prophet Abraham being called a 'bastard'.

The Muslims assume the fictional city of Jahilia is the holy city of Mecca. They do not like the description of Mahound's companions as a 'trio of scum' (incidentally featuring 'some sort of bum from Persia by the outlandish name of Salman'), nor the idea that he is an unscrupulous and manipulative hoodwinker of his flock.

Rushdie's narrative thrust is to re-imagine, through the dreams of the film star, the beginnings of the Islamic culture. Through Gibreel's human eyes, the prophet's original visions of heaven and earth materialize and are set down in the dissolving sands of an Unreal City.

The trouble lies in Rushdie's giving the fictional near-Muhammad a non-divine nature (he is a tyrant, a lecher, a man without scruple). Worse, Rushdie later suggests that the prophet included in the Koran certain verses that, on closer inspection, turn out to be the work of the Devil—the satanic verses.

Muslims believe the Koran is the direct word of God, as revealed by the archangel Gabriel to the scribes of Muhammad. They are thus passionate about the printed word and take seriously any suggestion that any of the Koran might be the work of the Devil.

There are also two passages in the book's fourth chapter (Return to Jahilia) which Muslim sensibility finds especially monstrous. In these the prophet Mahound reappears and is presented as a joke tyrant, whose disciples ('the followers of the new faith of Submission') fear him, but have begun to discover his weaknesses.

In the first passage, he is imagined (all this takes place in the everdreaming Gibreel's head) as inventing capricious and arbitrary laws. . . .

The revelation told the faithful how much to eat, how deeply they should sleep, and which sexual positions had received divine sanction, so that they learned that sodomy and the missionary position were approved of by the archangel, whereas the forbidden postures included all those in which the female was on top.

Scatology apart, Muslims take this passage as a symbolic assault on the Sheria, the law of Islam in the Koran.

Finally, there is an extended fantasy about 'the Curtain', Jahilia's most popular brothel, where the girls, to please a client, take the names of the prophet's 12 wives and are encouraged to whisper salacious details from their supposed earlier lives into the ears of their men friends. . . .

At no point in these imaginings does Rushdie refer to the prophet Muhammad by name, nor to the city of Mecca, nor to the Sheria law, nor anything directly concerned with Islamic faith.

All the fundamentalists' objections concern the *symbolic* representation of religious figures and events—as one might condemn

George Orwell's fictional Ministry of Love for satirising the Ministry of Defence.

What is altogether more odd is that the book's status as a novel cuts no ice with its Muslim critics. The grand sheikh of Cairo's Al-Azhar, the 1,000-year-old seat of Islamic theology, said when calling on all the nations in the Islamic Conference Organization to suppress the book that it contained 'lies and figments of the imagination' about Islam, which were 'passed off as facts', and that the Jahilia sequences were insulting distortions of Islamic history.

That Rushdie has always presented his material as fictional 'figments of the imagination' is not considered an excuse.

'What we are talking about here is an insult,' said M. H. Faruqi, editor of *Impact International*, the influential Muslim newspaper, whose selection of the book's offending passages has been widely disseminated.

'There is no problem about it being fiction or not. It doesn't matter if it's a fiction, a serious book, a dream—the point is that the language should be decent. The problem is the abusive and insulting way the Prophet is described in the most filthy language.'

Did Rushdie have any idea how his difficult, clotted, bewildering dramatisations of the mythical origins of Islam would be greeted? Surely not. But reading *The Satanic Verses* with the benefit of hindsight, one is constantly pulled up by Rushdie's teasing way with the idea of blasphemy and retribution, of flirting with the unsayable.

At one point (page 374) the betrayed prophet, Mahound, has his disciple, Salman, brought before him, whimpering, at knifepoint. He shakes his head: 'Your blasphemy, Salman, can't be forgiven. Did you think I wouldn't work it out? To set your words against the Words of God . . .'

It seems to be the authentic voice of 1,000m Muslims.

(*Sunday Times*, London, 19 Feb. 1989)

II

The Mounting Protest ~

The controversial nature of the book first emerged in public when two of India's news magazines, *India Today* and *Sunday*, published interviews with Rushdie in mid-September.

Both reports caught the eye of Syed Shahabuddin, an ambitious Muslim MP. As a member of the opposition Janata party, he immediately called on the government to ban the book.

With a general election due within a year, Rajiv Gandhi's increasingly unpopular Congress (I) party was well aware of the electoral importance of India's 100m Muslims. On October 5, soon after the book was published in Britain, the Indian Government telexed Penguin in London announcing the ban. Within weeks it was followed by Pakistan, Saudi Arabia, Egypt, Somalia, Bangladesh, Sudan, Malaysia, Indonesia, Qatar and South Africa, which has a vociferous Muslim minority.   (from *Sunday Times*, London, 19 Feb. 1989)

An irreverent journey
MAHDU JAIN
Review

    . . . This omnibus of a book dazzles like a kaleidoscope. It is studded with winged metaphors, parables, allegories, Hindi dialogues, sermons, smart one-liners of the advertising world and authorial interruptions, Hitchcock-like, with Rushdie in the guest role playing god with a small g. Like the kaleidoscope, each turn disorients. But taken together, the novel is, among several other themes, an uncompromising, unequivocal attack on religious fanaticism and fundamentalism, which in this book is largely Islamic. It makes

V. S. Naipaul's *Among the Believers* seem like an OK certificate for Islamic fundamentalism.

The root idea of the novel is that there are no absolutes. Heaven and Hell have no boundaries. It's almost impossible to tell angel and devil apart: Mahound the prophet has a tough time telling the difference between the voice of the angel and the *shaitan* (devil) up there on Mount Cone. In the process, Rushdie takes a very irreverent look at Islamic folklore and fact.

Shuttling between the Koranic-Biblical past and present, the past is a searchlight for the absurdities of the present. Ayesha, the youngest and most desirable of Mahound's 12 wives, appears in the middle of the book 'living chastely in the harem quarters of the great mosque at Yathrib'. She re-surfaces several chapters and centuries later—clad only in butterflies—to lead an entire village, lemming-like, into the Arabian Sea. The sea is expected to part and the pilgrims to go straight to Mecca—which provokes the famous deflationary Rushdie punchline. The affluent man in a Mercedes who tries to stop his cancer-stricken wife from taking the fatal plunge says, 'let me fly you to Mecca, pronto. . . . Why walk if you can go by Airbus?'

Angels and gods are dislodged from their heavens. Rushdie in person delivers the more deadly blows to the trumpeters of religion. 'Gibreel Farishta saw God. . . . Gibreel's vision of the Supreme Being was not abstract in the least. He saw, sitting on the bed, a man of about the same age as himself. . . . What struck him most was that the apparition was balding, seemed to suffer from dandruff and wore glasses. This was not the Almighty he had expected. Who are you? he asked. . . . "Ooparvala," the apparition answered. "The Fellow Upstairs." "How do I know you're not the other One," Gibreel asked craftily, "*Neechayvala*, the Guy from Underneath?"'

Pilgrim places get their mirror-image come-uppances. When Jahilia, the city of sand, begins to suffer after the camel trains start losing their business to the boats, the ruler Abu Simbel is convinced: 'Only the pilgrimage stands between the city and its ruin.' So the council searches the world for 'statues of alien gods, to attract new pilgrims'. But there is more competition. 'Down in Sheba a great temple has been built, a shrine to rival the House of Black Stone.' The rulers have no choice but to add 'the tempting spices of profanity to their religious practices.'

There is also in Jahilia, a Tent of Black Stone called The Curtain with 12 prostitutes who have given themselves the names of the 12 wives of Mahound in neighbouring Yathrib. 'For obvious reasons it was not politic to form a queue in the street, and so on many days a line of men curled around the innermost courtyard of the brothel rotating about its centrally positioned Fountain of Love much as the pilgrims rotated for other reasons around the ancient Black Stone.' Rushdie does not hesitate to name names, with the exception of the prophet. Here it is Mahound; but he has Hamza, Ayesha, and others straight from the Book. Moreover, the battles which the prophet had to win in order to convert people are very real. And characters like the idol goddesses Lat and Manat are part of Islamic folklore.

Migration is another major theme of this whirlpool of a book. The subcontinental migrants in England also undergo metamorphoses. Rushdie's contemporary mythic figures are not so different from the second generation British Asians finding their anthems in bhangra-discos—little islands within the larger islands of their homeward-looking parents and the Paki-bashing host community. 'From her Chamcha learned the fables of the new Kurus and Pandavas, the white racists and black "self-help" or vigilante poses starring in this modern *Mahabharaia*, or, more accurately, *Mahavilayet.*'

The magic carpet does take us places but sometimes, in the many twists and turns into dreamscapes, readers may find themselves temporarily off-loaded. If not vertiginous. As for the sentinels of Islam, they will get off at the first stop. *The Satanic Verses* is bound to trigger an avalanche of protests from the ramparts.

(from *India Today*, 15 Sept. 1988)

'My theme is fanaticism'

MADHU JAIN
Interviews Salman Rushdie

Do you see your new novel as the last in a trilogy after *Midnight's Children* and *Shame*?

Yes. I didn't when I was writing it. But having finished the book, I have begun to see the novels as a body of work. I also see my first novel, *Grimus*, as part of this. Metaphysical concerns were present in a different way in the first novel. With the last one I have come

to the end of the first movement in my work and I feel I can do very
different things now.

What are you doing now?

Being Zia's obituarist.

**Your book begins with an exploding aeroplane too. Aren't there
many coincidences between your work and events?**

There have been unbelievable coincidences. In my novels there
are five political figures. All have come to a violent end. Mujibur
Rahman in Bangladesh, Indira Gandhi and Sanjay Gandhi in India,
Bhutto and Zia in Pakistan. This whole generation either falls out
of planes, or gets shot or hanged. None of these people has had a
quiet end.

When did you actually begin *The Satanic Verses*?

Parts of the novel have been in my head since I first began to
study Islamic history at the university 20 years ago. But I started
work on the book in early 1984. I stopped after my first draft. I
wasn't very happy with it and the Nicaragua trip came as a godsend.
It gave me the chance to get away from my own internal situation.
When I returned the problems jamming me had gone away.

**The novel appears to be quite a fierce critique of Islamic fa-
naticism . . .**

Actually, one of my major themes is religion and fanaticism. I
have talked about the Islamic religion because that is what I know
the most about. But the ideas about religious faith and the nature
of religious experience and also the political implications of religious extremism are applicable with a few variations to just about
any religion. In the beginning and the end of the novel there are
other kinds of fundamentalism also.

**It is easy to recognise quite a few Bombay film stars in the
book.**

For the Indian readers there are many shocks of recognition. I've
taken little pieces out of many characters. There is something of
Amitabh Bachchan and something of N. T. Rama Rao, but these
characters are not supposed to be them. Some I made up, but the
film producer with a face like a knee-in-spectacles is partly based
on Ismail Merchant.

**Some of the names you use are straight out of the Book, based
on real characters in Islamic tradition; but others are made up.
Why did you do that?**

I have changed names. I have given the name of an Egyptian temple, Abu Simbel, to the leader of Mecca. I have not called the cities by their names. After all, this is a visionary thing: it happens in dreams. I wanted to distance events from historical events. Issues are being raised: it is not about whether they were historically true or not. The book is really about the fact that an idea or a new thing in the world must decide whether to compromise or not. Beyond that, the image out of which the book grew was of the prophet going to the mountain and not being able to tell the difference between the angel and the devil. The book is also about the wrestling match which takes place between the two.

Unlike some of your other novels, this one ends on some sort of an optimistic note.

Apart from this being my most serious book, it is also the most comic. I suddenly realised in the end of each of my books that the world disintegrates. But in this novel life goes on at the end of the story. No matter how terrible the events which have happened, at the end, it is not the end of the world. I do leave a few people standing at the end.

Do you fear a backlash from the mullahs?

Even *Shame* was attacked by fundamentalist Muslims. I cannot censor. I write whatever there is to write.

(from *India Today*, 15 Sept. 1988)

Of Satan, archangels and prophets

SHRABANI BASU
Interviews Salman Rushdie

Satanic Verses has caused a lot of controversy because of the references made to the Prophet Mohammad—there was even the possibility that it may not be published in India. Were you prepared for this?

That's news to me—I haven't heard it from Penguin. But it would be absurd to think that a book can cause riots. That's a strange sort of view of the world.

But then the situation in India is particularly delicate . . .

Well the point about the book is that there is a view in it that I take—and that is that everything is worth discussing. There are no subjects which are off limits and that includes God, includes prophets. I refuse to think that I should shut my mind off to subjects which are not just of interest to me but which have been my concern all my life.

The point is that I am not a religious person any more, formally; but I have remained all my life very attached to and interested in the subject of Islam. I studied it at university—indeed the place where I first heard about the satanic verses (of which a fictionalised version is in the book) is when I was studying Islam. So it's an image which has remained with me for 20 years.

I guess some people might get upset because it is not reverent, but the point is it is a serious attempt to write about religion and revelation from the point of view of a secular person. I think that's a completely legitimate exercise. Besides, Mohammad is a very interesting figure. He's the only prophet who exists even remotely inside history. He is the only one about whom there is some half-established more-or-less factual historical information. That makes him a human being and doubly interesting.

I don't believe that Mohammad had a revelation but then I don't doubt his sincerity either. Mohammad didn't make up the angel. He had that genuine mystical experience. But if you don't believe in the whole truth and you don't disbelieve him either—then what's going on? What is the nature of the mystical experience? Given that we accept it happens and we also don't believe in God and archangels. That's what I tried to write about. . . .

(from *Sunday*, India, 18–24 Sept. 1988)

Rushdie novel banned in India

FROM DAVID WIGG
In New Delhi

The Indian government, bowing to pressure from Muslim groups, yesterday banned Salman Rushdie's latest book.

Satanic Verses, which has been short-listed for the Booker Prize, was described by Syed Shahabuddin, an opposition MP, as an 'indecent vilification of the Holy Prophet'. The MP said Mr Rushdie had admitted the book was a direct attack on Islam. In one scene the Prophet's wives are portrayed as prostitutes. 'The Home Minister was shocked when I showed him the passage,' Mr Shahabuddin said. 'The book should also be restricted in England. No civilised society should permit it.'

Mr Rushdie, who was born in Bombay, came to prominence with *Midnight's Children*, a study of India's evolution since independence which won the 1981 Booker Prize. Like many Indian writers who moved to the West, he has become highly controversial here and is generally admired, albeit grudgingly.

Zamir Asari, who represents Penguin in India, had said he did not expect the book—which obviously had literary merits—to be banned, but Penguin would abide by the ruling. 'An unknown number' of copies of *Satanic Verses* have already arrived in India.

He said riots once broke out over an entry on Islam in the *Encylopaedia Britannica*. When a book was banned, which was rare, it sometimes led to a strange situation. '*Lady Chatterley's Lover*, for example, is still banned . . . but you can buy a pirated copy for 10 rupees [40p] and it is even recommended on some university courses.' . . .   (from *Independent*, London, 6 Oct. 1988)

An open letter to the Indian prime minister
SALMAN RUSHDIE
Writes to Rajiv Gandhi

Dear Rajiv Gandhi,

On Wednesday, October 5 the Indian Finance Ministry announced the banning of my novel, *The Satanic Verses*, under Section 11 of the Indian Customs Act. Many people around the world will find it strange that it is the Finance Ministry that gets to decide what Indian readers may or may not read. But let that pass, because at the end of the notification of the ban an even stranger statement appeared. The ministry—I am quoting from the Press Trust of India's report—'added that the ban did not detract from the literary and artistic merit of Rushdie's work'. To which I can only reply: Thanks for the good review.

The book was banned after representations by two or three Muslim politicians including Syed Shahabuddin, MP, and Khurshid Alam Khan, MP. These persons, whom I do not hesitate to call extremists, even fundamentalists, have attacked me and my novel while stating that they had no need actually to read it. That the Government of India should have given in to such figures is profoundly disturbing. No wonder the Finance Ministry's statement sounded confused and defensive.

At the weekend, a further official statement was brought to my notice. This explained that *The Satanic Verses* had been banned as a pre-emptive measure. Certain passages in my book had been identified as being capable of distortion and misuse, presumably by unscrupulous religious fanatics and such. The banning order had been issued to prevent this misuse. So now it appears that my book is not deemed blasphemous or objectionable in itself, but is being proscribed for, so to speak, its own good! This really is astounding. It is as though, having identified an innocent person as a likely target for assault by muggers or rapists, you were to put that person in jail for protection. This is no way, Mr Gandhi, for a free society to behave.

Clearly, your Government is feeling a little ashamed of itself, and, Sir, it has much to be ashamed about. It is not for nothing that just about every leading Indian newspaper and magazine has deplored the ban as, for example, 'a philistine decision' (The *Hindu*'s editorial) or 'thought control' (the title of the *Indian Express*'s leader). It is not for nothing that such eminent writers as Kingsley Amis, Harold Pinter, Stephen Spender and Tom Stoppard have joined International Pen, Index on Censorship and India's own association of publishers and booksellers in condemning the decision.

The right to freedom of expression is at the very foundation of any democratic society, and at present, all over the world, Indian democracy is becoming something of a laughing stock. When Syed Shahabuddin and his fellow self-appointed guardians of Muslim sensibilities say that 'no civilised society' should permit the publication of a book like mine, they have got things backwards. The question raised by the book's banning is precisely whether India, by behaving in this somewhat South African fashion, can any more lay claim to the title of a civilised society.

Let us try to distinguish truth from falsehood in this matter. Like my zealous opponents, you will probably not have read *The Satanic Verses*. So let me explain a few simple things. I am accused of having 'admitted' that the book is a direct attack on Islam. I have admitted no such thing, and deny it strongly.

The section of the book in question (and let's remember that the book isn't actually about Islam, but about migration, metamorphosis, divided selves, love, death, London and Bombay) deals with a prophet who is not called Muhammad living in a highly fantasticated city—made of sand, it dissolves when water falls upon it—in which he is surrounded by fictional followers, one of whom happens to bear my own first name. Moreover, this entire sequence happens in a dream, the fictional dream of a fictional character, an Indian movie star, and one who is losing his mind, at that. How much further from history could one get?

In this dream sequence, I have tried to offer my view of the phenomenon of revelation, and the birth of a great world religion, and that view is that of a secular man for whom Islamic culture has been of central importance all his life. Can the Indian Finance Ministry really be saying that it is no longer permissible, in modern, supposedly secular India for literature to treat such themes? If so, things are more serious than I had believed.

From where I sit, Mr Gandhi, it looks very much as if your Government has become unable or unwilling to resist pressure from more or less any extremist religious grouping, that, in short, it's the fundamentalists who now control the political agenda in India. You know, as I know, that Mr Shahabuddin, Mr Khurshid Alam Khan, Mr Suleiman Seit and their allies don't really care about my novel one way or the other. The real issue is, who is to get the Muslim vote? I deeply resent my book being used as a political football, and what should matter to you more than my resentment is that you come out of this looking not only philistine and antidemocratic but opportunistic and that's bad.

Mr Prime Minister, I can't bring myself to address finance ministries about literature. In my view, this is now a matter between you and me. I ask you this straightforward question: What sort of India do you wish to govern? Is it to be an open, or a repressive society? Your action in the matter of *The Satanic Verses* will be for many people around the world, an important indicator. If you confirm the ban, I'm afraid, I, and many others, will have to assume the worst. If, on the other hand, you should admit your Government's error and move swiftly to correct it, that will be an honourable deed and I shall be the first to applaud.

Yours sincerely,
Salman Rushdie
7 October

This letter appeared in various papers.

'You did this with satanic forethought, Mr Rushdie'

SYED SHAHABUDDIN

The ban imposed by the government of India, on the import and distribution of the novel, *Satanic Verses* by the overrated Eurasian writer Salman Rushdie, the imitation Garcia Márquez, has set into hectic motion the entire 'liberal' establishment in the country and outside. They are all set to overawe the government of India into surrendering its sovereign right and constitutional responsibility not to permit import of social turmoil of foreign origin into an already divided country.

What is shocking is not the protest of the 'irreverent minority' but the attitude of the Anglicised elite for whom a book by a writer of Indian origin nominated, sorry, shortlisted for the highest literary award in the *Vilayat* by the sahib's themselves—all pukka Sahibs, mind you—is the height of achievement and the mark of merit.

Perhaps it is just the sort of aphrodisiac needed to suit their perverted tastes. Not that many have read the book yet—they do not have to—from cover to cover—to boast about possession of a pirated edition or a smuggled copy. To have it is the thing, just the thing.

Even more shocking and saddening at the same time is the communication gap between the Muslim community and the so-called intelligentsia. There is no mental rapport, no instantaneous recognition of pain, no spontaneous sharing of anguish.

Our country is divided in many ways but can it survive such a psychological barrier? Can it overcome these intellectual divides which seem to preclude any possibility of speaking to each other in the language of the heart? It's unbelievable that what pains one section gives pleasure to the other. Are we really so estranged from each other?

As patriots and as nationalists we should not only be glad but grateful to the government for its sensitivity to the anguish felt by an important sector of our people at this deliberate offence to their religious feelings, for its readiness to share their sense of injury and to express its concern in the administrative idiom.

All that some Muslim MPs did was to caution the government on the reaction of the Muslim community to the book. They did not threaten violence; they did not incite mobs; they did not seek publicity; they did not wait till the storm broke; and the government listened to them with understanding and sympathy, got a copy, satisfied itself and acted.

An example of civilised interaction between the people and the government. No Mr Rushdie, contrary to your imagination, India is not being run by the 'fundamentalist lobby'. But if to seek redress of a religious grievance from the government which is the custodian of the dignity of all our people is fundamentalism in your lexicon, so be it.

One would like to ask the critics of the ban, whether it would be in the national interest, whether it will promote the process of national integration or aggravate the existing alienation if the government of the day remained a silent spectator to what the Muslim community, as a whole, was bound to consider an act of vilification, an exercise in blasphemy and an unpardonable insult to their religion. It would be nothing short of criminal negligence on the part of a responsible government.

The elite do not understand the dynamics of mass communication—how reports spread and how rumours, sometimes exaggerated and wild, fly and take possession of the minds of men. Translations, excerpts in various languages, comments in the local press, editorial reviews and, over and above them all, interviews (the most inflammatory being the brave statements by the writer himself) percolate down to form an emotional torrent and, given the religious context, reason and restraint are swept away in the current of passion.

Yes, Mr Rushdie, we are a religious people and we do not like our religious personalities—prophets, avatars, saints, rishis to be abused and vilified, directly or indirectly. Call us primitive, call us fundamentalists, call us superstitious barbarians, call us what you like, but your book only serves to define what has gone wrong with the Western civilisation—it has lost all sense of distinction between the sacred and the profane.

Life is not all that you live and what you can purchase with your royalty paid by a fatigued culture in exchange for your performance as a master of literary gimmicks and as a provider of cultural shock. It is something deeper. You have lost your sense of the supernatural. We have not. Why should you presume we have?

Civilisation is nothing but voluntary acceptance of restraints. You may hold whatever private opinion you like but you do not enjoy an absolute right to express them in public. As for a serious intellectual discussion, there is always a time and a place. But a logical argument cannot be on the basis of a piece of historical fiction.

In any case, you cannot claim to be the repository of absolute truths. Rest assured, Rushdies will come and go but the names of Mohammad, Christ or Buddha will last till the end of time. And soon your Satanic Verses will be laid aside, having served its literary purpose of generating excitement and forgotten, even by your champions (many of whom have not, I believe, seen or read it). But the Koran, the Bible and the Gita shall continue to be read by millions and not only read but revered and acted upon.

You are aggrieved that some of us have condemned you without a hearing and asked for the ban without reading your book. Yes, I have not read it, nor do I intend to. I do not have to wade through a filthy drain to know what filth is. My first inadvertent step would tell me what I have stepped into. For me, the synopsis, the review, the excerpts, the opinions of those who had read it and your gloatings were enough. Rushdie 'the Islamic scholar, the man who studied Islam at university' has to brag about his Islamic credentials, so that he can convincingly vend his Islam wares in the West, which has not yet laid the ghost of the crusades to rest, but given it a new cultural wrapping which explains why writers like you are so wanted and pampered.

Is any more evidence required in the face of your frank admission: 'I have talked about the Islamic religion subjects which are off limits and that includes God, includes prophets'? That is what you have said. The very title of your book is suggestively derogatory. In the eyes of the believer the Koran is the Word of God, and you plead innocence of the possible Muslim reaction. You depict the Prophet whose name the practising Muslim recites five times a day, whom he loves, whom he considers the model for mankind, as an impostor and you expect us to applaud you?

You have had the nerve to situate the wives of the Prophet, whom we Muslims regard as the mothers of the community, in a brothel, and you expect the Muslims to praise your power of imagination? You cannot take shelter behind the plea that after all it is a dream sequence in a piece of fiction. But tell us what compulsion you had to name the Prophet of your novel as Mahound (you are really too clever by half, not just naughty). Anyone conversant with the English language knows that Mahound is an archaic form for Mohammad, the name of the Prophet.

No, your act is not unintentional or a careless slip of the pen. It was deliberate and consciously planned with devilish forethought, with an eye to your market. Here in India, our laws are very clear. Though ignorance of law is no excuse, let me instruct you so that you are more careful if you wish to sell in India. Article 295 A of the Indian Penal Code says: Whoever, with deliberate and malicious intention of outraging the religious feelings of any class of citizens of India, by words either spoken or written or . . . otherwise, insults or attempts to insult the religion or the religious beliefs of that class, shall be punished with imprisonment . . . or with fine . . . or with both. I wish you were in India, Mr Rushdie, to face the music. And then there are other sections like 153 A, 153 B, 292, 293, 295 and 298 of the same Code which may be cited against you.

This is the legal system of a civilised society. We respect each other's religious beliefs. We do not intentionally outrage the religious feelings of others or insult their religion or ridicule the personalities to whom we are emotionally attached or mock our religious susceptibility. I would like to request the liberals on your side—the knights of freedom arrayed behind you in their shining armour—to launch a crusade to have the laws repealed before rushing to defend you, including the Customs Act under which our government banned the entry of your obnoxious product.

And take my word for it, Article 19 of the Constitution of India cannot come to your rescue either, because 'freedom of speech and expression' is subject to 'reasonable restriction' in the interest of, interalia, 'public order, decency or morality or in relation to a defamation, or incitement to an offence.' Incidentally, only citizens and not aliens can invoke Article 19. In any case, freedom to create is not the licence to abuse.

To sum up, your 'magnum opus' is objectionable on three grounds: it is a crime against human decency; it is an insult to Islam; it is an offence under the Indian law.

And tell your British champions and advisors that India shall not permit 'literary colonialism' nor what may be called religious pornography. Not even in the name of freedom and democracy, not even under the deafening and superb orchestration of your liberal band.

And also tell them not to have sleepless nights over our image abroad. Our image is not so fragile as not to survive this ban nor founded on the acceptance of the mores of your permissive society, but on what we can do as a nation to give a better life, a life of

dignity, to our people and how we can live with each other in peace, mutual respect and harmony.   (*Times of India*, 13 Oct. 1988)
Ellipses in this article are the author's own.

The Honourable Prime Minister,
C/o The Prime Minister's Secretariat,   Bombay.
South Block, New Delhi.   20th October 1988.

Dear Mr. Prime Minister,

We do not wish to add to the already considerable body of correspondence about the ban on Mr. Salman Rushdie's novel *The Satanic Verses*. But it is with deep disappointment that we learn that, without having read the book, you are not prepared to lift the proscription.

It has already been pointed out by a number of people that the ban was ill conceived and hastily executed, a sop offered to a handful of people, who themselves have not read the book. There has been considered opposition to the ban and we expected you to take note of it. Instead you have not only reiterated that you will not lift the ban but have hinted at possible forthcoming checks and controls on publishers.

Mr. Rushdie is alleged to have insulted Islam. It may be pointed out that Sufi poets like Rumi and Omar Khayyam, when their sect was ostracised in Persia, wrote of religion in a very veiled way, comparing God to an innkeeper and talking much of houris and wine. Mr. Rushdie is not, so far as we know, a Sufi, but he employs a 'host of fiery fancies' to build up a fantasy world of the conflict between good and evil. We repeat, a fantasy. Why should a fantasy hurt the feelings of any community? There are many Christians in the world. In a recent film, *The Last Temptation of Christ* [a film by Martin Scorcese that provoked controversy in Christian circles and demonstrations in front of cinemas around the world because of the way Christ is portrayed in the film], Jesus is depicted as dreaming of making love to Mary Magdalene. This film has not yet been banned in a Christian country. But it has been in India.

Many books that have been proscribed on publication, for one reason or other, have become modern classics: *Ulysses, Lady Chatterley's Lover, Dr. Zhivago* and the works of Solzhenitsyn. India is a secular democracy. We are not saying that *The Satanic Verses* will necessarily become a modern classic, but it is certainly a valuable work of literature. As such, it is neither secular nor democratic to deny the bulk of the literate population the opportunity to read this book. The members of the community it is supposed to offend should surely have the right to read it or not, as they choose, of their own free will.

Yours faithfully,

DON MORAES (*writer*)

ADIL JUSSAWALLA (*editor/publisher*)

A list of nineteen other signatories was appended.

Blackmail works

Islamic sentiment, whatever that is and wherever that is, is very hurt these days in our country. As if to bring some relief to it the Nobel Prize for Literature has gone to the Egyptian writer Mahfouz this year. We have been hoping to read something about him in our papers. As of the day of writing, apart from a line or two by the Nobel Prize Committee and a small file picture, we have not seen anything on or of Mahfouz. There must be at least twenty university departments of Arabic language and literature in our country. The national press hasn't yet found anyone to write on him. 'Islamic' sentiment here activates itself well when it is hurt but does not seem particularly excited that a writer in Arabic, the language of the prophet, has got the Nobel Prize. Fundamentalism and obscurantism have always gone with a certain illiteracy. . . .

Had Mahfouz been an European writer writing in some obscure European language, our press and our literary pundits would not have any problems in providing at least a sketch of his achievements. Unfortunately Mahfouz writes in an Asian language. He is not only a third world author but writes in a third world language. Two major literary events—and look at the contrast in their treatment. No one will read Mahfouz. A tiny section of our English-knowing elite will plod through Rushdie's massive novel if they are able to get hold of a copy. It won't be difficult either. Before long a copy would be available in one or the other of our major cities. There are some benefits of the famous Indian inefficiency. Even then apart from the chapter entitled 'Mahound' (which talks of the prophet) nothing else will probably get read. Syed Shahabuddin and Khurshid Alam Khan have achieved precisely what they did not mean to. They would have forced a small minority of the English-reading public which in turn is a minority itself, to read 'the blasphemy'. . . .

Rajiv Gandhi has made a laughing stock of himself for precisely this reason. He has not even bothered to consider the implications of the fact that Pakistan banned the Rushdie volume after India had done it. The whole issue of what is or is not there in the book is irrelevant. The finance ministry put it quite correctly (although Rushdie has expressed shock at that in his open letter to the prime minister) that the ban has nothing to do with the literary or artistic merit of the work. Indeed, that is so. The ban is a political decision the implications of which are so beyond what everyone is talking about. We found a letter carried by the national press signed by some writers and some radicals supporting the ban. They might as well keep a standard draft ready. For every other month now somebody or other is going to be hurt. Syed Shahabuddin's journal had carried an article by V. T. Rajshekhar on Hinduism, which if only Shahabuddin had been a Hindu would have angered him. The article was foolish in many ways. Why should V. T. Rajshekhar not say what he honestly felt was what I had thought. But these eminent writers and radicals are pursuing a line of argument which is shortsighted, to say the least.

The ban on Rushdie's book may or may not be lifted. It certainly will not be until the elections are through. What is amazing is the unscrupulous ways in which human lives are being treated as a useful argument in third world debates. What Shahabuddin has demonstrated (Rajiv Gandhi has merely capitulated, we must remember, the credit or lack of it goes entirely to Shahabuddin) is the efficacy of a threat strategy. If you don't do this or that I shall see to it that a few hundred or thousand people would be killed. . . .

In one sense the ban on an English book does not mean very much in India. A book priced at £12.95 and running into 547 pages in good English is not likely to be very avidly or widely read in India. A reflection of this is to be seen in vernacular journalism. There the ban has been portrayed as yet another concession to the Muslims. Nobody has even made the customary concession that Rushdie may be a good writer after all. Like the ministry of finance they will have nothing to do with the literary and artistic merit of the work. They are interested in projecting that by banning an English language volume the poor, starving Muslims of India are being pampered. Their poverty and starvation then become a non-issue. Shahabuddin and Khurshid Alam Khan, very much like the Hindu elite in India, would like Muslims to be busy breaking each others' or Hindus' heads over what an India-born writer might have written in a language which nobody understands here anyway. Quite proportionately to the spread of English education, English is declining in our country.

There is also the other factor. Shahabuddin and Rajiv Gandhi are typical colonials in their attitudes. What London might think of us coloured people is never absent from their thought. If it were an Indian writing in Argentina or somewhere the neo-Brahmins would not have been worried. They are now because they don't like the possibility that a white man may not like Islam. Shahabuddin cannot take it. Can you blame him?

(from *Economic and Political Weekly*, India, 22 Oct. 1988)

The Satanic Verses was launched with a publishers' party [on 26 Sept. 1988]. The novel had been short-listed for the Booker Prize and Viking, the publishers, were hoping for extensive press coverage. . . . Amid the euphoria the publishers should probably have paid more attention to a letter received from Harley Street dentist Hesham El Essawi, chairman of the Islamic Society for the Promotion of Religious Tolerance. After having read Rushdie's novel, he wrote on 2 October to say that he regarded it as an insult to Islam.

'I would like to invite you to take some kind of corrective stand before the monster that you have so heedlessly created grows, as it will do worldwide, into something uncontrollable.'

(from *Observer*, London, 19 Feb. 1989.)

Aslam Ejaz, of the Islamic Foundation in Madras, [had] already written to Faiyazuddin Ahmad, a friend in Leicester, telling him about the impending ban in India. A similar campaign, wrote Ejaz, should be mounted in Britain, which still remained largely oblivious to the blasphemous nature of the book.

Ahmad, who came to Britain from India five years ago, is public relations director of the Islamic Foundation in Leicester. His actions, as much as anything, were to spark the row in Britain.

He sent out a secretary to buy the novel for £12.95 at a local bookshop. The offending passages were photocopied and immediately sent on October 3 to the dozen or so leading Islamic organisations in Britain. Four days later copies were despatched to the 45 embassies in Britain of the member countries of the Organisation of Islamic Conference (OIC), including Iran.

Ahmad then flew to the Saudi Arabian headquarters of the OIC in Jeddah and canvassed the leadership. As a result, telexes were sent to all member countries calling for a ban. . . .

Back in London, one set of photostat copies arrived at the offices of Dr Syed Pasha, secretary of the Union of Muslim Organisations, an umbrella organisation for Islamic groups in Britain.

Pasha, sensing a serious problem for Britain's Muslim community, summoned the union's 19 council members to a crisis meeting on October 15. One of those present was Sher Azam, a representative from Bradford, whose 50,000 Muslims have since become the centre of protest in Britain against the book.

It was decided to start a campaign to get the novel banned. Pasha wrote to Penguin on October 20 but got no reply. At the same time he asked Margaret Thatcher to prosecute Rushdie and Penguin under the Public Order Act (1986) and the Race Relations Act (1976).

Pasha's letter to the Prime Minister set the tone for the Muslim assault on Rushdie: 'Never have we encountered such a ferocious and savage attack on our Holy Prophet, using abominably foul language,' he wrote. He added that 'the Muslim community is shocked and seething with indignation.'

The response from the Prime Minister on November 11 was detailed. Thatcher made it clear that 'there are no grounds in which the government would consider banning' the book. 'It is an essential part of our democratic system that people who act within the law should be able to express their opinions freely.'

Thatcher's only concession was to refer the matter to Sir Patrick Mayhew, the attorney-general, who decided the book constituted no criminal offence. But Pasha was not prepared to give up. He wrote to Lord Mackay, the Lord Chancellor, and the Home Office, demanding a ban. The responses were all negative. The Home Office said no change in the law of blasphemy was contemplated.

The early complaints went unheeded. Groups of offended Muslims met to decide how to proceed. One idea was to have the book prosecuted; a top London firm of solicitors, Kingsley Napley, were consulted, but advised that the law applied only to Christianity.

(from *Sunday Times*, London, 19 Feb. 1989)

Britain's 1,500,000 Moslems are being urged to boycott Salman Rushdie's new novel, *Satanic Verses*, by community and religious leaders who claim it is blasphemous.

Their action echoes that of Moslem leaders in India, who won a ban last week on the ground that the book, which has been short-listed for the Booker Prize, is offensive to the prophet Mohammed.

Dr Zaki Badawi, principal of the Moslem College and chairman of the Imams and Mosques Council, said yesterday: 'I would compare this with the film, *The Last Temptation of Christ*. We are all very unhappy about the book. It is an outrageous attack. He mocks our religion in many respects.'

Dr Badawi said he had written to all 382 mosques in Britain to inform them of his views and those of the council.

'There is no censorship in this country, but we have advised them of our views and, of course, we would hope that they don't buy it.'

Dr Badawi, who has read Mr Rushdie's book, continued: 'At one time, we were thinking of commissioning a play about Islam, perhaps looking at the dilemma of Moslems in Britain, and I had thought of asking him to write it, but I am afraid we can't do that now.'

Dr Syed Pasha, general-secretary of the Union of Muslim Organisations, said he intended writing to booksellers, asking them to withdraw the book from sale. He was considering an approach to Sir Patrick Mayhew, Attorney-General, to consider prosecution under race relations laws. . . .

(*Sunday Telegraph*, London, 9 Oct. 1988)

U.K. ACTION COMMITTEE ON ISLAMIC AFFAIRS
Representing: The Council of Mosques, the UK Islamic Mission, the Union of Muslim Organisations, the Islamic Foundation, The Islamic Organization for Media Monitoring, Jamiatul Ulema UK, the Union of Muslim Scholars of the London Central Mosque, Dar Uloom UK, Ahl Al Hadees.

28 October 1988

Dear Brother in Islam,

As salam alaykum wa rahmatullah wa barakatuh.

We hope that by now you have certainly heard about the recently published blasphemous and filthily abusive novel, *Satanic Verses*, by Salman Rushdie (published by Viking, a subsidiary of Penguin).

This work, thinly disguised as a piece of literature, not only grossly distorts Islamic history in general, but also portrays in the worst possible colours the very characters of the Prophet Ibrahim and the Prophet Mohamed (peace be upon them). It also disfigures the characters of the Prophet's Companions (Bilal, Salman Farsi, Hamza, Abu Sufyan, Hind, Khalid and several others) and the Prophet's holy wives and describes the Islamic creed and rituals in the most foul language.

This is the most offensive, filthy and abusive book ever written by any hostile enemy of Islam and deserves to be condemned in the strongest possible way. Various Muslim organisations and individuals have already shown their anger and protested to the publisher for publishing this Satanic book. Recently an Action Committee has been formed in London to stand against this sacrilege in a united and responsible way. It was not possible to invite all organisations and mosques at a very short notice especially those who are outside London. May we therefore request you to kindly form your local action committee comprising as many organisations as possible and demand at least three things:

1) To immediately withdraw and pulp all copies of the above mentioned title as well as to undertake not to allow to be published any future editions of this sacrilege.

2) To tender an unqualified public apology to the world Muslim community for the enormous injury to the feelings and sensibilities of the Muslim Community;

3) To pay adequate damages to an agreed Islamic charity in Britain.

Please also launch a signature campaign through the mosques and organise telephone calls to the publishers to register your protest demanding the above mentioned three things. Please liaise with the Action Committee in London and keep us informed of your action. We are contacting the Muslim Ambassadors to seek their help in blacklisting Penguin Books and banning its publication in Muslim countries.

We are also exploring to take all possible legal action. We will insha'Allah, keep you informed of all developments. Please do try to approach your local M.P.'s and police chiefs and tell them that the publication of this book has angered and outraged Muslims enormously and they should take up the matter with Scotland Yard to prosecute the publisher/author under criminal law, i.e. Public Order Act or Race Relations Act.

If you need any help or information, please do not hesitate to let us know. May Allah reward you for your efforts and give us *tawfiq* to face this challenge with courage and fortitude.

Yours in Islam,
DR. MUGHRAM AL-GHAMDI
Convenor
Action Committee.

Publishing sacrilege is not acceptable

M. H. FARUQI

... The Muslim community in Britain—and so would be others as information reaches them in the course of time—is shocked and outraged beyond any describable measure by the unprecedented enormity of this sacrilege and by the fact that a so far respectable publisher, Penguin, has been insensitive enough to lend its name in this extreme profanity.

Muslim organisations in Britain are, therefore, asking Penguin:

One—To withdraw and pulp all the copies of *The Satanic Verses* and to undertake not to reprint it in the future.

Two—To offer unqualified public apology to the World Muslim community.

Three—To pay damages equal to the returns received from the copies already sold in Britain and abroad.

Failing which they are asking Muslim authorities to freeze all Penguin and Viking business in their jurisdictions and to exempt from copyright law such titles as may be needed for educational purposes. The book should be banned in any case, but banning is meaningless unless it is accompanied by deterrent measures.

These demands have been supported by the Secretary General of the 46-nation Organisation of the Islamic Conference (OIC), Syed Sharifuddin Piozada, who has called upon member states to 'take strong measures to ensure that this book is withdrawn from circulation by its publisher immediately and its copies are destroyed' and 'the blasphemous book and its author must be banned from entry into all Islamic countries'.

Perhaps it would be more salutary if the author is allowed to enter into Islamic jurisdiction and prosecuted under relevant law.

Penguin have so far tried to maintain masterly indifference, telling people writing to them that they 'don't recognise Salman Rushdie's novel in your description', that it has 'been widely praised by critics' and that 'we have no intention of withdrawing the book.'

Surely they are counting on the legal security of the British law against blasphemy which applies only to Christianity. Probably they are hoping that few Muslim authorities would have the will or the courage to take on this powerful publishing house and PR network. Definitely they do not seem to be willing to think much of the deeply hurt feelings within the Muslim community.

The demands listed are neither unreasonable, nor unattainable. But it is time now for the Ummah to stand up for the honour and dignity of its Faith, of its Beloved Messenger of God (peace and blessings of God be upon him) and of his family and his companions (may God be pleased with them all). If they do not, then they should be prepared to receive more Rushdies and more Penguins.

We have never ever made an editorial appeal like this, but we are asking readers to pursue these demands both with the publishers and Muslim authorities through telegrams, letters, telephones, personal representations and through all civilised and legitimate means. But please leave Mr Salman Rushdie all to himself and to his charmed circle of 'literary critics'. We have to say this because we also sense a milling anger about the outrage committed by him. . . .

(from *Impact International*, London, 28 Oct.–10 Nov. 1988)

The same issue of Impact *contained the original list of purportedly blasphemous passages from* The Satanic Verses.

Moslems block 'blasphemous' Rushdie's trip to South Africa

STEPHEN ROBINSON
In Johannesburg

An invitation to Salman Rushdie, the Booker prize-winning novelist, to visit South Africa to speak out against censorship was withdrawn yesterday after Moslem extremists threatened him and the organisers with a 'holy war' in protest at his latest 'blasphemous' book.

The organisation which has been forced to gag Mr Rushdie is the *Weekly Mail*, the stridently anti-apartheid Johannesburg newspaper which on Tuesday was itself closed down for four weeks by government decree.

Mr Rushdie had been due to make the keynote speech on apartheid and censorship this weekend at a book fair organised by the paper. He was packing for last night's London-to-Johannesburg flight when told the news.

The paper he was due to deliver was entitled 'Wherever they burn books, they also burn people'.

Mr Rushdie's latest novel, *The Satanic Verses*, was shortlisted for this year's Booker prize, but has been condemned by Moslems around the world as blasphemous and an affront to their religion.

The book has already been banned in several countries, including India and Saudi Arabia.

The South African government also banned the book with unprecedented haste this week after Moslem groups followed up the international protests and lobbied the censorship board.

Some Islamic fundamentalist groups threatened a 'holy war' against the *Weekly Mail* should Mr Rushdie set foot in South Africa.

Several bomb threats were received at the paper's editorial offices in Johannesburg, as well as threats against Mr Rushdie himself.

His visit, which was arranged before his latest novel was published, fell victim to the murderous complexity of Left-wing South African politics.

Despite pleas from respected radical politicians, the Moslem fundamentalists, usually at the forefront of the struggle against apartheid and the erosion of free speech, refused to budge from their demands that the visit must be cancelled.

A large proportion of the *Weekly Mail*'s staff is Jewish, and, according to some journalists, there have been unpleasant overtones of anti-Semitism in several of the Moslem groups representations.

Mr Anton Harber, co-editor of the *Weekly Mail*, said the invitation had been withdrawn only because Mr Rushdie's physical safety could not be guaranteed.

The invitation was originally backed by the Congress of South African Writers, a literary group of radical authors sympathetic to the restricted United Democratic Front.

They reluctantly advised the *Weekly Mail* to withdraw the invitation yesterday afternoon.

Miss Nadine Gordimer, patron of the congress, said the organisation, which stood strongly against censorship and in favour of freedom of speech, was 'naturally very distressed to have to go back on this principle'.

She said: 'We have suffered all sorts of harassment and insulting accusations from extremists in the Moslem community.

'We were ready and willing to compromise with them, offered them a right to present their point of view at the meetings, but they were not prepared to be reasonable.'

(*Daily Telegraph*, London, 3 Nov. 1988)

Mr Rushdie said in a statement through Viking, his publishers, that he was sad not to be going because his visit was intended as an act of solidarity against apartheid.

From South Africa's banning order

Undesirable within the meaning of section 47(2)(b) of the Publications Act, 1974.

Reasons of ad hoc Committee of Publications for this decision:

After a thorough investigation into the matter the committee incorporating the experts report: 'This work, thinly disguised as a piece of literature, not only grossly distorts the Islamic history in general, but also portrays in the worst possible colours the very characters of the Prophet Ibrahim and the Prophet Muhammad (Peace be upon them).

'It may however be clarified that the Prophet Muhammed (Peace be upon him) is referred to in this novel as Mahound—a misnomer used about him. The work also disfigures the characters of the Prophet's companions (Bilal, Salman, Farsi, Hamza, Abie Sufyan, Hind, Khalid and several others—May Allah be pleased with them) and the Prophet's holy wives, and describes the Islamic creed and rituals in the most foul language.

'Based on the myth of the interpolation of the so-called 'Satanic Verses' into the Quran this novel stands out as the grossest sacrilege of all that is sacred for the Muslim . . .

'In view of the sinister nature of the novel and the irreparable damage it would inflict on the image of Islam the committee recommend that this publication be banned. The obscene language used in the novel for the most respected institutions and characters is disgusting not only to Muslims but to any reader who holds clear values of decency and culture . . .

'In reaching its decision the committee has taken due consideration of the literary merit of the publication and of the author's previously acclaimed works, literary distinctions, etc. It is however felt that these considerations do not outweigh the obvious offence which his latest work is likely to give to the strongly protesting Muslim community in South Africa who clearly regard the book as offensive to their religious convictions or feelings and likely to bring them as a section of the inhabitants of the Republic into ridicule or contempt, a point of view with which the Committee concurs.'

Salman Rushdie, whose prize-winning work, *The Satanic Verses*, has already been declared blasphemous in his native India, faces the prospect of a ban and legal proceedings throughout the Islamic world.

A ruling by Cairo's Al-Azhar, the most venerated Islamic institute, was delivered yesterday by the Grand Sheikh of Al-Azhar, Gad el-Haq Ali Gad el-Haq.

He called on all Islamic organizations based in Britain to join in taking legal steps to prevent continuing distribution there.

The sheikh, one of the most influential Muslim leaders, described the novel as containing 'lies and figments of the imagination' about Islam which were passed off as facts.

He demanded that the 46 nation Islamic Conference Organization should take concerted action against what he described as 'a distortion of Islamic history'.

The 1,000 year-old Al-Azhar institute, a combined mosque and university, is considered the seat of Islamic theology.

The strength of its ruling against *The Satanic Verses*, which is named after the verses the prophet removed from the Koran on the grounds that they were inspired by the Devil, will ensure that heavy international pressure is now aimed against the book.

(from *Times*, London, 22 Nov. 1988)

. . . After several weeks of behind-the-scenes activity, it seemed to the increasingly frustrated Muslim leaders that they had still failed to get their message across. A solicitor in the North of England suggested that if what they really wanted was publicity, they could always try burning the book in public; there was, he pointed out, no law against that.

(from *Observer*, London, 19 Feb. 1989)

Furious Muslims to stage mass protest

Thousands of angry Bolton Muslims will stage a protest march against a book 'insulting' Mohammed.

The furious Islamic community is calling on people of other religions to support the fight to stop the sale of Salman Rushdie's *Satanic Verses* in the town.

(from *Bolton Evening News*, 1 Dec. 1988)

In the event more than 7,000 people attended this 'peaceful' demonstration and burned copies of The Satanic Verses. *But the national press ignored the demonstration.*

A Bradford mosque representing 9,000 Muslims has joined the call to ban a novel which is claimed makes 'false and offensive accusations' against their faith Islam. . . .

But the Jamiyat Tabligh Ul-Islam mosque has written to Margaret Thatcher and Bradford West MP Max Madden urging them to ban the book published by Viking Press under Penguin.

Assistant secretary of the mosque, Mohammed Siddique said 'The book contains 547 pages and there is hardly a single page which does not reflect insult.' . . .

The Bradford Council for Mosques is holding an emergency meeting to discuss response to *Satanic Verses* at the Pakistan Community Centre tonight at 7.30pm.

(from *Bradford Telegraph & Argus*, 6 Dec. 1988)

Fury as book is set ablaze

STEVEN TEALE

More than 1,000 angry Muslims rallied in Bradford city centre today to protest about a novel which they claim attacks their faith.

They cheered and chanted as a copy of the book, *The Satanic Verses*, by Salman Rushdie, was burned outside police headquarters in the Tyrls.

Bradford councillor Mohammad Ajeeb told the crowd: 'This gathering today is an indication of the extreme anger which the Muslim community feels about the book.

'I am pleased that this demonstration is taking place in a peaceful manner because Islam is peace.'

He said he would try to persuade his fellow councillors to ban the book from Bradford libraries.

Many of the crowd waved banners and placards proclaiming 'Ban Satanic Verses', 'Rushdie Eat Your Words' and 'Rushdie Stinks'.

More than 20 police were present, but the meeting was marshalled by dozens of Muslim officials.

Sher Azam, president of the Bradford Council of Mosques, said they object to the book because it abuses Islam and is based on distorted facts about their faith.

He said, 'There are 65,000 Muslims in Bradford and they are angry and upset about the book. There is no doubt in our minds that it should be banned.'   (*Bradford Telegraph & Argus*, 14 Jan. 1989)

This time the national press did respond. The following two weeks were filled with commentary and debate.

Dangers of a Muslim campaign

If members of Britain's community of some two million Muslims do not want to read Salman Rushdie's novel *The Satanic Verses*, all they have to do is abstain from buying it or taking it out of the local library. They should not seek to impose their feelings about its contents—or, more probably, what they have been told about them—on the rather larger non-Islamic part of the population. Their campaign to have the book banned, on the grounds that it blasphemes Islam, led to a demonstration over the weekend in Bradford in which, following the example of the Inquisition and Hitler's National Socialists, a large crowd of Muslims burnt some copies of the book.

W H Smith, the booksellers, cannot be blamed for following police advice and temporarily withdrawing copies from display in their Bradford shop to avert serious danger to their staff and damage to their premises from the demonstrators. Having come under such pressure, they will have to be all the more careful to do nothing further which might be seen to be a surrender to it.

The Islamic campaign would be more understandable if Rushdie's novel were in any way trashy. But its literary merits are not in doubt. Shortly after coming near to winning this year's Booker Prize (which was awarded to Rushdie's *Midnight's Children* in 1981), it won this year's Whitbread literary prize, worth £20,000. It is hardly likely that the worthy and liberal-minded *literati* who sat on the panels awarding these prizes would have thought so highly of a book which was overtly blasphemous, even of another faith. *The Satanic Verses* was written as a moral parable, and that is how they interpreted it.

It may indeed be thought that Muslims are furnishing material for further moral parables about Islam by attacking Rushdie's fictional creation, not only throughout the Islamic world—it has been banned in the author's native India—but in Britain. Their crusade not just against the book but against Rushdie personally does them no credit.

The Muslim minority has contributed much to the nation's commerce and entrepreneurial spirit. Its members have been notably law-abiding, and their devotion to family values, hard work and personal integrity are rightly admired. It is important that their spiritual values should be respected, and that they should be spared from racial discrimination in all its forms.

They in turn, however, must not seek to impose their values either on their fellow Britons of other faiths or on the majority who acknowledge no faith at all. Their leaders should examine the implications of their war against the Rushdie novel. Do they really feel this book poses a serious threat to their followers? Is the Islamic faith not strong enough to withstand some controversial fictional analysis? Is their campaign not doubly counterproductive, first, in giving the book so much publicity, and second, in reminding Britons of the intolerant face which Islam has all too often shown abroad? There are enough pressures for censorship in Britain today without religious minorities endeavouring to suppress books which they find controversial or distasteful.   (*Independent*, London, 16 Jan. 1989)

FROM MR IBRAHIM B. HEWITT

Sir, Surely if, as your leader 'Islamic intolerance' (January 17), suggests, this country is a 'free democracy' the Muslims of Bradford have every right to demonstrate their displeasure over Salman Rushdie's book, *The Satanic Verses*, in whatever manner they see fit within the bounds of the law.

Since the demonstration last Saturday was obviously well publicised and, presumably, had police permission to proceed, why do you say that such a democratic show of feeling is not acceptable in a 'free democracy'?

If it is acceptable for one person to injure the feelings of millions by the use of his democratic rights of free speech and thought, then it must be equally acceptable for those so injured to voice their feelings.

As long as no laws are broken, how, in a 'free democracy', can you suggest otherwise without making a mockery of the supposed democracy in the first place? If laws were broken, why weren't the 'offenders' duly arrested?

The response of the media to this demonstration shows that there is only a pretence of democracy for all these days; it is very much a case of one set of standards for 'us' and another for 'them'. Your leader headline is an example of this.

> Yours faithfully,
> IBRAHIM B. HEWITT,
> The Islamic Organisation for Media Monitoring,
> 3 Furlong Road, N7.

(*Times*, London, 20 Jan. 1989)

AZIZ AL-AZMEH

Strange events are unfolding in Britain and elsewhere, unfortunately too late to have been the occasion for tragi-comic passages in Salman Rushdie's *The Satanic Verses*. Not only have several copies of the novel been publicly burnt in Bradford, doubtless in a rehearsal of Rushdie's fate in the hereafter, but Rushdie and his publishers have received thousands of letters from Muslim organisations and individuals, protesting against the publication of a book they consider blasphemous and insulting, and demanding its withdrawal from circulation, its reduction to pulp, and payment of 'appropriate damages'.

The Prime Minister, the Home Secretary, other politicians and many writers in Britain and abroad have been urged to intervene to ban the book. Michael Foot was castigated for his praise of it and an apology was demanded; he was also reported to the leader of the Labour Party for his misdemeanour. *The Satanic Verses* is banned in India, Pakistan, Malaysia, South Africa, Egypt and, of course, Saudi Arabia and local satellites. And while the book's critics have been shrill, though some affected a tranquil tone, some of the most eloquent declared they had not read it, claiming it to be filthy and thoroughly unworthy.

Even more improbable, protesters in the name of Islam, which insists on the sheer humanity of Christ, have joined forces with groups which protested against just this humanisation in Scorsese's *Last Temptation of Christ*. A symbiosis is also developing between sections of Britain's Muslims and extreme right-wing caucuses within the Tory party over social and moral issues. The fringes of the last Conservative Party conference were lobbied for (among other matters) the amendment of the blasphemy law to cover all religions.

Although some of this campaigning was waged by a body calling itself the Islamic Society for the Promotion of Religious Tolerance, author, publisher and booksellers alike have been threatened with murder, fire and untold destruction. So far only WH Smith have reacted, by deciding to remove the book from sale, but it is a moot point whether the company's resolve on matters of principle would have been more robust had the book been selling recently at a greater rate than their executives claim.

What is certain is that Muslim organisations in Britain, India, South Africa and elsewhere have succeeded in exerting pressure, arrogating to themselves the right to ban from the public domain ideas at variance with their own. They are prepared to allow only authorised discourse on certain topics over which they claim absolute proprietorship.

One such topic is early Islamic history, which Rushdie treats without much reverence, indeed, as fantasy, but with a decidedly realistic historical imagination. Rushdie's Islamic critics keep entirely out of sight the novelist's play with the literary and historical themes of cultural uprootedness, alienation, mutations, comfort and discomfort, focusing only on his putative treatment of Muhammad and Abraham.

All inquisitional procedures start with tearing specific statements out of context, and subjecting their rectitude to an examination which assumes that the inquisitional body has the final authority over these particular truths. And so it was with the Islamist reaction to *The Satanic Verses*. But far from being a throwback to earlier Islamic procedure, the methods used are borrowed from other minority groups who try to excise from the public domain ideas distinct from their own dearly held attitudes about the most profound issues of humanity, for both self-serving and other reasons. The Secretary-General of the Islamic Schools Trust underlined this when he compared Islamic protests against *The Satanic Verses* to the disgraceful campaign against Jim Allen's play *Perdition*, withdrawn after zionist pressure claiming the right to be the sole authorising body on Jewish history.

Just as any criticism of zionism or Israel can be made to look 'anti-semitic', so any non-authorised treatment of Islamic matters can be castigated as anti-Islamic.

At issue therefore are political questions of authority. What is at issue is who represents Muslims and who speaks in their name on a range of questions, including separatist sectarian education, intermarriage, ghettoes in which increasingly odd manners of dress and norms of behaviour are observed and affiliation to archaic politics in Pakistan, India and Saudi Arabia.

The claim to represent Muslims is in fact spurious. Few Muslims—even practising ones—are Islamists in cultural and political terms, although in Britain, as elsewhere, few are willing to contest the issue with cantankerous activists backed by deep (well-endowed) coffers. In fact this kind of political and cultural zealotry is very new in Muslim history, which only emerged from an insignificant subculture when its patrons, from some of the most archaic groups in the Muslim world, became spectacularly rich after the oil boom.

In Britain, Islamic organisations such as the Islamic Cultural Centre, the Islamic Council, the Union of Muslim Organisations in the UK and Eire, and the United Kingdom Action Committee on Islamic Affairs, have all managed an elaborate campaign against *The Satanic Verses* based on lobbying, petitions from mosques all over the country, and the Bradford *auto da fé*. The campaign's crescendo will be a demonstration in London on 28 January.

Yet this mass mobilisation is not attributable solely to money from Saudi Arabia and elsewhere; nor even to the officers of these organisations justifying their salaries. Nor can it be put down entirely to propitious conditions in Britain, where Muslim separatism is encouraged and aided by opponents of multi-culturalism such as the Parental Alliance for Choice in Education and the likes of Ray Honeyford and others.

Muslim organisations have a special appeal to Muslims in Britain. Speaking in terms of cultural enlightenment is all very well for those Muslims moving in sophisticated and relatively enlightened circles. But the majority of Muslim folk, first welcomed in Britain with the affability and warmth for which Albion is universally famed, have been reduced to hard times in inner metropolitan areas. They have been crushed by misery, uprootedness and disorientation, distracted by foul weather, confronted by both a hostile society and state, and forced to live in cramped and strangely organised houses.

Instead of the life they dreamed of in Britain, they find themselves regretting their migration. They are caught up in a civil society with its own polemic distinctions, including closed shops, lodges and clubs, both highbrow on Pall Mall and lowbrow at the Arsenal, all with their own emblematic ties, rings and scarves.

It is not surprising that they react by giving as good as they get. Under these conditions, religion aids the construction of trenches of collective help and self-defence, against the state, the educational system, and poverty. Islamic organisations provide an administrative and political means for the formation of these 'ghettoes' impervious to cultural relativism and multi-culturalism (though not to capitalism). But in the long run it can only serve to sustain a lowly position for Muslims in a labour market increasingly segmented and stratified, ethnically and regionally. It is paradoxical therefore that Muslim organisations here should have tried to invoke the Race Relations and Public Order Acts against *The Satanic Verses*. They want to excise from the body of Islamics anyone they believe is inimical to the claims by Muslim organisations to represent all Muslims. Rushdie in *The Satanic Verses* exposes this unfounded claim. In fact Muslims are as varied, multifarious, and discordant a body as any other.

In other countries, similar techniques of lobbying and clamour for the exclusive right to speak are adopted by Muslim organisations, though the overall score is somewhat different. In South Africa, intense political pressure, with evocations of the lynchmob, compelled the Congress of South African Writers to withdraw support for an invitation to Rushdie to speak against apartheid and censorship. Few writers, with the notable exception of Nadine Gordimer, spoke up for Rushdie.

In many third world countries, *The Satanic Verses* is characterised as the work of a self-hater eager to ingratiate himself with the coloniser simply because the novel challenges the most conservative instincts of those groups claiming Muslim 'nativism'. Such nativism is really a mirror image of Afrikaanerdom in South Africa: fully in keeping with a theory of separate development—*apartheid*—expressed in culturalist and religious tones. It also parallels, for instance, Jomo Kenyatta's pronouncement that infibulation was a precious component of Kenya's national heritage, and a bulwark against colonialism. In this way, many third world despotisms make the repression of colonial powers seem a very benign regime indeed!

In India, the other major arena where the controversy over *The Satanic Verses* is being fought, it is evident that the ban was prompted by electoral calculations by Rajiv Gandhi's ruling Congress Party in response to shrill demands led by the opposition politician, Syed Shahabuddin. As in Britain, Islamist Muslim politicians there hinted darkly about uncontrollable mobs if they were not appeased.

The totalitarian control over Islam and Muslims sought by such Islamic organisations is buttressed by a phenomenal supply of funds from Saudi Arabia and other Gulf states. They claim that what is at issue is the authenticity of Islamic ideas, as defined by them, versus the perfidies of a western world intent on emasculating this authenticity. The result is a retrograde social and cultural involution, which excludes universalist political philosophies of social and national emancipation. At the same time, these retrograde groups maintain excellent political and economic relations with this same perfidious west, avidly lapping up even its most trivial cultural products on television screens.

• *Aziz Al-Azmeh is Professor of Islamic Studies at the University of Exeter.*

(*New Statesman & Society*, London, 20 Jan. 1989)

Choice between light and dark

SALMAN RUSHDIE

Muhammad ibn Abdallah, one of the great geniuses of world history, a successful businessman, victorious general and sophisticated statesman as well as a prophet, insisted through his life on his simple humanity. There are no contemporary portraits of him because he feared that, if any were made, people would worship the portraits. He was only the messenger; it was the message that should be revered.

As to the revelation itself, it caused Muhammad considerable anguish. Sometimes he heard voices; sometimes he saw visions; sometimes, he said, the words were found in his inmost heart, and at times their production caused him acute physical pain. When the revelations began he feared for his sanity and only after reassurances from his wife and friends did he accept that he was the recipient of the divine gift of the Word.

The religion which Muhammad established differs from Christianity in several important respects: the Prophet is not granted divine status, but the text is. It's worth pointing out, too, that Islam requires neither a collective act of worship nor an intercessionary caste of priests. The faithful communicate directly with their God.

Nowadays, however, a powerful tribe of clerics has taken over Islam. These are the contemporary Thought Police. They have turned Muhammad into a perfect being, his life into a perfect life, his revelation into the unambiguous, clear event it originally was not. Powerful taboos have been erected. One may not discuss Muhammad as if he were human, with human virtues and weaknesses. One may not discuss the growth of Islam as a historical phenomenon, as an ideology born out of its time. These are the taboos against which *The Satanic Verses* has transgressed (these and one other; I also tried to write about the place of woman in Islamic society, and in the Koran). It is for this breach of taboo that the novel is being anathematised, fulminated against and set alight.

Dr Aadam Aziz, the patriarch in my novel *Midnight's Children*, loses his faith and is left with 'a hole inside him, a vacancy in a vital inner chamber'. I, too, possess the same God-shaped hole. Unable to accept the unarguable absolutes of religion, I have tried to fill up the hole with literature. The art of the novel is a thing I cherish as dearly as the bookburners of Bradford value their brand of militant Islam. Literature is where I go to explore the highest and lowest places in human society and in the human spirit, where I hope to find not absolute truth but the truth of the tale, of the imagination and of the heart. So the battle over *The Satanic Verses* is a clash of faiths, in a way. Or, more precisely, it's a clash of languages. As my fictional character 'Salman' says of my fictional prophet 'Mahound', 'It's his Word against mine.'

The Satanic Verses is not, in my view, an anti-religious novel. It is, however, an attempt to write about migration, its stresses and transformations, from the point of view of migrants from the Indian subcontinent to Britain. This is, for me, the saddest irony of all; that after working for five years to give voice and fictional flesh to the immigrant culture of which I am myself a member, I should see my book burned, largely unread, by the people it's about, people who might find some pleasure and much recognition in its pages. I tried to write against stereotypes; the zealot protests serve to confirm, in the western mind, all the worst stereotypes of the Muslim world.

How fragile civilisation is; how easily, how merrily a book burns! Inside my novel, its characters seek to become fully human by facing up to the great facts of love, death and (with or without God) the life of the soul. Outside it, the forces of inhumanity are on the march. 'Battle lines are being drawn up in India today,' one of my characters remarks. 'Secular versus religious, the light versus the dark. Better you choose which side you are on.' Now that the battle has spread to Britain, I can only hope it will not be lost by default. It is time for us to choose.   (from *Observer*, London, 22 Jan. 1989)

*Media coverage, described by a leading Muslim magazine, as 'gra-
tuitous advice, part patronising, part intimidating' (Impact, 27 Jan.
1989), did not soothe the Muslim community. Over the next month
there were an increasing number of demonstrations and book burn-
ings throughout the country, which culminated in a Hyde Park rally
on 28 January.*

More than 8,000 Muslims from all over Britain flocked to march
against Salman Rushdie's book, *The Satanic Verses*, because they
feel it is blasphemous.

Passionate chants of Allah Akbar (God is Great) maintained the
momentum of the rally despite the damp conditions.

Athar Hussain, editor of *Muslim Voice* Newspaper, based in Har-
row, said: 'Rushdie picked a theme that would win the biggest market by being controversial, courting publicity, and thus becoming a
best seller.

'The people who are reacting against it are simply generating
publicity, the book will not affect people who follow Islam.'

However, the Islamic Defence Council has vowed to continue
the fight against the book which it has described as sacrilegious.

A spokesman for the Islamic Council said: 'It is not civilised to
insult the religious sanctities of any people.

'We do not object to anyone writing critically about Islam there
are hundreds of such books in our libraries—but as you see these
Satanic Verses belong to an entirely different genre.'

More than 250 police were on duty at the demonstration with 18
just outside the Iranian Embassy just off Hyde Park.

Ali Mohammed Azhar, a barrister, announced that papers had
been filed with Bow Street magistrates' court as the march moved
off through Kensington, and on to a rally at Shepherds Bush.

He said: 'We believe the book infringes the blasphemy laws. If
we do not succeed here, we will go to the supreme court, the House
of Lords. We are prepared to go all the way to the European Court.
My duty is to see that my faith is protected.'

Small groups broke off to petition Downing Street and Penguin
Books, who publish *The Satanic Verses*.

Objections to the book include Abraham being allegedly called
'the bastard', and Muhammad being given the middle ages name of
'Mahound' meaning 'devil' or 'false prophet.'

The Islamic council is calling for the withdrawal and pulping of all remaining copies of the book, and an unqualified apology to the world Muslim community.

(*Chiswick, Fulham & Hammersmith Recorder*, 8 Feb. 1989)

During the demonstration the following petition was presented to Penguin Books.

Memorandum of Request
From: The Muslim Community in Britain
To: The Owners of Penguin Books Ltd
27 Wrights Lane, London W8 5TZ

Having noted with regret and dismay the attitude of the Penguin Editorial in turning a completely deaf ear to innumerable requests, pleadings and protests from all over the world to withdraw your imprint Viking's most outrageous ever sacrilege, the so-called *Satanic Verses* and to tender unqualified apology, we feel we had no option but to adopt this extraordinary way of delivering this note to you.

We have tried to understand your company spokesmen's oft-repeated explanation that literary critics and reviewers have perceived the book as a major and serious literary work; that it was short-listed for Booker and had won Whitbread Prize; that Muslim perception of the book being blasphemous and sacrilegious was based on 'failure to read in its entirety, what is after all, a work of fiction' and; that to withdraw the novel 'would be wholly inconsistent with our position as a serious publisher who believes in freedom of expression etc.' But, with respect we do not find them relevant except that we too want to believe that Penguin is a 'serious publisher' otherwise we would not have tried to reason with your company.

The issue is plain and simple:

That no individual much less a whole world community can accept to be abused and insulted in the filthy way that this 'novel' work has sought to do; and no 'serious publisher' can take shelter behind the undisputed right of freedom of expression in order to publish such dirty work.

For example:

The book calls Abraham, the revered Prophet of Jews, Christians, Muslims alike, 'the bastard'.

The Blessed Prophet Muhammad is given the Middle Ages' name of 'Mahound' (The word means 'devil' or a 'false Prophet').

—He is a man who 'had no time for scruples'.

—He was 'no angel, you understand . . . !'

—The revelations he received were well-timed to suit him when 'the faithful were disputing'.

—His companions are described as 'bum' and 'scum'.

—The namesakes of his wives are sited in a brothel with all the literary pornography that would go with such a locale.

—The Islamic Holy City of Makkah is a city of Jahilia—of ignorance or darkness.

—The Muslim 'God . . . sounded so much like a businessman' and 'the Islamic Shari'ah was about every damn thing'.

—Sodomy and the missionary position were approved by the archangel'.

It, therefore, mattered little what praises or prizes are lavished on such a work. It is also not obligatory to pocket such outrageous insult because one had not wasted his time (and money) on reading this book 'in its entirety'.

We wish we did not have to repeat it again and again that it is neither honourable nor acceptable to publish insult. We are not objecting to anyone writing critically or irreverently about Islam or Muslims. Hundreds of such works have been published in the past and hundreds more are going to be published in the future.

Islam stands on its own merits and we have no tradition of burning and banning such works.

We, therefore, urge that instead of seeking comfort in the fact that sacrilege against Islam was not indictable under the law of this country, you would please listen to this request of ours and at least

1) Withdraw and pulp all remaining copies of the book and undertake not to publish any future editions or translations of the title.

2) Tender unqualified apology to the world Muslim community, in fact to all those people of faith or no faith who believe in decency of expression, no matter the differences in their beliefs and outlook.

As Muslims we believe in the inborn goodness of human nature and we, therefore, still hope that reason and decency will prevail and we will be able to close this painful chapter. Insha-Allah!

THE ISLAMIC DEFENCE COUNCIL
101 Windsor Road, London E7
Dated 28th January 1989.

In addition to this petition, Penguin Books received threats and 'hate mail' in unprecedented quantity.

Although the affair had already opened up worrying questions about competing freedoms and multi-cultural misunderstandings, it seems quite possible that the immediate concentration on the question might have died down.

The next incidents took place not in the UK at all, but in Pakistan and Kashmir on 12 and 13 February 1989.

Five killed in Pakistan anti-Rushdie protest rally

Islamabad—At least five people were killed and dozens injured yesterday when police opened fire on Muslim fundamentalists protesting against Salman Rushdie's novel, *The Satanic Verses*, who tried to storm the US Information Centre in the centre of the Pakistani capital.

More than 2,000 protesters screaming 'American dogs' and 'God is great' threw stones and bricks and drove away scores of police trying to guard the building. Some police were beaten by the crowd. 'Hang Salman Rushdie,' one man yelled. Police repeatedly fired rifles, semi-automatic weapons and pump action shotguns at the protesters during three hours of fierce clashes.

Some of the protesters broke into the centre, smashing windows and starting a number of small fires. US officials had no immediate word on the extent of the damage. Several demonstrators climbed on top of the two-story building and pulled down the US flag, which was burnt along with effigies representing Rushdie and the United States, as the mob cheered and chanted. 'America and Israel are enemies of Islam,' one banner proclaimed.

(*Independent*, London, 13 Feb. 1989)

The following day another person was killed and over 100 were injured in a similar riot in Kashmir. It seems to have been those deaths that directly provoked the until-now relatively silent Ayatollah Khomeini to issue his fatwa, *which in turn helped to escalate the Rushdie affair into an international issue.*

III

The Khomeini *Fatwa* ~

... The announcement came on Radio Tehran just before the 2 p.m. news [on 14 February, 1989]. It was a 'fatwa' or decree from Ayatollah Khomeini, the revered spiritual leader of Iran's 50 million Shia Muslims.

'In the name of God Almighty,' intoned an announcer. 'There is only one God, to whom we shall all return. I would like to inform all the intrepid Muslims in the world that the author of the book entitled *The Satanic Verses*, which has been compiled, printed and published in opposition to Islam, the Prophet and the Koran, as well as those publishers who were aware of its contents, have been sentenced to death.

'I call on all zealous Muslims to execute them quickly, wherever they find them, so that no one will dare to insult the Islamic sanctions. Whoever is killed on this path will be regarded as a martyr, God willing.

'In addition, anyone who has access to the author of the book, but does not possess the power to execute him, should refer him to the people so that he may be punished for his actions. May God's blessing be on you all. Ruhollah Musavi Khomeini.'

(from *Observer*, London, 19 Feb. 1989)

Iran's Majlis speaker says publication of
***The Satanic Verses* was 'worse than an**
officially declared war'
Tehran home service 1030 gmt 15 Feb 89.
Text of recording of remarks by Hashemi-Rafsanjani at a
session of the Majlis on 15th February.

In the name of God, the Merciful, the Compassionate. The way in which our women and men have (?reacted) to the process of [word indistinct] which the global infidelity has planned for the world of Islam is the right way. They are following specific targets with specific motives in their insult to Islamic sanctities.

It is possible that some rascals and Satanic people existing within our society may mar the mind of the people by making insinuations along the lines of asking what importance a book or a writer, who has done something wrong, has to merit such a sensation, (?measure) or public holiday in society, or to cause demonstrations in the world of Islam. Therefore, this point deserves to be thrashed out. It is necessary to do so because if our nation was exposed to such temptations, it must know that the problem is not that of [words indistinct].

What can be surmised from the events—the events which prompted our great leader, the Imam of the Ummah, to embark on such a spirited confrontation with it and also outraged the deputy leader [Montazeri] the grand ayatollahs, the clerics and people throughout the world—is that such outrage and confrontation are caused because of what goes on out of sight, behind the scenes.

What one can discern through these events is that there has been planning and organisational work aimed at bringing about a very dangerous move—which is worse than an officially declared war. Following the blows they received from Iran after the Islamic revolution, as well as following the might of Islam which they saw in Lebanon and Afghanistan and the dynamism and awareness they saw of Muslims all over the world, they arrived at the conclusion, in their analysis, that all this stems from the holiness which covers everything which is sacred in Islam. This keeps the minds of the Muslims clean and gives dynamism and happiness to the world of Islam.

Materialism and all kinds of political forces failed to break such holiness. So they chose this method of action—choosing a person who seemingly comes from India, apparently is separate from the Western world and who has a misleading name. They begin their work in this fashion. Money had been given to that person, in advance, as royalties. They appointed guards for him, in advance, as they knew what they were going to do. One notes that Zionist publishers are involved and that translations have already been prepared in countries like America and Italy. Such publicity is aimed at preparing the people to buy the book.

All this speaks of an organised and planned effort. It is not an ordinary work of which one might say that, well, many books have been already written, insults to Islam have been frequent, many others have said bad things against God and everything else and that this is the way in history. Yes, this [is] true. But I believe that there has never been such a well planned act the way it is being done now. This is a confrontation to break the sanctity of Islam and all that is sacred in Islam.

Therefore, the importance of the issue merits our great leader—who usually does not involve himself in personal issues—involving himself in force to express his anger. It is always incumbent upon us to obey his orders. We always know that he raises issues related to Islam in a timely manner and that he makes a confrontation in due time.

It is incumbent on the world of Islam to regard this issue seriously so that the enemies of Islam may learn that such a method does not lead them anywhere and also those who lend themselves to be manipulated for such acts by the enemies of Islam may learn that they are involved in dangerous issues.

The logic of Islam is clear. The Koran, from the very early days, instructed Muslims not to befriend those who leave the faith. [Several Arabic words indistinct] This is the logic of the Koran—not to indulge in bad language, in insulting ways in the sacred schools and in anything which is sacred to the nations. The Koran does not indulge in bad language, nor does it accept it, nor does it shrink from opposing insults to the sacred things of other peoples. For us that applies to other religions. If today somebody insults His Holiness Moses, Abraham, or Jesus, then we must stand up against such insults with the same intensity. These are sanctities in which the majority of people believe. You see how the Koran campaigns against accusations inflicted on Her Holiness Mary.

Such a method is an unreasonable one. We expect the world's Christians and Jews—those who do not espouse Zionism—to protest seriously to obstruct such a foul move. The issue is more serious than the mere publication of a book or a novel. . . .

(*BBC Summary of World Broadcasts*, 17 Feb. 1989)

• *The Summary of World Broadcasts is a BBC monitoring service which transcribes broadcast material.*

Commentary on 'Satanic Verses'
Tehran Domestic Service in Persian 0545 GMT 15 Feb 89.

. . . Existing facts show that *The Satanic Verses* was published at the request of British Intelligence services by a hireling of Indian origin who lives in England and is known as Salman Rushdie. After its publication, it was introduced by these very intelligence services as the book of the year in Britain. It should be noted that Salman Rushdie is a member of Britain's Royal Academy of Literature. The republication of this anti-Islamic book is in its last phases in the United States, and reports from Italy indicate that preparations are being made to translate and publish it in Italian.

The hands of the intelligence services of world arrogance can be clearly seen in this. They are trying to start a poisonous and disgraceful propaganda campaign against Islam and the Koran on the basis of an impudent program.

Arrogance has had blows inflicted on it by Islam, and it is greatly terrified by the growth of the Islam-seeking wave throughout the world. However, it wants—by investing in this—to distort the face of Islam and of the Koran. Arrogance wants to tarnish the active role of Islam and to gradually divert attention to Islam with vexatious propaganda and by insulting the sanctities of the Muslims.

It is not accidental that this book has been introduced in Britain as the book of the year. This is actually an effort to confront Islam and the Muslims.

However, fortunately the Muslims showed, with their rage and serious reaction, that they have fathomed well the depth of the plot and that they are trying to neutralize it.

This act is an insult to the most major common point among all the Muslims of the world, and arrogance has specifically made respect for Muslims its target in this attack.

A basic point which should be noted here is that Britain and the United States form one of the pillars of any mischief against Islam and the Muslims, and they overtly or covertly support and fan the

flames of such mischievous acts. The duty of Muslims in the midst
of this has great importance because if we remain silent or indifferent, we should expect more such incidents—and we definitely have
more of them. The role played by Britain and the United States in
the midst of this should be precisely noted, and effective methods
should be found to crush the inhuman and anti-Islamic characteristics of these two governments.

(from *Foreign Broadcast Information Service*, 16 Feb. 1989)

Iranian President's sermon at Friday prayers attacks British policy on *The Satanic Verses* issue

Tehran home service 1528 gmt 17 Feb 89.
Excerpts from recording of second sermon at Friday prayers at
Tehran University by President Khamene'i.

In the Name of God, the Compassionate, the Merciful. [Koranic
verses] Today there are various issues, and the vast gathering of the
people to express their hatred and disgust about the evil arrogant
conspiracy has given a special character to today and our great prayer
gathering. . . .

The important issue of the day is the cultural conspiracy of world
arrogance, about which I will say a few words.

World arrogance has utilised every means to destroy the revolution and its institutions. Political, military, economic, cultural, propaganda and all other means at the disposal of arrogance have been
used. The method which received more attention right from the
start, and which was considered more effective for arrogance, was
the cultural method. We Muslims should be as wary of the enemy's
cultural front as we are of the enemy's military front. As the enemy's attack on our frontiers brings us into action, the enemy's attack on our cultural frontiers should evoke a reaction from us at
least to the same degree, if not more. That is a lengthy discussion
about which I spoke during the Friday prayers one or two years ago.
We should talk to the people about this issue at greater length to
evoke a reaction and awareness in the face of the enemy's cultural
attacks, which is an extremely important and dangerous issue.

However, sometimes arrogance makes a mistake and, when resorting to a course of action, miscalculates and does something which backfires. An example of this can be seen in the book, *The Satanic Verses*, which is no doubt one of the verses of the Great Satan [USA] or one of his surrogates, where one member of the British royal literary society was forced to write a book. The book is of course a fictional novel; it is a story. He makes out that the story takes place in modern times. In the story and in the description of the heroes and characters in the story he relates some of the issues and incidents pertaining to the Great Prophet and the early days of Islam, but with such ugly and offensive interpretations, which are no doubt worthy of a base and impolite person like the author of the book, and insults the Great Prophet and some of his close allies, such as Salman, Balal and his wives.

A reminder of what he [Rushdie] said makes one's blood boil. They have created such a filthy thing and put it on the media market and advertised it. Such a book does not stand a great chance of becoming a best-seller in various circles. Thousands of books are written in the world every year. There are good stories written by famous and talented authors with artistic value. Many years pass before these books are translated into another language, or become widely known in the countries in which they were written. However, by spending money, advertising, using the media and their mercenary newspapers and magazines they hurriedly and prematurely propagated the book. They publicized its title and the name of its publisher, they printed the photograph of its publisher, first in the British and then in the American press. A few weeks ago I saw it with my own eyes in two American magazines. He [Rushdie] took advantage of the situation and gave interviews and adopted an impartial and cool attitude; but at the same time, he repeated his insults and filth-spreading in other forms. Aside from being a sin in the eyes of the law, religion and humanity, this dirtying of literature and arts was an ugly deed. It would be fitting for the world's literary men and scribes and those involved in this field to banish this ugly, cursed and evil person. Because for a person to taint the shining period of history which is admired by one billion human beings in the world, to receive some money or to become famous, is one of the basest deeds that a writer could commit. . . .

(from *BBC Summary of World Broadcasts*, 20 Feb. 1989)

Rushdie and 'the world devourers'
Tehran home service 1030 gmt 23 Feb 89.
Text of the Ayatollah Khomeini's message, read by announcer.

In the Name of God, the Compassionate, the Merciful. To their eminences the clergymen throughout the country, the illustrious maraj'i [sources of emulation, or supreme religious authorities] of Islam, honourable instructors and dear students of religious seminaries and esteemed Friday and congregational imams, may their blessings continue. The benediction and salutations of God and the Prophet of God upon the pure souls of the martyrs, especially the dear martyrs of the religious seminaries and members of the clergy. Greetings to the trustees of the inspiration and martyred custodians of prophethood who carried the pillars of the greatness and pride of the Islamic revolution upon the shoulder of their crimson and blood-stained commitment. Salutations to the everlasting epic-makers from among the members of the clergy who have written their theoretical and practical epistles with the crimson of martyrdom and the ink of blood, and who upon the pulpit of guidance and preaching and leadership of the people, turned the candle of their existence into a luminous pearl. . . .

Salutations to those who rushed forward for the sake of the discovery of the inner meaning of jurisprudence, and who became sincere sentinels to their nation and community; whose complete sincerity was attested by the drops of their blood and the torn-off pieces of their bodies. In truth, nothing except that could be expected from the true divines of Islam and Shi'ism: that they offer the first sacrifices in the call to truth and in the bloody path of the struggle of the people, and whose final testament is their martyrdom. . . .

There is no doubt that in the course of the history of Islam and Shi'ism, the religious seminaries and committee clergy have formed the most important and fortified base of Islam in the face of onslaughts, distortions and perverseness. The great ulema of Islam throughout their lives tried to propagate those things which have been made lawful or unlawful by God without any amendment or distortion. Were it not for the beloved clergy, it would not be clear today what kinds of sciences would be fed to the masses as sciences of the Koran, Islam and the Prophet's family, peace be upon them.

The collation and safeguarding of the Koranic sciences and the esteemed Prophet's traditions and writing and those of the esteemed immaculate ones [the Imams], God's peace be upon them, and the compiling, editing and codification of that material under difficult conditions when facilities were very scarce and when kings and tyrants used all their means to eradicate such material, has not been an easy task. . . .

For hundreds of years the Islamic clergy has been the shelter of the deprived people. The oppressed people have always drunk their fill from the pure fountain of the gnosis of illustrious jurisconsults. Even if we set aside their scientific and cultural endeavours, which are in some respects truly nobler than the blood of the martyrs, in every age they have experienced hardships and bitterness for defending their religious and national sanctities. Side by side with enduring captivity, banishments, imprisonments, hardships, sufferings and malicious talk, they have also offered noble martyrs to the holy present of the Truth [God]. . . .

Truly, if anyone thinks that colonialism has not and does not persecute the clergy which has so much greatness and honour and influence, is this not naive? The issue of the book *The Satanic Verses* is that it is a calculated move aimed at rooting out religion and religiousness, and above all, Islam and its clergy. Certainly, if the world devourers could, they would have burnt the roots and the title of the clergy. But God has always been the guardian of the sacred torch and, God willing, he will continue to be so on condition that we recognise the tricks, ploys and deceptions of the world devourers. Of course this does not mean that we should defend all clergymen, since those dependent, pseudo and ossified clergy have not been and are not too few in number. . . .

God wanted the blasphemous book of *The Satanic Verses* to be published now, so that the world of conceit, arrogance and barbarism would bare its true face in its long-held enmity to Islam; to bring us out of our simplicity and to prevent us from attributing everything to blunder, bad management and lack of experience; to realise fully that this issue is not our mistake, but that it is the world devourers' effort to annihilate Islam, and Muslims; otherwise, the issue of Salman Rushdie would not be so important to them as to place the entire Zionism and arrogance behind it. The clergy and the dear hezbollahis and the respected families of the martyrs must be on guard, not to allow the blood of the dear ones to be wasted through these writings and wrong thoughts. . . .

[Signed] God's peace and blessings be upon you, [dated] 3rd Esfand 1367 [22 February 1989], Ruhollah al-Musavi al-Khomeini.

(BBC Summary of World Broadcasts, 24 Feb. 1989)

IV

The International Response ⌒

UNITED KINGDOM AND WORLD ROUNDUP

Rushdie in hiding after Ayatollah's death order

Mr Salman Rushdie was in hiding under police protection last night and unrepentant about his novel, *The Satanic Verses*, which provoked the Iranian religious leader, Ayatollah Khomeini, to call for his execution. (from *Guardian*, London, 15 Feb. 1989)

SALMAN RUSHDIE

'Frankly I wish I had written a more critical book. A religion that claims it is able to behave like this, religious leaders who are able to behave like this, and then say this is a religion that must be above any whisper of criticism—that doesn't add up.'

IQBAL SACRANTE
UK Action Committee on Islamic Affairs

'Death, perhaps, is a bit too easy for him . . . his mind must be tormented for the rest of his life unless he asks for forgiveness to Almighty Allah.' (*Guardian*, 15 Feb. London)

HESHAM EL-ESSAWI
Chair, Islamic Society for the Promotion of Religious Tolerance

'We very much regret and denounce Khomeini's statement. Threats like this, or any violent response, is not the correct religious response. It is a very dangerous development and will give Rushdie sympathy where it is not deserved.'   (*Independent*, 15 Feb. London)

DAVID WILSHIRE MP (CON.)
Tabling a Commons Motion

'It is a positive outrage to civilised standards throughout the world.'

SIR ELDON GRIFFITHS MP
Chair, All Party Parliamentary Anglo-Iranian Group

'The Ayatollah's splenetic reaction is a demonstration that he is losing his marbles.'   (*Times*, 15 Feb. London)

SIR GEOFFREY HOWE
Foreign Secretary

'The death sentence is a matter of grave concern. It illustrates the extreme difficulty of establishing the right kind of relationship with a manifestly revolutionary regime with ideas that are very much its own.'   (*Daily Mail*, 15 Feb. London)

SON OF THE FORMER SHAH OF IRAN

'I, too, cannot countenance an offence to Islam, particularly if it should be a deliberate one. But equally, I can't excuse pronouncements which repudiate the basic principles of human rights. However great the injury Rushdie may have done to Islam, it bears no comparison with the damage Khomeini is doing.

'The campaign against Rushdie is a calculated one. Khomeini's regime can only survive as long as it produces permanent critics. A politics of opening towards the West would be tantamount to a loss of power for the present regime.

'The monarchy is beyond ideology; it is an institution. I engage in politics because I believe that due to the historic meaning of my position, I can exercise great influence. My origin, my descent is only the means, not the end. When freedom and democracy are to hand, then the people will decide: if they want a monarchy, fine; if they want a republic, that's fine, too.'

(from *Salzburg Kronen Zeitung*, 11 March 1989)

ANTHONY BURGESS

'. . . Evidently there is a political element in the attack on *The Satanic Verses* which has killed and injured good if obstreperous Muslims in Islamabad, though it may be dangerously blasphemous to suggest it. The Ayatollah Khomeini is probably within his self-elected rights in calling for the assassination of Salman Rushdie, or anyone else for that matter, on his own holy ground. To order outraged sons of the prophet to kill him and the directors of Penguin Books on British soil is tantamount to a *jihad*. It is a declaration of war on citizens of a free country and as such it is a political act. It has to be countered by an equally forthright, if less murderous, declaration of defiance.'   (from *Independent*, 15 Feb. London)

£1,500,000 TO KILL HIM—by order of that Mad Mullah
(Headline from *Daily Mirror*, London, 16 Feb. 1989)

HARVEY MORRIS, HEATHER MILLS AND COLIN HUGHES

The Government faces strong pressure today to pull Britain's diplomats out of Iran after a crowd of demonstrators, shouting 'Death to England' and 'Death to America', broke windows at the British embassy in Tehran yesterday. The 1,000 demonstrators gathered in support of Ayatollah Khomeini's edict calling on Muslims to carry out a sentence of death on Salman Rushdie and his associates for the alleged blasphemy against Islam contained in his novel, *The Satanic Verses*.

The Revolutionary Guard Corps yesterday announced its readiness to carry out Khomeini's order, and an Iranian cleric who heads a wealthy Islamic charity organisation offered a $1m reward to any foreigner 'who would punish this mercenary of colonialism for his shameful act'—and nearly three times as much if an Iranian did the job. The offer was made by Hassan Sanei of the Fifth of Khordad (5 June) Foundation, which was set up to care for the relatives of demonstrators killed in an anti-American protest in 1963 and now runs supermarkets and other businesses in Iran.

Margaret Thatcher's response to the inevitable appeals at Commons question time today for firm action to be taken is expected to be coloured by the outcome of a meeting in Tehran this morning between the British chargé d'affaires, Nicholas Browne, and Iranian foreign ministry officials. Mr Browne will ask for clarification of Khomeini's edict and about the announcement, also on Tuesday, that Roger Cooper, held in jail in Tehran for more than three years, had been given an unspecified heavy sentence for spying.

The demonstration at the embassy was relatively peaceful and police kept the protesters to the opposite side of Ferdowsi Avenue in the centre of town. Windows were broken, however, when the crowd hurled rubbish across the road. Mr Browne was quoted as saying that at no time were British or local staff in any danger. . . .

The embassy demonstration was part of a day of mourning in Iran to protest against Mr Rushdie's book. Senior officials of the regime announced their support for the Ayatollah Khomeini's execution edict, broadcast by Tehran radio; Iranian President Khamenei said: 'The brave and pious youth across the Muslim world needs no other message.'   (from *Independent*, London, 16 Feb. 1989)

Rapprochement heading for rocks

PETER MURTAGH

Relations between Britain and Iran have virtually been at rock bottom since Ayatollah Khomeini came to power in 1979. Only recently has there been any indication of an improvement and that now appears to be in jeopardy.

When the Shah left Tehran in January 1979, in ignominy and just ahead of the Ayatollah's incoming plane from Paris, Iran entered an era in which it has been cast as a leper among the nations of the world. . . .

Last year, however, both sides agreed to normalise relations; the Foreign Secretary, Sir Geoffrey Howe, and his Iranian counterpart agreed to reassign diplomats and reopen the Tehran embassy amid hopes that 'moderates' were gaining the upper hand in Iran and hostages in the Lebanon might be released.

It is that process of re-establishing confidence and mutual trust— a process barely four months old—which now appears to be in jeopardy as Anglo-Iranian relations totter.

(from *Guardian*, London, 16 Feb. 1989)

Iran also declared a ban on the sale of all Viking Penguin books,
although Viking apologised for the offence the book had caused.

The Dutch were the first European nation to treat the fatwa *as*
an event of international diplomatic significance by cancelling their
Foreign Minister's visit to Iran.

Writers rally to Rushdie

PETER MURTAGH

Members of the literary community rallied to Salman Rushdie
yesterday as publishers abroad, shocked at the ferocity of Muslim
opposition to *The Satanic Verses*, began to have second thoughts
about bringing out translations of the book. . . . A group of writers,
literary agents and publishers led by the playwright, Mr. Harold
Pinter, delivered a letter to Mrs. Thatcher expressing outrage at Ayatollah Khomeini's order. . . . Mr Pinter said, 'A very distinguished
writer has used his imagination to write a book and has criticized
the religion into which he was born and he has been sentenced to
death as well as his publishers. It is an intolerable and barbaric state
of affairs.

'The Government . . . should confront Iran with the consequences
of its statement and remind the Islamic community that it cannot
incite people to murder.'

(from *Guardian*, London, 16 Feb. 1989)

Iran was actively seeking allies, both within the Muslim nations
and in the West.

The Iranian embassy to the Vatican demanded that the Pope
should join the crusade against *The Satanic Verses*.

But a senior Vatican official said later: 'I doubt very much
whether the Holy Father will take any action.

'After all, he is not a defender of the Moslem faith. In fact this
move by the Iranian diplomats is rather out of place.

'It's their problem, not ours. we have enough of our own, especially with all the books and films which cast doubts on Jesus Christ
himself. We have never asked for Moslem help in curbing their
sale.'   (*Telegraph*, London, 16 Feb. 1989)

On February 15, the embassy of the Islamic Republic of Iran made public an appeal to Pope John Paul II to intervene to block the publication of Salman Rushdie's book The Satanic Verses *in Italy. The following day, at 1 p.m., the Iranian Ambassador to the Holy See, Salman Ghaffari agreed to an interview with 30* DAYS. *As usual, he was friendly and courteous. As usual, his views were sharp and harsh.*

You have asked the Pope to act 'energetically' to prevent the publication of the book *The Satanic Verses* in Italy. What type of intervention by the Pope did you have in mind?

The Pope certainly knows better than anyone else how he can intervene—whether through the Italian government or through the Mondadori publishing house—to block the publication of this blasphemous book, which offends religion. The Pope has a great spiritual influence, and he can bring it to bear effectively.

Perhaps some Catholics can understand the reason for your indignation, but how can you imagine that Catholics could sanction a manhunt in the name of God?

For those who know the sacred texts of the monotheistic religions, this is something very easy to understand: in the sacred scriptures, in the Hebrew Torah, there are numerous examples of sinners who are punished with death, for example for the sin of homicide or adultery (in the latter case, by stoning). The sin of this English writer is much graver than that of adultery because adultery has only a personal dimension while the writer's sin has a social dimension. Catholics should understand this argument well. We have the same roots.

In the appeal you made to the Pope on February 15, you describe the Pope as a 'defender of spirituality and of religion'. Are you thinking perhaps in terms of a kind of Holy Alliance between the Catholic Church and Islam against modern unbelief?

This holy union existed from the beginning. Islam has always hoped for this collaboration. Our history shows that Islam and Christianity can live together like brothers. Let us leave aside the ideological conflicts of the past. We hope that Christianity, with the help of Islam, can carry this world toward God and toward faith, preventing all oppression. . . .

Finally, I'd like to ask a hypothetical question about the Rush-

die affair, as one man to another. If Mr. Rushdie were in this room, unarmed, and you were armed with a pistol, would you pull the trigger without any hesitation?

Yes, certainly I would. The law of God is clear. The specific law in this case is also. But why do you find this behavior strange? If God orders and allows that someone be executed, the carrying out of this divine precept serves to teach all of society. It is as if you asked me if I would hesitate to carry out a death sentence for the big drug dealers. Why hesitate? Their execution would prevent evil and corruption from spreading among young people. And this is a good for all society.   (from *30 Days*, March 1989)

JOHN BULLOCH AND HEATHER MILLS

The Government reacted with studied moderation yesterday to Ayatollah Khomeini's 'sentence of death' on Salman Rushdie, who was still in hiding last night and reported to be under armed guard.

The Cabinet decided Britain would not go ahead with its plan to upgrade its embassy in Tehran, reappointing an ambassador, but would maintain diplomatic relations, for the time being at least. The decision was taken on the strength of a brief telephone call by Nicholas Browne, the chargé d'affaires in Tehran, as he came out of a meeting with the head of the European desk at the Iranian Ministry of Foreign Affairs.

Over the crackling line to Whitehall, Mr Browne reported that he had got 'no satisfaction' in response to his strong protest at Khomeini's statement. That message was immediately passed to the Cabinet, which was holding its usual Thursday session.

The Iranian chargé in London, Mohammed Mehdi Basti, was summoned to the Foreign Office to hear Britain's protest. He was warned that no new applications for visas for diplomats to reinforce the Iranian embassy in London would be issued, although permission has already been given for a second Iranian diplomat to join Mr Basti.

After the Cabinet meeting, Sir Geoffrey Howe, the Foreign Secretary, said Britain recognised that Muslims and others might have strong views about Mr Rushdie's book, *The Satanic Verses*: 'But nobody has the right to incite people to violence on British soil or

against British citizens . . . Ayatollah Khomeini's statement is totally unacceptable.'   (*Independent*, London, 17 Feb. 1989)

*Other governments were now prepared to take up positions. The
USA and several EC countries were 'shocked' or 'appalled' by the
death threat.*

The Government of Pakistan called in foreign ambassadors to
convey concern about the publication. A foreign ministry spokesman also said that Pakistan was considering court action against
the novel . . . and told reporters that Pakistan wanted [its] destruction and an apology from Mr. Rushdie and his publishers, as well
as assurances that no further similar books would be published.

(from *Independent*, London, 17 Feb. 1989)

Other Muslim countries were less certain.

A spokesman for Kuwait, the current chairman of the Islamic
Conference Organisation, said he opposed an Iranian request for an
emergency meeting of the organisation: 'Many newspapers and demonstrations criticise [the novel], but to get forty-five countries to
discuss this matter is too much.'

Article 19, the London based international centre on censorship,
expressed its concern at the threat to Mr Rushdie, saying: 'Any
denunciation of acts of the imagination by secular or religious authorities strikes at the very heart of freedom—the freedom to imagine. As such, the order seeking Mr. Rushdie's death is the ultimate
and most extreme form of censorship and must be universally
condemned.'   (from *Independent*, London, 17 Feb. 1989)

*Three early letters, in what was to become a month-long volumi-
nous correspondence, set the tone.*

The life of a British citizen has been threatened by a foreign
government leader with whom the British government has been
trying to re-establish diplomatic links. It is to be hoped that Sir

Geoffrey Howe will immediately withdraw his envoy in Tehran until the threat to Salman Rushdie has been authoritatively repudiated.

DAVID SPILSBURY
Birmingham 12.

Ayatollah Khomeini's call for Salman Rushdie to be killed because his novel *The Satanic Verses* is blasphemous makes it even more important that socialists are clear about the issues. Everyone regrets the genuine offence caused to thousands of ordinary Muslims because of what they have been told is in Mr Rushdie's book. And Muslims in Britain are entitled to resent being lectured on tolerance by a society which has often shown its ethnic minorities cruel intolerance and whose prime minister bans books, programmes and interviews at will.

But censorship is wrong and any calls for censorship by any fundamentalist religious leaders should be resisted. Not because of any lack of respect for anyone's sincerely held personal faith. But because it cannot be right to have one set of views imposed on everyone else by force, punishment and the censor.

Thatcher has made liberalism and tolerance deeply unfashionable. But they are still values worth taking a stand on. Not least, because they afford the only real protection for Britain's religious and ethnic minorities.

DIANE ABBOTT
(Lab, Hackney North and Stoke Newington).
(*Guardian*, London, 16 Feb. 1989)

Dear Sir,

Himself a Muslim until recently, Salman Rushdie has committed acts of apostasy by writing what he did in his *Satanic Verses* and later on in his interview with Channel 4 (*Bandung File*, 3 February). It is a very serious crime against the Muslim Ummah (universal brotherhood of Muslims), much more serious than high treason is against a state of which one is a citizen.

Like the many secular states that provide the death penalty for high treason, several schools of Islamic thought deem the blood of an apostate a fair target (Halaal) for Muslims. Ayatollah Khomeini, therefore, did his duty as a religious leader when he pronounced the death sentence against Salman Rushdie for his crime of high treason against the Muslim Ummah.

Had he called his own biological parents bastard and prostitute, his brothers and sisters would have been the most likely to be infuriated. By writing these blasphemies against a messenger of God and the wives of the Prophet of Islam, whom the Muslims revere and love more than their own biological parents, he has earned the wrath of the entire Muslim world.

As for the publishers of his *Satanic Verses*, they are accessories in his crime, of blasphemy, if not of apostasy as well. That the publishing of books is their business is not a valid defence; in the same way as the business of innkeeping is no valid defence for harbouring an outlaw. The Ayatollah's verdict against these publishers, too, is just and fair.

Even though these criminals against Islam are being protected by the British police, this protection can only delay the execution of the sentence. Who is destined to be the executioner, and when, is something that neither the police nor the fugitives can know. . . .

There is only one way out of this rat-like existence for him. By recanting his blasphemies publicly, he can win a reprieve to make amend for the wrong he has done. God *is* oft-forgiving, most merciful.

Yours sincerely,
INAYATYLLAH ZAIGHAM
Gravesend, Kent.
15 February
(from *Independent*, London, 17 Feb. 1989)

Zaigham did not, however, speak for all British Muslims.

SULTAN SHAHIN

The religious leadership of British Muslims has expressed strong opposition to the idea of any individual murdering Salman Rushdie for having written the controversial *The Satanic Verses*, which is alleged to be sacrilegious to Islam.

Asked if he supported Iranian spiritual leader, Ayatollah Khomeini's order to his followers to murder Salman Rushdie, the chairman of UK Action Committee on Islamic Affairs, Dr Mughram Ali

Al-Ghamdi, said: 'We have learnt over the years to treat media reports with a good deal of scepticism.

'We do not know what the Ayatollah has actually said. But we are a minority living in this country and we do intend to fully abide by the law. We are not above the law. We do not condone violence of any kind by anybody under any pretext.'

Explaining the Muslims' view on Salman Rushdie's latest work to the press at London's central mosque this week, Dr Ghamdi said: 'There is widespread anguish in the Muslim community all over the world.

'This book has caused real, genuine and universal hurt. We are doing all we can within the legal framework of the country to get it banned and the author punished for blaspheming Islam.

'But Britain is not a Muslim country. Islamic laws do not apply here and even in Islamic countries it is not for individuals to take the law in their hands.

'Only courts and governments can deal with offending authors.'

Calling the book the 'filthiest-ever sacrilege against Islam', Dr Ghamdi continued: 'It is described sometimes as pure fantasy and fiction and sometimes as a serious secular critique of Islam; in our view, it is a mere collection of insults, sacrilege, blasphemy and obscenity against Islam. No individual with the slightest grain of self-respect can accept being insulted and it is a more serious matter when a whole world community is subject to outrageous abuse of its inviolable sanctities.

'In asking for the withdrawal of this sacrilege, Muslims are neither showing intolerance, imposing censorship, nor infringing any one's freedom of expression'.

(*New Life*, London, 17 Feb. 1989)

Feature articles attempted to explain both the principles at stake and the background to the affair.

Khomeini's scapegoat
AMIR TAHERI

The apostate Salman Rushdie must die. That was how Tehran Radio opened its main news bulletin yesterday afternoon. The decision to have the Indian-born novelist 'eliminated' did not come from an ordinary court. It came in the form of a *fatwa* (edict) from Ayatollah Khomeini in his capacity as the self-styled Imam or Supreme Guide of the world's estimated 1,000 million Muslims.

The Ayatollah pronounced Rushdie, author of *The Satanic Verses*, as *mahdur ad-damm* (he whose blood is unclean). In other words it is now incumbent on all true Muslims to eliminate him.

A demand for Rushdie to be judged by Khomeini is believed to have been made by a number of British Muslims in a petition sent via the Islamic embassy in London several weeks ago. Once he received the demand, Khomeini could not remain silent. As Imam he is responsible for guiding his flock on all issues.

He was told of the contents of *The Satanic Verses* through an aide and decided that Rushdie was guilty on all three charges, any one of which would carry the death penalty under Islamic law. He was found to be 'an agent of corruption on earth', one who has 'declared war on Allah' and, last but not least, a *murtad*—a born Muslim who has abandoned his faith and crossed over to the enemies of Islam.

This is not the first time that Khomeini has exercised what he regards as his legitimate right, indeed, his duty to call for the punishment of the enemies of Islam. His first such edict was in 1947 when he sentenced an Iranian education minister to death. The minister was gunned down a few days later.

The Ayatollah subsequently ordered the murder of several other prominent politicians and intellectuals from his exile in Iraq. After the 1979 revolution his authority was used to cover the execution of thousands of political opponents and the assassination of several people abroad, two in London.

The fact that Khomeini's edict seems like a relic of the dark Ages in the West must not hide another equally disturbing fact. Almost all Muslims, including the most enlightened, feel offended by Rushdie's novel or, rather, by reports they have read or heard about it. Very few people have actually read the dense and tortuous book, but they do not have to.

The very idea of using the prophet Muhammad as a character in a novel is painful to many Muslims. The entire Islamic system consists of the so-called *Hodud*, or limits beyond which one should simply not venture. Islam does not recognize unlimited freedom of expression. Call them taboos, if you like, but Islam considers a wide variety of topics as permanently closed.

Most Muslims are prepared to be broad-minded about most things but never about anything that even remotely touches on their faith. 'Better that I be dead than see Islam insulted,' said Ayatollah Majlisi in the last century. An Arab proverb says: 'Kill me, but do not mock my faith.'

To Muslims religion is not just a part of life. It is, in fact, life that is a part of religion. Muslims cannot understand a concept that has no rules, no limits. The Western belief in human rights, which seems to lack limits, is alien to Islamic traditions.

A telling example of the limits in question has been provided by the Partisans of Allah who still hold a number of Western hostages in Lebanon. As soldiers of the Imam, they are prepared to deprive innocent men like Terry Waite and John McCarthy of their freedom. But they will never mock the religious beliefs of their captives. All the hostages who have been released say they were instantly provided with a Bible and allowed time each day to say their prayers.

Muslim states through much of their history imposed a social head tax on their non-Muslim subjects. But Islam seldom ordered or condoned the destruction of non-Islamic places of worship.

The duty to 'propagate the good and combat evil' is a responsibility incumbent on every true Muslim. The Muslim who sees wrong being done and who does nothing to stop it becomes a partner in that crime.

Sometimes, true believers must act even before any harm is done to Islam. The prophet is quoted as saying: 'Kill the harmful ones before they can do harm.' Reports about Rushdie having claimed that part of the Koran, Islam's holy book, was not dictated to Muhammad by the Archangel Gabriel but by Satan masquerading as an emissary of Allah have inflamed passions throughout the Muslim world. Muslims are especially sensitive to anything even remotely questioning the authenticity of the Koran for they take a special pride in the belief that they alone have a holy book that was directly dictated by Allah himself.

The fact that Rushdie propagated his heresy in a book is of especial significance to Muslims. Islam is the religion of the book *par excellence*. Few cultures hold the written and printed word in so much respectful awe as Muslims, even though the vast majority are illiterate. When a Muslim wants to clinch an argument he says, 'It is written'.

What is written and printed must, ideally, confirm the teachings of the Koran or at least conform with them. Christians, Jews and Zoroastrans are accepted as believers because they, too, have holy books and are the people of the book (*Ahl Ketab*). Any attempt to use a book to demolish or even cast doubt on the authenticity of even a small part of what is *the* book is intolerable to most Muslims.

Does all that mean that a majority of Muslims would approve of the death sentence passed by Khomeini on Rushdie? The honest answer is probably yes. To be sure, Muslim intellectuals, especially the tiny liberal and leftist wings, have been justly outraged both by Khomeini's order and by the book-burning antics organized in Bradford and Islamabad. But the mass of Muslim poor, who feel their religion and culture have been humiliated in the West for too long, are unlikely to consider the complex issues involved in this very complex case.

Most of them live in conditions of misery unimaginable in the West and feel that all they have in this world is their religious faith. Today they are being told by the mullahs that even this is being threatened by the American 'Great Satan' and its allies.

Rushdie says that one of his aims in writing the novel was to try to fight prejudice and fanaticism by establishing a dialogue with Muslims. He has manifestly failed. He is not the first Muslim-born Westernized intellectual to dream of helping to extricate the Muslim masses from the straitjacket of fanaticism imposed by the mullahs. He is not the first to fail, either. Nor is he the first to be sentenced to death for having dreamed that dream. And as things stand today he might not be the last.

Khomeini's motives for giving his order are not entirely religious. In the last few months he has suffered a number of humiliating setbacks: the ceasefire with Iraq, the election of a woman prime minister in Pakistan and, with the Soviet withdrawal from Afghanistan, the failure of his protégés to secure a prominent role in the assembly organized by the Mujahidin in Rawalpindi. He also wants to point a finger at Pakistan and Saudi Arabia as half-hearted defenders of the faith.

He has therefore been looking for an issue likely to stir the imagination of the poor and illiterate masses, the so-called *mustadhafin* or 'the feeble ones', among whom he recruits his most devoted 'volunteers for martyrdom'. Waving Rushdie's novel, the Ayatollah hopes to tell his supporters that plots against Islam have not ceased, and that if one war has ended another is about to begin.

• *Amir Taheri is an Iranian journalist and author of* Spirit of Allah, *a biography of Khomeini.*

(Times, London, 13 Feb. 1989)

The hubris of the hidden imam
MALCOLM YAPP

If Salman Rushdie repents may he be forgiven? President Ali Khamenei said yes. Ruhollah Khomeini said no. Who is correct in Islamic law? Since Khomeini bears the title of ayatollah and the President only that of Hojatoleslam one may think that the former is more likely to be correct, but that is not necessarily the case. Other ayatollahs have held views different from those of Khomeini. For example his old associate of the early days of the Islamic Revolution, Ayatollah Motaheri.

Motaheri considered a problem relevant to that of Rushdie. What, he asked, should be done with those who attacked Islam? If they attacked Islam openly, he replied, they should be answered in the same way—book against book, opinion against opinion. Only if they attacked deceitfully, intending to mislead the believers, should they be dealt with violently. But, he said, even then, if the attackers sincerely repented they should be forgiven.

Muslim jurists often differ from each other in the interpretation of Muslim law. And it is important to understand that the Rushdie affair, for all its important political aspects, comes down to a matter of the interpretation of the law. Many commentators have suggested that Khomeini speaks in the Rushdie affair as leader of the Islamic Republic of Iran. In fact he speaks as a *mujtahid*, that is as one recognised by Shia Muslims to be qualified to interpret Muslim law. Sunni Muslims have similar authorities known as *muftis*.

Muslim jurists work from a body of material which consists of the Koran and the Traditions, although they differ about what traditions are to be admitted as valid, and from the commentaries of their predecessors on that material. They work by using strictly defined rules of reasoning, giving opinions concerning the law in answer to queries submitted to them.

The opinions of some Muslim jurists are considered better than those of others. Before 1979, several ayatollahs were generally thought to be wiser than Khomeini in matters of Muslim law. Ayatollah Shariat-Madari quarrelled with Khomeini because he thought Khomeini was laying claim to authority far beyond his desserts. Among others, many scholars would think Ayatollah Gulpaygani in Qom and Ayatollah Khoy in Najjaf to be Khomeini's superiors as mujtahids.

So why is it that we have Khomeini's opinion and not that of the others? The answer is that he was asked for his opinion. Shia go to the mujtahid of their choice: those who went to Khomeini rather than to another mujtahid may have gone to him because they wanted the answer they knew they would get. It would be open to another Shia to go to another mujtahid and perhaps obtain a different opinion. Or a Sunni could go to a mufti of one of the four schools of Sunni Islam. Of course these might agree with Khomeini, in which case there would be what is called a consensus. The reported declaration of the Tehran *ulema* is an attempt to create the impression that there is a consensus about what many think to be a very controversial decision. But Tehran is not considered a major centre for mujtahids.

A mujtahid gives an opinion on a point of law. It remains an opinion even when it is regarded as authoritative. Before it can be applied to a case under Islamic criminal law, there must be a trial under proper procedures. Here there is something of a puzzling discrepancy between Khomeini's two reported statements. In the first he seemed to be delivering an opinion in the traditional manner, although many took it to be verdict and sentence against Rushdie as well. But in his second statement about the inutility of Rushdie's repentance he seemed to be adopting the role of judge. Of course it could be argued that Rushdie's expression of regret amounted to an admission of responsibility and therefore dispensed with the need for a trial.

Khomeini has gone outside traditional Shia practice in another way. Muslim jurists make a clear distinction between the Dar al-Islam where Muslim law (sharia) rules and the Dar al-Harb where it does not protect Muslims. Those Muslims who have emigrated to the Dar al-Harb must be deemed to have voluntarily withdrawn themselves from the protection of Muslim law. In his opinion, verdict and sentence on Rushdie, Khomeini appears totally to have ignored the argument that the Muslims' law does not apply to Rushdie.

Khomeini's second judgement against Rushdie appears at odds with traditional Muslim thought in other ways. One may argue about whether the crime of which Rushdie is accused is a crime for which genuine repentance may be admitted as a reason for lifting the sentence. It is contended that for some crimes the criminal must suffer the earthly punishment even though, through repentance, he may escape eternal damnation. But Muslims have always claimed that only God can decide whether to admit repentance. But Khomeini is reported as having made the decision, on behalf of God, that Rushdie should go to Hell.

On the evidence we have, it would seem that Khomeini is going very far beyond the traditional province of the mujtahid. Of course the concept of the government of the learned which he introduced into the Islamic republic does assume that he exercises the powers of the real ruler of Shia Islam, the Hidden Imam. Until now, one did not realise how extensive those claims were. The traditional Shia view is that, after the Twelfth Imam went into hiding in 874 AD, there was no one left to exercise the powers which belonged to him, although the next four leaders of the Shia community claimed to be in touch with the Hidden Imam and therefore to possess special powers. But since then mujtahids have claimed only to exercise limited powers of interpretation. Khomeini's claims are quite staggering in their scope.

To an outsider, the oddest feature is the way in which Khomeini's controversial pronouncements are taken by Muslims to be authoritative statements of law. Any of them may seek other views. Shia traditions urge that, if there is doubt, one should always choose the most cautious opinion. But Sunni and Shia Muslims have chosen the most radical interpretation, or so we are led to believe, perhaps by those who would wish us to do so.

Muslim law appears to have undergone a dramatic change. The opinion of one man appears to have replaced all the elaborate mechanisms by which opinions were formed and consensus achieved. It is difficult to believe that this can really be so: 1,300 years of the work of Muslim jurists, which has created in Islamic law one of the most remarkable of the intellectual achievements of man, can hardly be expunged overnight. It must be possible for a Muslim to have a different, valid opinion to which Rushdie could appeal.

To appeal to Muslim law would destroy or weaken the most fundamental of all Rushdie's protections, namely English law. England is Dar al-Harb: the sharia does not rule here and may be applied only when English courts choose to apply it to the personal affairs of Muslims. Those Muslims who have withdrawn from the protection of the sharia must put up with English law.

(Independent, London, 22 Feb. 1989)

MIHIR BOSE

For the past 20 years I have seen Britain come of age as a multicultural nation. Born a Hindu in India, educated in Jesuit schools, but growing up amongst Moslems, I have seen the society in which I have lived for most of my adult life accept and tolerate a wide variety of people and opinions. The multi-culturalism is not perfect, but it is the best we have and needs protection.

The murderous reaction of Moslem fundamentalists to Salman Rushdie's book threatens to destroy this tender plant. Even before the occurrences of the past few weeks, the activities of some members of the Moslem community had suggested that they would prefer to live in an exclusive society, to have their children taught in their own schools, eating their own food, living the lives of an unassimilated, self-protective sect. But the outburst which has greeted *The Satanic Verses* is altogether more damaging and dangerous. At one extreme it may confirm among some a reactionary prejudice that Moslems, and by extension other, non-white, non-Christian people, are prone to be barbarous and brutal, delighting in inflicting medieval punishments on those they consider their enemies. At another extreme it provokes dismay and confusion, even from friends and co-religionists, that just 11 years away from the twenty-first century there are human beings who can still speak the language of the Seventh, who burn books and incite people to commit murder.

How should those of us non-Christians who live in this country and who have embraced its values, in particular how should moderate-minded Moslems, react?

We know all too well that Islam provokes strong passions; but those who accept Western secular society also believe that religion should be a private matter between a consenting adult and his or her chosen God.

So far, it looks as though attempts to launch a signature campaign, amongst Asians in Britain—both Moslems and non-Moslems—may come to nothing. Most moderate Moslems feel confused and disorientated by the sheer ferocity of the reaction to Rushdie's book. But even they find it difficult to voice dissent within the context of a culture that has never acknowledged tne right to dissension.

Although it is no excuse for the fundamentalists' behaviour, it is worth trying to understand the tremendous emotions the Koran arouses among Moslems. All religions venerate their holy books, but Islam's attitude towards the Koran is of a unique and unbending reverence. Every Moslem, whether fundamentalist or liberal, believes that the Koran is literally the very word of God, preserved in heaven and transmitted by the Archangel Gabriel through Mohammed.

Even among Christians who might be described as fundamentalists, it is accepted that a whole school of textual criticism has grown up, convincingly suggesting that human hands were involved in the making of the Bible. To a Moslem any such thought about the Koran would be blasphemous. In Islam, even today, there is simply no tradition of theological criticism or inquiry.

In many ways this is at the heart of the debate about the Rushdie book. Rushdie's argument is that while the Koran is sacred, Mohammed has no divine status. It is the powerful tribe of clerics, in Iran and elsewhere, he implies, who are acting as contemporary thought police turning the human prophet into a perfect being, his life into a perfect life.

Even those Moslems who do not share Khomeini's murderous instincts share a deep unease at Rushdie's humanising of Mohammed, in that the very act casts doubts on the Koran. In the Islamic faith, the messenger is also very much part of the message, as Dr Moojan Momen, an expert on Shia Islam, has pointed out: 'Neither liberal Moslems nor the fundamentalists seriously question the authority or the infallibility of the Koran. This is not a debate in the Islamic world and has never been.'

Worse, Rushdie has kindled old fears that this is another in the long line of Western attempts to denigrate Islam. The peculiar mixture of envy and hatred with which the West has viewed Islam can be traced back through the centuries to the very birth of the religion. In the hellish circles of Dante's *Inferno*, 'Maometto' is placed only just above Judas and Satan himself. Dante's vivid description of Mohammed's punishment turns the strongest of stomachs even today, and perhaps provides a cautionary reminder of times when cruelty formed a part of Christian culture too.

It would be tempting to dismiss all this as ancient history; but even Moslems who are appalled by the reaction to Rushdie's book point out that the Mahound character in his novel is the abusive name given to Mohammed in medieval western caricature.

This perhaps helps to explain why a faith that is growing so fast not merely in the Third world but also in the West—where its allure is that it provides a rock of certainty amid chaos and confusion—can nevertheless behave in such a beleaguered and aggressively defensive fashion.

Such an attitude is reinforced by a deep-seated fear of being culturally overwhelmed by the West. The culture and the religion of Islam leave no room for individualism. Even the great Moslem schisms are national and sectarian rather than theological. Organised religion for Moslems is not a matter of individual conscience and private practice.

The limited attempts at textual criticism of the Koran have always met with extreme resistance. Even Maxime Rodinson's classic biography of Mohammed attracted vituperation and efforts were made to ban it. Rushdie seeks to go much further than almost any previous Moslem writer. 'I have tried to give a secular humanist vision to the birth of a great world religion,' he states apologetically. He has combined this with writing 'about migration, its stresses and transformation, from the point of view of immigrants from the Indian sub-continent to Britain.'

What he has not appreciated is the near impossibility of doing anything like this. The migrants whom he seeks to portray are in most cases unlikely to read his book, and the history of the Indian sub-continent has shown over and over again that in any conflict between the humanist and the religious vision, religion will always triumph.

Indeed, the Moslems of the sub-continent have never been able to organise a secular movement of any importance. 'Islam in danger' has always been the cry to arouse them. In the one movement which brought the Moslems and the Hindus together, at the end of the First World War, what enticed the Moslems to join forces was their fear that the Western powers would strip defeated Turkey of the Caliphate and remove the great symbol of Islam.

'Islam in danger' is still the cry today, from Beirut to Bradford. Moslems have always had a special horror of apostasy, and Rushdie, who confesses that he 'has a god-shaped hole, unable to accept the unarguable absolute of religion', attracts anger with all the greater passion. Liberal Moslems are privately appalled by what is happening to Rushdie. Now it is time for them to stand up publicly and say so. Only they can truly civilise the more barbarous instincts of their co-religionists.

• *Mihir Bose is an Indian-born writer and journalist living in Britain.*

(Daily Telegraph, London, 16 Feb. 1989)

It seemed as though the low-key response of the British Government might prove effective in calming the situation, and allowing the more liberal elements in the Iranian Government to rally; especially as it appeared that Iran was not going to receive very strong support from the rest of the Muslim world.

President Ali Khameini suggested that if Rushdie apologised, 'this wretched man might yet be spared'. He also gave a very strongly worded instruction that the British Embassy in Tehran was not to be damaged or attacked.

The British Government meanwhile announced its intention of seeking support from the European Community at the regular Brussels meeting of foreign ministers.

Other nations, however, now seemed to want to treat the affair even more urgently than either Britain or Iran. West Germany recalled its chargé d'affaires, and in Pakistan and India the demonstrations continued.

Rushdie expresses regret

As author of *The Satanic Verses* I recognise that Moslems in many parts of the world are genuinely distressed by the publication

of my novel. I profoundly regret the distress that publication has
occasioned to the sincere followers of Islam. Living as we do in a
world of many faiths this experience has served to remind us that
we must all be conscious of the sensibilities of others.

(Full text of Rushdie's statement, 18 Feb. 1989)

*This 'carefully-worded statement' seemed only to increase the
'chaos' in Iran—the apology was rejected ('falling far short' of what
was needed) then accepted ('generally seen as sufficient enough to
warrant [Rushdie's] pardon by the masses') and then rejected again.*

*Muslims in Britain seemed equally uncertain as to how to re-
spond.*

Mr. Hesham El Essawy said 'I regard it as an apology and it should
pave the way out of this crisis.' The Council for Mosques, however,
described the author's statement as 'not a sincere apology but a
further insult to the Muslim community as a whole.'

(*Sunday Times*, London, 19 Feb. 1989)

*The British press, on rather different grounds, were more likely to
side with the Council of Mosques than with Mr El-Essawi:*

Works of art need no apologies

It is not the job of the artist to make life more comfortable for
societies or governments. It *is* the job of democratic governments
to protect the artist's right to free expression and the liberty of
life. That is what all the sound and fury over Salman Rushdie's
novel, *The Satanic Verses*, is fundamentally about—not whether life
would have been easier if he had never written it, nor whether it is
an offensive or even readable book, nor whether its publication en-
dangers our hostages or our international interests.

'Writers and politicians are natural rivals,' Salman Rushdie once
wrote. 'Both groups try to make the world in their own images; they
fight for the same territory.' In his case the fight to possess—or
reinterpret—the imaginative territory of Islam got him into deeper
waters than even he could have anticipated, including a death warrant personally issued by the spiritual leader of Iran and the Shia
Muslims, the Ayatollah Khomeini.

The politicians' response has been to try and reclaim the territory for diplomatic compromise. After two days of humming and hawing and wait-and-seeing, Sir Geoffrey Howe finally made some discreet complaints to the Iranian Government and called on his fellow Ministers of the European Community to fall into line. After an equal period of silence which may have reflected some internal differences, the Iranian Government, too, sought to limit the damage, to separate politics from religion, calling on Rushdie to apologise to the Muslim world—a demand which led the embattled author to issue a statement profoundly regretting 'the distress that publication has occasioned to sincere followers of Islam.'

One hopes this statement of regret will defuse the situation, and last night's immediate Iranian response was encouraging in this respect. But the campaign against the book may not end so easily, especially if confusing signals continue to emerge from the rival factions in Tehran. In any event, an act of repentance or humiliation in order to gain 'pardon' is hardly appropriate in the wider moral context of the case. Neither Britain nor the author has anything to apologise *for*.

Both can, as Rushdie has done, regret the offence caused or the anger stirred, but not the act itself. For the right to perform that act, to create and publish a book, has been fought for too painfully to be tossed aside in a desire for a quieter life. Those who ask that it should be are forgetting their own history—from Socrates to Stalin. Galileo is admired for his intellectual courage, not his retractions before the Inquisition.

In this light the British Government's response has been cautious and late. . . .

The harsh lesson of the pasta lesson that thousands of people have died to defend—is that it never pays to compromise. In the end, Mr Rushdie must have the right to publish his book and the freedom and security to publicise it. He is entitled to nothing less.   (from *Observer*, London, 19 Feb. 1989)

AYATOLLAH KHOMEINI

Even if Salman Rushdie repents and becomes the most pious man of time, it is incumbent on every Muslim to employ everything he has got, his life and his wealth, to send him to hell.

(*Irna Iranian News Agency*, 19 Feb. 1989)

On 20 February at his meeting with the EC Foreign Minister Sir Geoffrey Howe was 'taken by surprise' at the strength of feeling shown by his colleagues.

When the EC ministers assembled it quickly became clear that several member states, West Germany and France in particular, were keen to go a step further than mere condemnation. The 12 Ministers issued a joint statement undertaking to recall ambassadors from Tehran and freeze all high level visits between their countries and Iran. In addition they condemned the 'incitement to murder' as an 'unacceptable violation of the most elementary principles and obligations which govern relations among sovereign states'.

(from *Independent*, London, 21 Feb. 1989)

Too tolerant for too long

The diplomatic sanctions taken yesterday against Iran by the European Community are welcome, as are the belated measures announced by the British Government. Until lunchtime yesterday it had appeared that this country did not take particularly seriously murderous threats to freedom of expression. The Foreign Office seemed more interested in protecting what remained of its exercise in *rapprochement* with Tehran than in demonstrating that Iran's adherence to the norms of civilised international behaviour was essential to that exercise. There was something particularly unseemly about the fact that France, Germany and Holland had last week reacted more rapidly and more firmly than Sir Geoffrey Howe deemed appropriate to Ayatollah Khomeini's call to assassinate a leading British writer.

Sir Geoffrey's apologists adduced supposedly weighty reasons to justify his caution. Different groups are undoubtedly competing for influence in Tehran and there was nothing to be gained, it was said, by playing into the hands of the fundamentalist radicals in Tehran who have no desire for improved relations with the West. Next, the British businessman Roger Cooper remains effectively a hostage. Others, including Terry Waite, are held in Lebanon by Iranian surrogates and their survival, and ultimate release, depend to some extent on relations between London and Tehran.

Moreover, this country has a large and currently unhappy Muslim population, composed overwhelmingly of British citizens. It is important for the future of good race relations that their beliefs are treated with respect. This is why the offence of blasphemy should either be extended to embrace other major religions or abandoned.

The events of the weekend demonstrate, yet again, the consequences of appeasement. The ayatollah contemptuously rejected Salman Rushdie's statement of profound regret for any offence caused to 'sincere followers of Islam' by his book, *The Satanic Verses*. Neither Mr Rushdie's statement—extracted under the most appalling of threats—nor Sir Geoffrey's studied moderation had eased the crisis or improved the position of supposed pragmatists in Tehran. Mr Cooper faces a long prison sentence and the fate of the hostages remains unknown.

Yesterday, however, in a further attempt to calm the atmosphere, the Archbishop of Canterbury issued an unprecedented message of understanding in which he stressed that he regarded offence to other religions as being as wrong as offence to the religious beliefs of Christians. This must surely meet the legitimate worries of the Muslim community in this country. It contrasts sharply with the shocking and unislamic lack of compassion or mercy demonstrated by the ayatollah when he rejected any possibility of 'repentance' on the part of Mr Rushdie, and called on Muslims to bend every effort 'to send him to Hell'. It is for those who lead Britain's Muslims to respond with tolerance and maturity to the archbishop's direct appeal and to ensure that their zealots obey the law of the land—not the dictates of a bloodthirsty medieval bigot.

(*Independent*, London, 21 Feb. 1989)

The Archbishop of Canterbury, Dr Robert Runcie, yesterday implicitly called for a strengthening of the law against blasphemy to cover religions other than Christianity, in a statement which condemned incitement to murder.

Dr Runcie said that only the utterly insensitive could fail to see that the publication of Mr Rushdie's book, *The Satanic Verses*, had deeply offended Muslims both here and throughout the world. 'I understand their feelings and I firmly believe that offence to the religious beliefs of the followers of Islam or any other faith is quite as wrong as offence to the religious beliefs of Christians. But however great the grievance, I utterly condemn incitement to murder or any other violence from any source whatever.'

(*Independent*, London, 22 Feb. 1989)

TO THE INTERNATIONAL COMMITTEE
FROM SIR SRIDATH RAMPHAL
Secretary General Commonwealth Secretariat

'Nothing is more important at the moment in the issue over Salman Rushdie's *'The Satanic Verses'* than that those in authority in Iran should be left in no doubt that directing and rewarding the killing of Rushdie is wholly unacceptable to the rest of the world. There is no country in the Commonwealth that supports or acquiesces in such conduct. Even countries that have banned the book's publication draw the line at incitement to its author's assassination. Iran must not believe that this is a quarrel only with Britain. All people, all countries, that value the norms of free societies and look for a world governed by law, are outraged by Tehran's incitement to murder and join in demanding its withdrawal.'

(London, 20 Feb. 1989)

DECLARATION OF UNESCO'S DIRECTOR-GENERAL,
MR FEDERICO MAYOR

For Unesco, as a world-wide forum for dialogue and understanding, freedom of creation, of opinion and of expression, with respect for convictions, beliefs and religions, is essential.

A house of freedom, Unesco is troubled whenever the fundamental right of the individual to express his or her thoughts is threatened. A house of creativity, it has a sense of loss whenever the human imagination is condemned to silence. A house of peace, it suffers whenever violence is unleashed.

It is every person's duty to respect other people's religions; it is also every person's duty to respect other people's freedom of expression. Whatever the offence may be, no incitement to violence, from whatever source, is admissible.

The human community thrives on its differences, be they of race, language, belief or culture. Such differences are our common wealth; respect for them by one and all is the guarantee of our survival.

(Paris, 20 Feb. 1989)

There were other kinds of responses.

THE SPORT SAYS

By any reasonable yardstick we reckon that Ayatollah Ruhollah Khomeini has broken the law of his country by inciting his followers to murder author Salman Rushdie.

The religious ruler of an impoverished land has even promised £2 million to carry out the execution.

It is outrageous and unlawful—and he ought to be made to answer for it.

That's why we are offering £1 million to anyone directly responsible for bringing him to face a fair trial in this country.

We are not against Islam, or, indeed, any other religion. We are not supporting Rushdie or his boring book. In fact, the Ayatollah has done more to sell it than the best-orchestrated campaign.

And we are certainly not sinking to Khomeini's level by demanding his execution.

In Britain we believe in live and let live. We might not agree with what Rushdie wrote, but we defend his right to say it. Moslems, Hindus, Buddhists and Rastafarians are all welcome to our tolerant society. But there is only one law for all of us.

Those who say their deep religious convictions prevent them from obeying the law of this land should quit Britain immediately and go to live in a country where the conflict does not exist.

(*Sunday Sport*, London, 19 Feb. 1989)

ROBERT MAXWELL
Chairman, Maxwell Communications

We need waste no words on this barbarian . . . Let us deal with the barbarian in his own coin, the only coin that so diseased and underdeveloped a mind can understand, the coin of a price on his head . . . I will offer $10m to the man or woman who will, not kill, but civilise the barbarian Ayatollah, the test of which shall be that Khomeini shall publicly recite the Ten Commandments, with special reference to the sixth ('Thou shalt not kill') and ninth ('Thou shall not bear false witness against thy neighbour').

(*Bookseller*, London, 24 Feb. 1989)

JOSEPH BRODSKY
Russian Nobel Laureate

... There is nothing surprising about the Ayatollah Khomeini, who is theoretically the top authority on Islam, commenting on the book. The death sentence he issued amounts, as it were, to a review of the book. As for Khomeini himself and what he has under his turban, I'm quite surprised that nobody thus far has put a price on that as well. It would be the only comparable response. If men of letters feel so indignant about the whole affair they should have pooled their resources and come up with the price. Mind you, it shouldn't be too big. On the whole this lifts the veil on Islamic fundamentalism. They execute people left and right and nobody gives a squeak.'   (*New Statesman*, London, 31 March 1989)

After the 'tough' EC statement, Western-aligned countries came to their support. On 21 February, USA, Sweden, Canada, Australia, Norway and Brazil all committed themselves to the EC position.

In Britain, Howe received the unqualified support of the Opposition and the Conservative Party.

Iran responded to this unanimity by an increasing solidarity between the different factions. Hashemi Rafsanjani, the Iranian Parliamentary Speaker and leading moderate, said: 'The EC's decision will have absolutely no effect on us as we are used to being on our own ... and the present confrontation will end once again with our victory.'

UN diplomats involved in the Iran-Iraq peace talks were worried that the whole saga would undermine Iraqi confidence in Iran, stiffen the resolve of Iranian radicals and threaten the progress of the peace talks.

In Britain, the West Yorkshire police confirmed that they would not be bringing charges of incitement to murder against Muslim

leaders in Bradford. The Crown Prosecution Service had concluded
that there was insufficient direct evidence, but said that one of the
factors it took into account was whether such a prosecution would
be in the public interest.

More moderate Muslim leaders, who claimed to represent the
majority view of the British Muslim community, spoke out against
Khomeini's death threat.

As Britain's one remaining diplomat in Iran prepared to leave
yesterday, strong support for the Government stand against Ayatollah Khomeini came from Chancellor Helmut Kohl of West Germany
and President Mitterrand of France.

Chancellor Kohl called on the 'entire civilised world' to take
action against Iran's threat to kill Salman Rushdie. His cabinet decided to halt preparation for high-level economic talks with Tehran.

In Paris, President Mitterrand told his weekly cabinet meeting:
'. . . All dogmatism which through violence undermines freedom of
thought and the right to free expression is, in my view, absolute
evil. The moral and spiritual progress of humanity is linked to the
recoil of all fanaticisms.'

Britain's chargé d'affaires in Tehran, Mr Nick Browne, returned
to London with two colleagues yesterday saying he feared it would
be some time before relations with Iran could be repaired.

'We did not call for this affair. The Iranians unfortunately started
it,' he said. 'Statements by Ayatollah Khomeini gave us no choice
but to leave. We asked them to state clearly that they rejected the
threat which had been made, that they rejected all forms of violence and that they stood by considered norms of international behaviour. Unfortunately they were not able to do that.'

In London, the Iranian chargé d'affaires, Mr Mohammad Basti,
and his staff have yet to state when they will return to Tehran.

Further support for Mr Rushdie came yesterday from 800 Dutch
authors, artists, publishers, and journalists who urged their government to break diplomatic ties with Iran if it failed to rescind the
execution order.

The Nigerian Nobel laureate, Mr Wole Soyinka, condemned the
threat against Mr Rushdie as cowardly, criminal, and blasphemous.

(from *Guardian*, London, 23 Feb. 1989)

1987 IRAN'S MAIN TRADING PARTNERS

Iranian Imports	(%)	Iranian exports	(%)
W Germany	19.4	USA	14.6
Japan	12.9	Japan	13.0
Italy	6.2	Italy	8.8
UK	6.2	Netherlands	8.1
Turkey	5.4	India	6.0
Netherlands	3.5	Turkey	5.8
Brazil	2.0	Spain	5.8
Spain	1.3	W Germany	4.2
India	1.0	Singapore	3.8
Singapore	1.0	Brazil	3.1
USA	0.7	UK	2.6
Total (in dollars)	9.0 billion	Total (in dollars)	10.9 billion

Source: Economist Intelligence Unit

Iran leaders unite to attack West

The Iranian President, Ali Khamenei, who last week hinted at the possibility of pardon for a repentant Salman Rushdie, yesterday proclaimed the monolithic unity of Iran's clergy behind the decision to sentence the author to death. 'The arrow has been launched towards its target. It is now flying towards its aim,' he said. . . .

President Khamenei, who is on a tour of eastern Europe, said there was no difference between himself and Ayatollah Khomeini over the Iranian spiritual leader's twice-repeated death sentence against the author of The Satanic Verses. 'The Western analysis of this matter is funny and mistaken,' he said.

The latest statement by the Ayatollah Khomeini, broadcast by Tehran Radio yesterday, nevertheless reinforced the view that his intervention in the Rushdie affair marked a definite shift towards the radical wing of the ruling clerical hierarchy, which opposes better relations with the West. 'As long as I am alive I will never allow liberals to come to power again, nor shall I allow any deviation from our policy of "neither East nor West," and I will continue cutting off the hands of all Soviet and American mercenaries. . . .'   (from *Independent*, London, 23 Feb. 1989)

On 23 February, Iranian members of Parliament, like their European counterparts, demanded that Iran lead the way in breaking off diplomatic relations with Britain and take reprisals against her EC allies.

A further 10 people died on 24 February, and about 50 were injured, during anti-Rushdie rioting in Bombay—the first deaths since the fatwa *was pronounced.*

As was only to be expected, Ayatollah Khomeini's call for 'Shaitan' Rushdie's head has begun to draw blood. That the killing field has for the moment turned out to be the most cosmopolitan city of the country which was the first to ban *Satanic Verses* is another matter. It is not likely to unduly upset the Iranian leader who, worried about the prospects of his revolution taking a U-turn, appears to have belatedly seen in Rushdie's book a god-sent opportunity. It has not only helped him upstage his opponents within Iran who are harking for change, but also in realising an impossible dream—through his kill Rushdie fatwa, he has succeeded to some extent in cutting across the Shia-Sunni divide and assuming the posture of the tallest leader within the global Muslim fraternity, forcing more level-headed Islamic leaders to stand up and be counted.

If anything, in Friday's bloody battle on Bombay's streets the Ayatollah will see a vindication of his notion of religion in which Muslims are for Islam and not the other way around—they must kill or be dead rather than live with any affront to their faith in a multi-religious and even non-religious world community. In this din of battle, there is the danger that the voices of moderation and reason may not be heard by many. It is necessary to register that Islamic Egypt, Indonesia, Oman and to some extent even Saudi Arabia are talking a language quite different from that of Khomeini. . . .

In India, apart from the immediate concern over how the Rushdie saga will end, there is the more pressing issue of what the fallout of the unfortunate episode portends for the communal cauldron that the country has become. Earlier, reacting from hurt religious sentiments, virtually the entire Muslim community in India had condemned *Satanic Verses* and demanded its ban. In that they received the support of a section of the non-Muslim liberal intelligentsia. But following Khomeini's call, the community appears to have become polarised between those pro-mercy and those who want to move in for the kill. Now, the Imam of Delhi's Jama Masjid and Syedna Burhanuddin have lent their voice to the vociferous backing to Khomeini's murderous fatwa by some fringe Muslim organisations.

A Muslim college student from Bombay fears that Khomeini's firman will generate feelings amongst fellow Hindus that all Muslims are after all blood-thirsty fanatics. A journalist from Delhi and an executive from Bombay told this paper that in the wake of *The Satanic Verses* and its aftermath, a plethora of prejudices against Muslims are surfacing to the fore.

Will Rushdie's book—Khomeini's call—recharge the reservoirs of communal prejudice amongst Hindus and Muslims in India? Will Muslims' anti-Rushdie sentiments be exploited for anti-Muslim ends by Hindus' consciousness that Indian Muslim leaders who have dubbed Khomeini's dictat as 'un-Islamic' far outnumber those who have risen to his support? Or that the call for the Bombay bandh and a protest march received only a lukewarm response from the city's Muslims—even organisations such as the Muslim League and the Jamaat-E-Islami maintained a studied silence on the issue? . . .

(from *Observer*, Bombay, 26 Feb. 1989)

In Britain angry Muslims shouted 'Where do we go for justice!' while the Home Secretary, Douglas Hurd, told a meeting in Birmingham that under British law there was nothing he could do about The Satanic Verses. *The bulk of his speech was on the obligation of immigrants to integrate.*

Rushdie row in Israel

YORAM KESSEL
Jerusalem

Israel now has its own Salman Rushdie row, after a local publisher announced that he was rushing to translate *Satanic Verses*, the Rushdie book which Moslems feel is blasphemous.

Ignoring the fact that several Western publishers have cancelled plans to publish the book after death threats against the author and publisher by Ayatollah Khomeini of Iran, the Keter publishing house in Jerusalem said that it was unperturbed.

Keter has also ignored complaints by local Moslem leaders who say that publication of the book constitutes a direct offence to Islam.

All 100 copies ordered by Steimatzky's, the country's leading bookseller, have been snapped up, and more have had to be ordered.

Not only Moslems have complained about the book. Rabbi Avraham Ravitz, the leader of the strictly Orthodox Degel Hatorah Party, said this week that Salman Rushdie needed to be condemned.

His book had portrayed Mohammed as going to a prostitute. 'Imagine what the response would have been if someone had written that about Moses.'

(*Jewish Chronicle*, 24 Feb. 1989)

Ahkundazeh Basti, the Iranian Chargé d'affaires, finally left London on 1 March 1989 lamenting that the British 'government has taken the lead in making this matter purely political. The more they take this line, it will have a disastrous effect for the whole world.'

Events took a new turn, however, with a suggestion from the Soviet Union that they might be able to mediate in 'this very delicate and sensitive issue'.

World writers' statement

On February 14th the Ayatollah Khomeini called on all Muslims to seek out and execute Salman Rushdie, the author of *The Satanic Verses*, and those involved in its publication worldwide. We, the undersigned, insofar as we defend the right to freedom of opinion and expression as embodied in the Universal Declaration of Human Rights, declare that we also are involved in the publication.

We are involved whether we approve the contents of the book or not. We appreciate the distress the book has aroused and deeply regret the loss of life associated with the ensuing conflict. We call upon world opinion to support the right of all people to express their ideas and beliefs and to discuss them with their critics on the basis of mutual tolerance, free from censorship, intimidation and violence.

We request all world leaders to continue to repudiate the threats made against Salman Rushdie and those involved in the book's publication worldwide, and to take firm action to ensure that these threats are withdrawn.

Thousands of literary figures across the world have put their names to this statement. These are some of them:

Dannie Abse
Said Aburish
Chinua Achebe
Kathy Acker
Larry Adler
Joan Aitken
Eric Ambler
Babakh Amir-Khosravi
Phuong Anh
Alan Ayckbourn
Paul Bailey
Sebastian Barker
Stan Barstow
Nina Bawden
Samuel Beckett
Sybille Bedford
Giaconda Belli
Alan Bennett
Rachel Billington
Claire Bloom
Robert Bolt
Malcolm Bradbury
Melvyn Bragg
Richard Brain
Joseph Brodsky
Nicholas Byam Shaw
Nigel Calder

Simon Callow
Mel Calman
Patrick Campbell
Denis Cannan
Robert Caro
Angela Carter
Amarjit Chandan
Robin Chapman
Caryl Churchill
John Coetzee
Lettice Cooper
William Cooper
Peter Curman
Don DeLillo
Anita Desai
Andre Deutsch
Joan Didion
Mohammed Djalali
E L Doctorow
Margaret Drabble
John Gregory Dunn
Nawal El Saadawi
Per Olov Enquist
Ruth Fainlight
Moris Farbi
Elaine Feinstein
Eva Figes

Penelope Fitzgerald
Frances Fitzgerald
Ken Follett
Michael Foot
Margaret Forster
Antonia Fraser
Michael Frayn
Carlos Fuentes
Juan Gaoytisolo
Jane Gardam
Leon Garfield
Giovanni Giovannini
Victoria Glendinning
William Golding
Nadine Gordimer
Mary Gordon
Giles Gordon
Andrew Graham-Yooll
Simon Gray
Graham Greene
Antony Grey
Christopher Hitchens
Russell Hoban
Richard Hoggart
Alan Hollinghurst
Michael Holroyd
Sereydoyun Hoveyda
Edward Hower
Shirley Hughes
Kazuo Ishigura
Peter Jay
Roy Jenkins
Kjell Olaf Jense
Judith Kazantzis
H R F Keating
Dhabiya Khamees
Ismai Kho'i
Francis King
Doris Lessing
Frederic Lindsay
Penelope Lively
David Lodge
Elizabeth Longford
Anthony Lukas
Alison Lurie
Manoocher Mahjoobi

Norman Mailer
Robert Massie
Ian McEwan
Larry McMurtry
Ved Mehta
Stanley Middleton
Artur Miedzyrzecki
Arthur Miller
Rodney Milnes
James Michener
Penelope Mortimer
John Mortimer
Iris Murdoch
Peter Nichols
Deborah Owen
David Owen
Parviz Owsia
Caryl Phillips
Harold Pinter
Agneta Pleijel
Igor Pomerantsev
Dennis Potter
V S Pritchett
Lenka Prochazkova
Frederic Raphael
Piers Paul Read
Ruth Rendell
Jasper Ridley
Tom Rosenthal
Philip Roth
Marya Rozanova
Bernice Rubens
Anatoly Rybakov
Amina Said
Edward Said
Anthony Sampson
Paul Scherer
Tom Sharpe
Alan Silitoe
Milan Simecka
Andrei Sinyavsky
Joan Smith
Joran Sonnevi
Susan Sontag
Drago Stambuk
George Steiner

Robert Stone
Susan Strachan
Geoffery Strachen
Anthony Summers
Behruz Suresrafil
Rosemary Sutcliff
Graham Swift
Amir Taheri
Gay Talese
Colin Thubron
Anthony Thwaite
Ann Thwaite
Lionel Tiger
Pavel Tigrid
Mazhar Tirmazi
Tatyana Tolstaya
Jeremy Treglown
Diana Trilling

Birgitta Trotzig
Joran Tunstrom
Milan Uhde
Uo Van Ai
Mario Vargas Llosa
Jan Vladislav
Kurt Vonnegut
Marina Warner
Stuart Weir
Arnold Wesker
Francis Wheen
Hugh Whitemore
Nigel Williams
Charles Wintour
Manoucher Yektai
Alan Yentob
Philip Ziegler
Juliusz Zulawski

Sponsoring organisations include:

Article 19
Booksellers Association
    of Great Britain and
    Northern Ireland
Charter 88
English Centre of Pen
International Independent
    Publishers Guild

Index on Censorship
NUJ
New Statesman and
    Society
Society of Authors
Theatre Writers Union
Writers Guild of Great
    Britain

HOMI BHABHA

The tragic events surrounding the publication of *The Satanic Verses* have so polarised public opinion that it seems difficult to produce a political and cultural initiative that will promote responsibility, understanding and reconciliation. But difficult or not, an intervention is urgently needed. Without one we find ourselves in the eye of the storm, at once becalmed and embattled. *We are embattled in the war between the cultural imperatives of Western liberalism, and the fundamentalist interpretations of Islam, both of which seem to claim an abstract and universal authority.* What results is an implacable antagonism that is continually rehearsed in the media, sometimes by journalistic reportage, at other times as informed opinion or intellectual debate. On the one hand there is the liberal opposition to book burning and banning based on the important belief in the freedom of expression and the right to publish and be damned—and emphatically not to be condemned to death. On the other side, there exists what has been identified as a Muslim fundamentalist position. This seems to include everything from the Ayatollah's death edict and the internal politics of Iran, to the more problematic position of British Muslims who may feel that Rushdie has violated the received wisdom of the Koran, but are resolute that this should not lead to illegal acts of incitement and violence. The blind rage through which these positions are increasingly acted out on the international stage has its own agenda, but meanwhile the lives of Rushdie and of others, in India and Pakistan, are further endangered. Some are already dead. The complex vision of *Satanic Verses* is fast losing its reality. Both literature and humanity are being reduced to empty symbols: symbols that at the same time are the prisoners of a Western liberal conscience and hostages to an Islamic fundamentalist orthodoxy.

For those of us, who, like Salman Rushdie himself, belong to the black communities, and have worked in various ways for the rights of migrants, refugees and ethnic groups, neither of these two perspectives is adequate. They do not represent the social and political values of the multiracial society that we identify with, either as a political idea or as a social reality. Our experiences in the classroom, in community work and the media, have made us aware of the problems of the liberal democratic state and its sense of cultural supremacy and historical sovereignty. Having experienced forms of racial and cultural discrimination, and having engaged with its social effects, we can only deplore the anti-Muslim statements and anti-third world sentiments that have emerged in the escalation of international tension. Such political positions are profoundly at odds with Salman Rushdie's own beliefs and the causes to which he has dedicated his entire writing life. There can be no accommodation between racist, cultural stereotypes and the narrative of *Satanic Verses*, which attempts to reveal the hidden injuries of social democratic complacency, while unsettling the pieties of Eurocentrism and ethnocentrism. Equally, those of us who have experienced the authoritarian and patriarchal conditions of orthodox communities, of any colour or creed, and have witnessed their attempts to stifle dissent and discussion, can never endorse demands for censorship and unquestioned conformity. Such quiescence serves and preserves the traditional hierarchies of power and knowledge. So where do we turn, we who see the limits of liberalism and fear the absolutist demands of fundamentalism?

This is ironically the central problem in *The Satanic Verses*. It is Rushdie's painful and problematic encounter with the most intractable and intimate area of his imaginative life. What the book uniquely reveals is a life lived precariously on the cultural and political margins of modern society. Where once we could believe in the comforts and continuities of Tradition, today we must face the responsibilities of cultural Translation. In the attempt to mediate between different cultures, languages and societies, there is always the threat of mistranslation, confusion and fear.

The Satanic Verses is a post-colonial work that attempts the onerous duty of unravelling this cultural translation. The book is written in a spirit of questioning, doubt, interrogation and puzzlement which articulates the dilemma of the migrant, the émigré, the minority. It is by turning back to the social and political experience of these communities—multi-ethnic and minority—whose historical fate requires them to construct their cultural identities from contesting traditions and imperatives, that we shall be able to re-evaluate the message of *The Satanic Verses*. If there were no doubt, no confusion or conflict, would religion or literature have any place in our lives? Would *The Satanic Verses* have been written?

• *Homi Bhabha, a lecturer at Sussex University, presented the view that emerged out of the first meeting of the 'Black Voices in Defence of Salman Rushdie'.*

(*New Statesman*, London, 3 March 1989)

Meanwhile Margaret Thatcher joined her Foreign Secretary in criticising The Satanic Verses: 'We have known in our own religion people doing things which are deeply offensive to some of us . . . and we have felt it very much. And that is what has happened in Islam.'

Salman Rushdie contacted Paddy Ashdown, the Liberal and Social Democrat Party leaders expressing his concern that the Government was 'weakening in its resolve'.

Rude, as in rudimentary

It was presumably someone else at the Foreign Office who went through *The Satanic Verses*, picking out the naughty bits which led Sir Geoffrey Howe to conclude on Thursday that the book was 'extremely rude' about Britain. The result was not a great success, either as an exercise in literary criticism or as a covert signal to the moderates in Iran. . . .

There is something rather worrying too, on the principled front, about the way that Sir Geoffrey delivered his latest judgement on behalf of 'the British Government (and) the British people.' Aren't we supposed to be against governments saying that they disapprove of books—let alone making up other people's minds for them? It was also a somewhat philistine judgement. Not only was the book 'rude' but, said Sir Geoffrey, it 'compares Britain with Hitler's Germany.' It does nothing of the kind. It does portray, as our reviewer Angela Carter wrote before the great row began, 'the mean streets of a marvellously evoked eighties London.' And since most of its characters, like Mr Rushdie himself, are 'displaced persons of one kind or another,' it also confronts in its surreal narrative images of racism which are not Nazi-like at all but very definitely British. The Foreign Office may take offence at the surreal scene when 57 uniformed policemen on the Sussex coast gleefully arrest a suspected—expletive deleted—Pakistani immigrant. They may dislike the description of the death in custody of Dr Uhuru Simba, the suspected Granny Ripper, who broke his neck (said the authorities) falling out of his bunk. They may take even graver exception to the references to Her Majesty, the Prime Minister and the Falklands. But *The Satanic Verses* is no more about Thatcher's Britain than it is about Khomeini's Iran. And on any rational scale of offence-giving, its phantasmagoric dreams about the Prophet and his teachings can and do upset many Muslims—as Mr Rushdie has now accepted—to a degree which his less fantastic picture of British illiberality cannot reasonably provoke. . . .

Mr Rushdie seems to have broken his silence yesterday to express concern about Sir Geoffrey's statement; and, regrettably, one can see why.   (from *Guardian*, London, 4 March 1989)

Over the next few days the success of the radical faction in Iran became clear—a success which finally resulted in the resignation of the liberal Ayatollah Hossein-Ali Montazeri, Khomeini's heir designate, on 30 March 1989. Pakistani fundamentalists put increasing pressure on Mrs Bhutto's regime; pro-Khomeini demonstrations took place in South Beirut; while Ahmed Jebril of the Popular Front for the Liberation of Palestine-General Command volunteered to carry out the Ayatollah's fatwa. The Russian intervention had not proved successful.

Islam turns its sights on Marxists

DAVID HIRST

Amazing though their impact on international relations have been, Salman Rushdie and his Satanic Verses cannot claim credit for the extraordinary honour which Ayatollah Khomeini bestowed on the Soviet union last week.

True, they lent additional significance to his two-hour tête-à-tête with Eduard Shevardnadze—apparently the first foreign minister he has ever received—and the accompanying intimations that the Islamic republic would now turn, in a big way, to its mighty, much feared northern neighbour in compensation for its deepening divorce with the West.

But the shift was already underway: the Ayatollah had already decided that perestroika was nothing less than proof that Islam was the only answer, and that the time had come to persuade that citadel of 'godlessness and irreligion', the Soviet union itself, of this self-evident truth. . . .   (from *Guardian*, London, 9 March 1989)

Le Monde criticised the UN for its 'timidity and silence' and the British Library placed The Satanic Verses *in its 'restricted', locked shelves.*

JOHN HARRIOT

Monday's report that a Vatican official had condemned Salman Rushdie for blaspheming and spoken in curiously ambivalent tones of the threat to his life was, for those aware of the present climate of opinion in Rome, like hearing the second boot drop. It seemed only a matter of time before someone was bound to say something of the sort.

Since the Vatican's official newspaper, *Osservatore Romano*, reverted to publishing unsigned articles, it has indicated the seniority of writers only by the number of attached asterisks so both the identity of the writer in question and his degree of authority remain obscure. The article carried three stars, which can mark statements by the Pope himself, so it was certainly someone of very high rank.

As this system permits coded messages, kite-flying and easy disclaimers, the motive behind the article is also obscure. It may be partly political. Though the Vatican recognises that dialogue with the ayatollah's fundamentalist regime is impossible, it has shown over a long period a strong inclination to be on good terms with the Muslim world: partly to reach a better religious understanding with Muslims (and other non-Christian believers) as the Second Vatican Council urged; partly to protect Christian minorities in Arab countries, notably in Egypt and Lebanon; . . . and partly to maintain its status, should occasion arise, of diplomatic honest broker.

The present Pope has consistently spoken out forcefully and eloquently in defence of human life and human dignity and against abuses of state authority. It is incredible that he or anyone who shares his mind would actually endorse the savage threats to Mr Rushdie's life. Is it conceivable that these political considerations can explain why the Vatican and its Secretariat of State in particular, might wish to soft-pedal its direct criticism of the Iranian regime? It has no wish to be caricatured as yet another Western enemy of Islam.

Thus far the *Osservatore Romano* article is at least intelligible, even rationally defensible, however ignoble it may be thought, smacking more of institutional calculation than religious principle. What to many Catholics and fellow-Christians is most alarming is its readiness to add its own condemnation and intolerance to the already intolerable anguish of Mr Rushdie. It is not simply that the charge of blasphemy against an unbeliever is a contradiction in terms. Only a believer can deliberately insult the God in whom he believes. It is the suspicion of a link between the affronted tone in this particular instance and the hostility towards any expression of religious dissent within the Catholic Church which characterises the Vatican at the present time. . . .

The Second Vatican Council seemed finally to have marked the end of this long dark night of obscurantism. It explicitly recognised that the Church must not invade areas of learning and activity where it has no competence. It explicitly recognised the intrinsic value of democracy, tolerance, including, for the first time, the innate rights of the non-believer and free speech. It expressed not just the right but the duty, in certain circumstances, of dissent within the Church itself. . . .

During Pope John Paul's papacy, however, that ground is steadily being eroded. 'John Paul,' said one Vatican observer recently, 'is good for the world but bad for the Church.' Leading Catholic theologians such as Metz, Schillebeeckx, Kung and the Brazilian Franciscan, Leonardo Boff, have found themselves silenced, censured or penalised. . . .

It is against this background that the Vatican article takes on wider significance. . . .

• The author is a Roman Catholic commentator and a regular columnist for The Tablet.

(from *Independent*, London, 8 March 1989)

On 7 March Iran formally broke off diplomatic relations with Britain and appealed to all Muslim nations for a united anti-British front.

Islamic states refuse to back Rushdie death sentence

Islamic foreign ministers in Riyadh yesterday called for *The Satanic Verses* to be withdrawn but refused to back Iran's call for the author, Mr Salman Rushdie, to be killed. . . .

The ICO told member states to boycott Mr Rushdie's publishers if they did not withdraw the book, and urged the international community to pass laws protecting the beliefs of others.

(from *Guardian*, London, 17 March 1989)

Countless letters to the press, many of them from writers and writers' organisations, appeared throughout these weeks, as did editorials.

Norman Podhoretz's statement (Guardian, February 22) that the British literary establishment has been 'slow' to support Salman Rushdie, is, as readers of your paper know, totally untrue where English Pen is concerned. For the record, we sent a telegram to Rajiv Gandhi protesting against the banning of the book in October and in the same month attempted to engage in a dialogue with the Muslim Council for Religious Tolerance on the subject of free speech; protested against the Bradford book-burning in letters to the press on February 2. Lastly, on February 15, immediately after the Ayatollah's death threats, we sent a letter to the Prime Minister calling for protection for our distinguished member Salman Rushdie while Harold Pinter, a vice-president of English Pen, went on nationwide (and US) television to the same effect.

English Pen would like to take the opportunity of this letter to pay tribute to the heroic determination of Salman Rushdie's publisher not to be cowed by threats and above all to the steadfastness of British booksellers, who have continued to make *The Satanic Verses* available. That is after all the whole point: freedom to publish, sell and read (or not read) within the law.

It should be recorded that our firm but non-inflammatory position has received widespread Muslim support.

ANTONIA FRASER.
President, English Pen,
London SW3.

(*Guardian*, London, 25 Feb. 1989)

10 Downing Street
London SW1A 2AA
16 March 1989

From the Private Secretary

Dear Lady Antonia

The Prime Minister has asked me to thank you and Mrs Pullein-Thompson for your letter of 15 February about the Iranian threats against Mr Salman Rushdie and his publishers, and to reply on her behalf.

The Government have left the Iranians in no doubt that Britain is not prepared to tolerate such threats. The European Community has withdrawn its Heads of Mission from Tehran and put a moratorium on high-level visits to and from Iran. We have recalled our diplomats from Tehran and closed our Embassy. At our request, the Iranians have done the same with their Embassy and diplomatic staff in London. We have taken further measures following the Iranian decision of 7 March to break relations and their refusal to withdraw their threats. A number of Iranians are being expelled, and the Iranian Consulate-General in Hong Kong is being closed. There has been widespread support in many countries for the stand that we and the Twelve have taken.

We would like to have a normal relationship with Iran, but this is absolutely out of the question while that country is threatening the life of our citizens. We recognise the offence to Islamic sensitivities which Rushdie's book has caused. But nobody has the right to advocate the use of violence in support of their opinions. Our commitment to the protection of the rights and freedoms of our citizens, including freedom of expression, is unshakeable. Before Britain's relationship with Iran can be repaired, Iran must show clearly that it is willing to meet its international obligations and to renounce the use or threat of violence against the citizens and interests of other countries.

Yours sincerely,
DOMINIC MORRIS

IAN DAVIDSON

Three weeks have now passed since Ayatollah Ruhollah Khomeini issued a religious edict calling for the death of Mr Salman Rushdie, author of *The Satanic Verses*, and a peaceful settlement of this appalling affair appears as far away as ever.

Iran has now broken off diplomatic relations with Britain, and is attempting to whip up support for its holy war from other Islamic states at the forthcoming conference in Riyadh. Moderate Arab states will probably turn a deaf ear to the Iranian campaign; but whatever the immediate diplomatic outcome, there can be no doubt that the Iranian threat to Mr Rushdie's life remains as serious as ever.

In the circumstances, one can only be dismayed at the figure cut by the British Government in its response to Iran's monstrous attempt to defy the rule of law in Britain. It is Iran which has broken off relations with Britain; and yet Britain is being threatened by what amounts to a declaration of terrorism, and in logic it ought to have been Britain which broke off relations.

Moreover, the British government went to demeaning lengths to avert such a diplomatic rupture. Mrs Thatcher and Sir Geoffrey Howe both attempted to appease the Iranians by issuing their own criticisms of the Rushdie book. Yet it must surely have been obvious that the Government could not do or say anything which would be consistent with British law and would also satisfy the Iranians. Mealy-mouthed expressions of distaste for *The Satanic Verses* merely served to make the Government look obsequious and cringing. . . .

The implications are unmistakable and alarming: in the hope of avoiding a break in diplomatic relations, the British Government was fully prepared to adopt the posture of an equally injured party, even if it meant endorsing (in modified terms) the Ayatollah's attack on *The Satanic Verses*. If Mr Rushdie felt he was in danger of being dumped by the British Government, he may have had good reason.

Whether Sir Geoffrey or Mrs Thatcher thinks *The Satanic Verses* is a nice book or a nasty book, whether they believe it is offensive to Moslems, or whether they consider it is unfair to the British people, are entirely irrelevant questions. In any case, they are wholly unqualified, in their capacity as elected politicians, to have a useful opinion on any of these subordinate issues.

Under the Iranian gun, the only questions which are immediately relevant are whether Mr Rushdie was legally entitled under British law to write and publish his book, and whether Ayatollah Khomeini is entitled to incite the murder of Mr Rushdie.

(from *Financial Times*, London, 9 March 1989)

Despite the pressure, individuals on all sides struggled to pave the way towards peaceful co-existence.

BHIKHU PAREKH

A political crisis is like a magnifying mirror reflecting some of the deepest trends and tendencies developing in society. A wise nation meditates on it, and uses it as a means of self-knowledge. The Rushdie affair has raised issues likely to preoccupy us for a long time, and has highlighted some of the limitations of the British Press and Muslim leadership which we can only ignore at our peril.

British Muslims began to complain against *The Satanic Verses* in October last year, but it was striking that hardly any national newspaper thought it necessary to publish a detailed list of the passages involved and explain why they were considered offensive, let alone run articles by Muslim spokesmen. When the desperate Muslims decided to burn the book to 'draw attention to the intensity of their feelings', as one of their spokesmen put it, they were viciously attacked for behaving like the Nazis, but again no newspaper took their case seriously enough to enter into a reasoned dialogue with them. It was only when Ayatollah Khomeini issued his notorious *fatwa* that the quality newspapers published some of the offending passages and gave expression to the Muslim feeling of deep hurt.

Several factors seem responsible for this poor reporting. Muslim opposition was largely led by religious fanatics whose strident tone and lack of intellectual satisfaction alienated a large body of public opinion. Since only a few national newspapers have ethnic minority reporters with their ears close to the ground, or arrangements for periodic digests of ethnic minority papers, they remained insensitive to the forces at work within the Muslim community.

The influence of racism and anti-Muslim feeling should not be underestimated. The bulk of influential public opinion in Britain tends to dismiss most Muslims as fundamentalists and fundamentalism as a new form of barbarism. Thus they are infantilised, ridiculed as illiterate peasants preferring the sleep of superstition to liberal light, and placed outside civilised discourse.

This lack of sensitivity and imagination was evident also in the way Muslim statements and actions were widely construed. The notorious book-burning in Bradford was automatically equated with the Nazi acts of book-burnings. No one paused to inquire if book-burning had the *same* meaning and significance in Islamic traditions, or whether the Bradford incident was largely symbolic, an expression of impatience rather than intolerance, and the result of misguided advice rather than hatred of Rushdie.

Again, *all* Muslims were implicated in the book-burning. No one asked why it took place in Bradford or what special factors led up to it. As a result, Muslim opinion—which was deeply divided—was forced to rally round the Bradford *mullahs*, and the latter were allowed to acquire new prestige and importance.

The intensity of Muslim reaction can only be understood in the context of the deep suspicion and alienation prevailing between the Asian community as a whole and its intellectuals. Rightly or wrongly, the large masses of Asians have long felt that those Asians who write, make films and television programmes or engage in instant punditry about them do not understand their innermost hopes and fears, and that they earn a handsome living and white acclaim by selling tired stereotypes and biased stories. Many Asians view their intellectuals as being as racist as the whites.

This is broadly how the Hindus felt about Nirad Chaudhury's idiosyncratic writings on India, the Bangladeshis about Farrukh Dhondy's television play *King of the Ghetto* and the Muslims about Hanif Kureishi's film *My Beautiful Launderette* and recently about Rushdie's *The Satanic Verses*.

The Muslims instinctively concluded that Rushdie was 'like the rest of them', and that they knew what the book 'was bound to say'. When he summarily dismissed their complaints, they felt them amply confirmed. There is an important lesson here for Asian intellectuals to learn from the Afro-Caribbeans. We must never hesitate to criticise our people, but should do so with respect and affection without ever forgetting that we *belong* to them.

On the other hand, Britain's Muslim leaders must also accept their share of blame for allowing the Rushdie affair to get out of control. Middle-class and Western-educated Muslims have rarely shown the courage to speak up on important matters and guide their community along sensible lines. I know quite a few who privately oppose religious and single-sex schools, refuse to send their children there, yet publicly maintain the opposite. As a result, the most orthodox Muslims have taken the lead. That religious orthodoxy has become a source of considerable indigenous and foreign money, international influence and political power means that the much-needed spirit of tolerance and dissent will never grow unless the Muslims throw up a more enlightened leadership.

The question of Muslim leadership in Britain is crucial. It is only during the last 20-odd years that they have become a significant minority in Britain, West Germany, France and the United States. They therefore need to consider carefully such vital issues as their place in these societies, the way they should educate their children and run their domestic affairs, and the kind of life they can hope to lead. Since they have never faced these questions before, painful choices are bound to be involved.

As an integral part of this debate, British Muslims need to confront the dilemma of their divided loyalties. Whatever the provocation, the eagerness with which some of them fell for Khomeini's horrendous *fatwa* is deplorable. It is unacceptable that they should even debate whether Rushdie 'deserves' to be killed. The very question shows the level to which Muslim consciousness has fallen. If British Muslims do not treat the *fatwa* as it deserves, they will remain open to the legitimate charges of violating the integrity of the British state and failing to live up to their minimal obligations as its citizens. The *fatwa* violates the Koranic stress on mercy and ignores the Prophet's lifelong practice of tolerance and forgiveness.

Britain cannot afford to have a large, proud and law-abiding minority smarting under treatment as barbarians, or withdrawing in a mood of deep sulk. For their part, the Muslims cannot expect to live in peace and dignity in a proud and self-confident country unless they attend closely to the way their actions and utterances are received by the majority community. Both sides must assess the impact of the Rushdie affair and react in a spirit of generosity and understanding.

• *Bhikhu Parekh is professor of political theory at Hull University and deputy chairman of the Commission for Racial Equality.*

(*Independent*, London, 23 Feb. 1989)

JOHN EZARD

Dismissing 'fellow writers, who are supporting you to the last drop of their ink,' one of the earliest Muslim campaigners against *The Satanic Verses* asked Mr Salman Rushdie last night to 'end the suffering' and withdraw the book.

The appeal came in a mostly friendly and respectful open letter to the author from Dr Hesham El-Essawy, chairman of the Islamic Society for Religious Tolerance in the UK. Dr Essawy objected to passages in the book shortly after it was published last year.

His letter was delivered to the publishers, Viking Penguin, and says in part: 'It is not very easy for me in a place of relative freedom to write to you in your place of relative captivity, but I must. You will remember that on our train journey back from the BBC debate in Birmingham on January 30, I went to you, extending my hand in peace and asking you to bring this matter to an end by agreeing to a simple erratum for historical and factual mistakes. You refused, saying: "You want me to apologise. I will never apologise. I said what I said and will never stand down."

'The half-apology that you later offered was quickly accepted by this society and myself as a full one . . . Unfortunately by then it wasn't my acceptance that mattered . . . I do not think that it will make you happy to stay where you are and watch people die. I do not think you will be happy to see a crisis of an unprecedented nature.

'Your fellow writers, who are supporting you to the last drop of their ink . . . are making it much more difficult for you to make a brave move. They seem to be driving you into a position of enforced martyrdom. For them, freedom of expression has become a fetish. To them that alone is sacred, but if this crisis has proved anything to us it is the fact that it will never do to divorce what you say from your freedom to say it. Both you and the Imam Khomeini have demonstrated that very adequately. Please do not be tempted to indulge their cause—first take good care of your own.

'As the holder of the copyright of *The Satanic Verses*, please put an end to all the suffering. Instruct your publishers here and abroad to stop publishing.'   (*Guardian*, London, 7 March 1989)

Dear Sir,

Now that the media discussion on *The Satanic Verses* is drawing to a close, it may be well to attempt a healing of the wounds which still afflict our society.

Long before the publication of this book, Muslims in Britain were trying to gain the same rights and protection accorded to other religious communities in our multi-cultural society. The Rushdie book, which Muslims regard as blasphemous, is only one aspect of a society showing itself to be insensitive to the needs and pain in which Muslims find themselves. The courts have now ruled that the law of blasphemy is inapplicable, but the need to discuss this problem with inter-faith dialogue is even more urgent.

We deplore all calls to violence which contravene the highest aspirations of all religious traditions. Muslims in Britain have shown themselves to be peace-loving and law-abiding citizens, and responsible Muslim leaders are resolved to approach this problem within the framework of law. It is our hope that inequalities in that law

will be redressed and that all minority religions will be fully protected.

The World Conference on Religion and Peace associates itself
with our Muslim friends, and would like to move from the present
debate to a more sympathetic appraisal of Islamic life in our society.
It is our hope that writers and publishers will now exercise more
self-discipline in dealing with the most sacred beliefs of their religious neighbours.

We are deeply concerned that the end result of the affair could
lead to persecution of the Muslims in the Western world. If any act
of terrorism were to take place this would be a tragedy, and we can
only affirm our belief that non-violent protest is a more effective
and religious response.

Everyone must join together in challenging extremism and in
creating a climate of free discussion.

> Yours faithfully
> Canon GORDON WILSON (Christian),
> Rabbi ALBERT H. FRIEDLANDER (Jewish),
> Mr B. KONNUR (Hindu),
> Dr SYED AZIZ PASHA (Muslim),
> Professor HARMINDAR SINGH (Sikh),
> Mr PANKAY VORA (Jain)
> World Conference on Religion and Peace
> London, E1
> 14 March

(*Independent*, London, 17 March 1989)

*But over the next weeks, various events proved that the Ayatollah's
exhortations continued to carry weight.*

Imam in Rushdie row is killed

JULIE WOLF
In Brussels

The spiritual leader of Belgium's Islamic community was shot
dead with an assistant last night in an incident believed to be linked
to the controversy about Mr Salman Rushdie's novel, *The Satanic
Verses*.

The two men, shot in the head with a 7.65 calibre weapon, were named as Imam Abdullah Al-Ahdal, a 36-year-old Saudi Arabian, and his aide, a 40-year-old Tunisian, Salem el-Behir.

A police spokesman said the Imam had received threats after an apparently lenient statement he made on Belgian television about the Rushdie issue. . . .

(from *Guardian*, London, 30 March 1989)

Rushdie motive feared in bomb attack on bookshops

SARAH BOSELEY

The ground floor of Collets Penguin bookshop in London was destroyed by a firebomb on Sunday night and a Dillons store in the capital similarly attacked, apparently because they stocked Salman Rushdie's novel, *The Satanic Verses*.

Collets' managing director, Ms Eva Skelley, said yesterday it was likely the Charing Cross Road store would stop stocking the book. 'We feel that it is an important issue and we'd like to carry on selling it, but it is a special one where the safety of people and property has to be considered.'   (from *Guardian*, London, 12 April 1989)

By 8 May, British police had stepped up security for bookshops. Salman Rushdie remained in hiding under police guard and the pressure on Penguin Books, similarly under guard, continued unabated. Meanwhile the international Muslim community continued their protest.

Rushdie protest 'to pull 500,000'

DAVID ROSE

Muslim leaders are mobilising support from mosques throughout the country for a demonstration against Salman Rushdie's novel, *The Satanic Verses*, which is likely to be the biggest held in Britain this century.

The many sects and organisations within the Muslim community have united for the first time to back the organisers of the demonstration, the British Muslim Action Front.

Some of the front's regional co-ordinators claimed last night that up to one million would attend the march, a figure which can confidently be discounted. But senior officials of the Commission for Racial Equality said that 500,000 'would not be an unreasonable guess.'

The Metropolitan Police's belief that 10,000-plus were expected appears certain to be a wild under-estimate.

The march, which will assemble in Hyde Park at 1.30pm on May 27 and proceed to Parliament Square and Downing Street, will call for Mr Rushdie's publishers, Penguin, to cease printing the novel, which Muslims hold to blaspheme the prophet Mohammed, and for the Government to widen the scope of the blasphemy laws to bring the book within the scope of the criminal law.

Mr Rushdie remains in hiding, guarded by armed police, as a result of the death threat made against him by Ayatollah Khomeini last February.

The chief organiser of the demonstration is Mr Abdal Hussain Choudhury, who is based at the big East London mosque in Whitechapel.

He confirmed that imams throughout the country were telling their congregations to go on the march, because the novel was 'an attack against the Koran,' and that all mosques had been supplied with leaflets.

Mr Choudhury said that he was also mobilising support from Muslims in Europe. He is to meet religious leaders in Holland and Belgium and assist with transport arrangements.

Mr Choudhury said: 'I think this will be the biggest Muslim demonstration in the world: you've never had anything like this. On this issue, everyone can mobilise.'

Some Muslim organisations have scrapped their own protests in favour of supporting Mr Choudhury and his committee. The demonstration's representatives include Bangladeshis, Pakistanis and Indians.

Professor Bhikhu Parekh, the deputy chairman of the Commission for Racial Equality, said that there was still little appreciation how far the Rushdie affair had united British Muslims. There are about 850,000 British Muslims, according to the CRE.

The Campaign for Nuclear Disarmament claims the record for the biggest demonstration this century. Organisers said 250,000 were on a march in 1983, although police said 100,000. About

300,000 people attended a May Day trade union march in London
in 1890.   (*Guardian*, London, 2 May 1989)

*As the summer of 1989 progressed, the controversy continued, as
did threats to bookstores. The pros and cons of the paperback edition of the book made their way into political debate.*

Issue of softcover edition of *Satanic Verses* splits Labour party

The increasingly contentious issue in Britain of a paperback edition of *The Satanic Verses*, reportedly planned for fall, has become
a subject of heated debate within the opposition Labour Party. Party
leader Neil Kinnock, who revealed recently that he has met with
Salman Rushdie since he went into hiding, publicly defended Rushdie's right and that of his publishers to release subsequent editions.

But deputy leader Roy Hattersley and a number of other senior
Labour figures have voiced their belief that Rushdie should come
out against publication of a paperback edition. Referring to the novel
as an "intentional blasphemy" in an article in the *Independent*
newspaper, Hattersley commented: "Mr. Rushdie is entitled to
abuse the religion in which he was reared and must be protected
against those who want to intimidate him into silence. But the idea
that we all have a duty to applaud his calculated assault is a novel
interpretation of the liberal obligation."

A number of Labour members of Parliament, several of them
representing constituencies with large Muslim populations, have
warned that unless the party presents a united front and encourages
Rushdie to withdraw the book, or prevent softcover publication, it
stands to lose a substantial number of seats at the next general
election in about two years' time.

(*Publishers Weekly*, 4 Aug. 1989)

FRANCE

*After receiving threats to himself, his family and his staff, Christian
Bourgois, Rushdie's publisher, announced on 15 February 1989 that*

the French publication of The Satanic Verses *would be suspended for security reasons.*

114 French writers issued a statement on 16 February against the 'menace of fanaticism':

'The freedom of opinion, of publication, the right to irony vis à vis authority and dogma have been paid dearly enough for us not to have to accept threats to them by fanaticism, whatever its source. The critical function of literature is a condition of everyone's freedom. For this reason, and because intolerance is a symptom from another age, we express our whole-hearted solidarity with Salman Rushdie and his publishers.'   (*Le Monde*, 19–20 Feb. 1989)

On 20 February, the French Foreign Minister joined with other European Community Foreign Ministers in condemning the Ayatollah's fatwa.

On 21 February, French intellectuals protested against the Ayatollah's fatwa:

'In England, the country where the first declaration of rights and of habeas corpus took place, a book has been burned, Salman Rushdie's *The Satanic Verses*: and death threats, echoing the condemnation ordered by a tyrant who reigns 1000 leagues away, have been made against the author and his publishers. . . .

'We will not be resigned to these pyres being lit for the third time in history. Recent examples remind us that fundamentalist violence of whatever degree can take place anywhere, even in French cinemahouses. . . . We call on human kind to defend its life and its soul.'   (*Le Monde*, 22 Feb. 1989)

French cardinal joins attack on 'insulting' novel

'*The Satanic Verses* is an offence against religious faith,' according to Cardinal Decourtray, Archbishop of Lyons, who is the president of the French bishops' conference. In a public statement, Cardinal Decourtray, who has not read Salman Rushdie's novel, said: 'Once again the faith of believers is insulted. Yesterday it was the Christians who were offended by a film which disfigured the face of Christ. Today it is the Muslims by this book about the Prophet.

'. . . Leaving aside fanatical reactions, which are in themselves an offence against God, I express my solidarity with all those who endure this pain in the spirit of dignity and prayer.'

The Cardinal's statement provoked President Mitterrand into making his first public comment on the Ayatollah Khomeini's week-old call for Salman Rushdie to be put to death. M. Mitterrand said yesterday: 'All dogmas which, through violence, violate the freedom of the human spirit and the right to self-expression, represent, in my eyes, absolute evil.' He added that 'the moral and spiritual progress of humanity is dependent on the decline of all forms of fanaticism'.

(from *Independent*, London, 23 Feb. 1989)

MONCEF MARZOUKI
Tunisian author

The Ayatollah Khomeini has rejected Salman Rushdie's apology and maintained the death sentence which he pronounced against him.

He made this sentence in the name of Islam and Muslims, that is, also in my name. I deny him this right for all sorts of reasons. First of all, there is no papacy in Islam and even less is there infallibility. Only a qualified tribunal has the right to pass judgement on a would-be crime. Secondly, Islam, like all the great religions, is one and diverse. Khomeini represents only a fraction of the whole, Shi'-ism, and only one group in this fraction, the clericalism of the extreme right.

In condemning Rushdie in the name of Islam and Muslims, he is usurping a representative function which is far from his and which the majority has never conceded him.

Of course, Khomeini expresses the legitimate indignation of Muslims, but he is amplifying it and exploiting it. That Rushdie has insulted us is evident. More than that, this author takes us for imbeciles when he maintains that Mahound is not the prophet. . . . Of course, the rights of the individual, notably to free expression, are inalienable. Those of the community, notably the respect of its beliefs, are no less so.

. . . But Rushdie has apologised and since I believe in this God who defines himself as lenient and merciful, I have no difficulty in accepting his apologies and considering the matter closed. Moreover, even if Rushdie hadn't apologised, Khomeini claims himself to be the spokesman of God. But this God is bereft of his two principal attributes. It is thus as Muslims that we must unreservedly condemn the call to murder which has come from Tehran.

On behalf of Arab intellectuals and Muslims, the position to take must be clear and firm, because we are what is at stake. We haven't forgotten that it was these very same intolerant priests who assassinated El Hallaj, Ibn El Mugaffa, Adelhamid El Kateb, and condemned the great Ibn Rochd to exile. We know they bear a heavy responsibility for our cultural backwardness and that they are always poised to suffocate our nascent liberties.

If it came to Rushdie's assassination, may it not please God, we would all be covered in shame. May people of good sense then say that it wasn't Muslims who committed the crime, but fanatics who on top of it all were paid.   (*Le Monde*, 25 Feb. 1989)

One thousand Muslim fundamentalists demonstrate in Paris

A thousand people—Indians, Pakistanis, Turks, North Africans, Afghans, etc.—demonstrated on Sunday 26 Feb. in Paris, from Barbès to the Place de la République, to protest against Salman Rushdie's book. They marched to cries of 'we are all Khomeinists' and 'death to Rushdie'. The demonstration was organised by the association 'La voix de l'Islam' and had been announced in leaflets handed out on Friday outside the mosques . . .

(*Le Monde*, 27 Feb. 1989)

A blow to Islam in France

. . . After the appearance of Rushdie's book, the indignation of the French Muslim community, numbering some two-and-a-half million, was undoubtedly under-estimated. It was known that the community was seeking to be represented and was more worried about moderation and respectability than excess.

Rushdie's book is a godsend to those who, in the name of the defence of an offended Islam, dream of taking control in the West of communities who are often disoriented, badly integrated, both in social and religious terms.

This is notably the case in France, where competition between fundamentalist associations and external forces (Algerian, Saudi Arabian) restrains initiatives towards unification and organisation made by the Muslim community itself. . . .

(from *Le Monde*, 28 Feb. 1989)

A demonstration, numbering some 1000 people and organised by SOS-Racisme, took place in front of the Palais de Chaillot on 2 March, protesting against fundamentalist extremism.

Comments

MICHEL ROCARD
Prime Minister

'All new calls to violence or to murder' will result in immediate judicial prosecutions . . . 'The laws of the Republic affirm and guarantee the liberty to express opinions, even information'.

(*Le Monde*, 1 March 1989)

GISCARD D'ESTAING
Former President of the Republic

The reactions of the Europeans to the Rushdie affair 'could have been stronger and more concrete . . . The displacing of ambassadors or high-level visits, these do not touch public opinion.'

(*Le Monde*, 28 Feb. 1989)

JACQUES CHIRAC
Mayor of Paris

'I am not confusing Muslims with fanatics, but I cannot imagine that in Paris we will accept desperadoes who call for murder. If they are French they need to be pursued; if they are foreigners, they should be expelled. Foreigners, once they are on our soil, must respect our laws, and we cannot tolerate calls for murder in the capital of human rights.' (*Le Monde*, 2 March 1989)

JEAN-MARIE LE PEN
President of the extreme right-wing National Front:

'What Khomeini has just done with revolting cynicism is exactly what I fear for France and Europe, that is the invasion of Europe by a Muslim immigration.'   (*Le Monde*, 28 Feb. 1989)

Indecision marks world publishers

In France, Christian Bourgois, a member of the Presses de la Cité group, announced that he was delaying indefinitely publication of a French edition of *The Satanic Verses*. Although his feeling that his staff must be protected in a country with a Muslim population of four million was understood, his decision was nonetheless widely condemned by authors, intellectual circles, some other publishers and many newspapers.

A statement from the French publishers association (Syndicat national de l'Edition) expressing solidarity with Rushdie, his intended publisher and his staff, and protesting against "this return to barbarity," called on the International Publishers Association and Gelc (the EEC publishers' association) to "take the initiative of instigating worldwide action in favor of respecting the right to freedom to publish." This statement was condemned in some quarters as passing the buck.

Bourgois's statement led to a call from several national newspapers and magazines for a joint edition of the book to be published by several French publishers, as a gesture of solidarity. Two small publishers, Quai Voltaire and Arléa, promptly offered to join in such an enterprise, and several of the larger publishers were thought to be prepared to be involved.

At the same time several small publishers pressed Bourgois to sell them the French translation rights, claiming that they were prepared to bring out their own edition. However these initiatives have generally been dismissed as publicity-seeking moves. At any rate Bourgois has not as yet shown any sign of being willing to sell the rights, and a translation is not yet available, though there is talk of a "pirated" version being produced rapidly.

Meanwhile 114 writers were quick to publish, February 16, a manifesto proclaiming their support for freedom of expression. They included several writers who are also publishers, such as Tony Cartano, novelist and editorial director of the Presses de la Renaissance, and Régine Deforges.

In other parts of the world, Mondadori in Italy said it would continue with its publishing plans. In Spain Seix Barral was postponing its decision. In the Netherlands, where the English-language edition is sold out, Veen said it would consult with government authorities and Islamic organizations before deciding. In Norway, William Nygaard, publisher of Aschehoug, said he had received death threats and had not yet made a decision. The Danish publisher, according to PEN, intends to proceed with publication, as does the Finnish publisher. In Germany Kiepenheuer & Witsch is still undecided. And in Japan, authorities have banned the sale of the English-language edition.

(Publishers Weekly, 3 March 1989)

Bourgois publishes *Satanic Verses* in pseudonymous translation

The French edition of *The Satanic Verses* was released July 19 in a pseudonymous translation, using an anagram of his own name that François Rabelais had used when he was feeling the heat. But the original holder of translation rights, Editions Christian Bourgois, took full responsibility for publication, its logo appearing alone on front cover and title page, contrary to earlier announcements that several Paris houses would join in sponsoring the book. The names of 21 publishers who offered "friendly support" to publication are listed on the back cover, along with the French Ministry of Culture.

The Bourgois edition had a first printing of 65,000 copies, and was delivered only to booksellers who ordered it in advance, publisher Christian Bourgois having decided to bypass the usual automatic servicing of book outlets, which in this case might have upset retailers who did not wish to take a risk. Confirming that security precautions initiated early in the year remain in effect at his company, Bourgois told an interviewer that the book could have been released earlier, but was held back so as not to complicate security arrangements for the French Revolution bicentennial.

No bookseller in Paris was displaying the book prominently and most of the bigger outlets such as department stores were not carrying it. But the best literary shops such as La Hune, Gallimard and Le Divan stocked it, as did the upmarket FNAC chain outlets, where sales were so brisk the book couldn't be kept in stock.

Muslim groups were divided in their reactions, ranging from threats of violence if the book is placed in a window to silent prayers and a suit to have the book seized. In rejecting the Muslim complaint a Paris court nevertheless requested that the publisher respect a commitment not to promote the book. This is perhaps the first such official interference with distribution of the Rushdie novel outside the Third World.   (*Publishers Weekly*, 11 Aug. 1989)

WEST GERMANY

Soon after the Ayatollah's fatwa, Rushdie's West German publishers, Kiepenheuer & Witsch, who had planned to bring out The Satanic Verses *in October to coincide with the important Frankfurt Book Fair, announced that they were stopping publication so as not to endanger the lives of their employees and inflame the numerous Islamic communities in and around Cologne, who had morally condemned the book without sanctioning Khomeini's death threat. Led by Hans Magnus Enzensberger, writers, intellectuals and journalists protested this decision. Plans are now under way for the book to appear as soon as the translation is complete under the joint imprint of some 70 authors and publishers, grouped under the name Article 19.*

On 23 February 1989, a group of West German writers called on Chancellor Kohl to ask the German government to intervene with the Iranian authorities.

A public reading of The Satanic Verses *took place in Berlin on 9 March. Outside, some fifty Muslims protested in orderly fashion. It had been planned that the reading should take place in the Akademie der Künste which had refused its premises for security reasons. Günter Grass, a former president of the Academy, resigned over this refusal, and stated that the Academy had already given way to political pressure once in the past: during the Nazi period. 'In denying the use of its premises, [the Academy] is bowing to*

terrorist pressure . . . and taking a stand which sets a bad example,'
he said.

The Middle Ages are overtaking us
GÜNTER GRASS
Interviewed by Völker Hage

How far can tolerance go? Think of the television talk shows.
Should one allow an arsonist who advocates a call to murder on
the air?

. . . As long as there is an opponent debating with him on screen
who can counter the fundamentalist's demagogy—as was the case
here—it is right to allow people to speak out. I am for openness;
and the more hidebound the opposition is, the more we must insist
on openness. Unfortunately our government up till now has believed
that terrorist provocation should be met with the withdrawal of
rights, which I think is wrong. Our liberal system has suffered not
because terrorism was so strong, but because the state was so weak
that it felt it needed to impose restrictions. With the Rushdie case,
we have the opportunity to see how a Conservative state will behave
in such an instance. When in England people publicly reflect on
whether the laws should be changed, amongst them Labour MPs
who are worried about their voters, that is naturally a victory for
Fundamentalism. . . .

When one reflects on all this, it would seem that the flame of
the Enlightenment is waning.

But there is no other source of light. The tendency, which I also
observe in our press, of being frivolous and prepared to do down an
Enlightenment which is always endangered, is therefore all the more
censurable. But the Enlightenment is not at an end. When the idea
grows narrower, then we have to fight for its broader definition, fight
with all the means of Enlightenment.

(from *Die Zeit*, 24 Feb. 1989)

ITALY

On 16 February 1989, Mondadori, Rushdie's Italian publisher, de-
clared that despite threats and initial reports to the contrary, the

publication of The Satanic Verses *would take place in a few day's time and on schedule. While affirming his total respect for the Islamic religion, the publisher felt that* 'any restrictive decision concerning publication of the work of Mr Rushdie would be in contradiction of the rules of freedom of expression practised by the international publishing world'.

Mondadori's statement came after the Iranian Ambassador to the Vatican had caused a sensation by announcing that should he find himself next to him he would be prepared to execute Rushdie. Publishing headquarters and key bookshops were put under 24-hour guard.

A Mondadori bookshop was set on fire in Padua on 5 March, and Muslims in Ravenna, calling themselves the 'Guardians of the Revolution', threatened to blow up the monument to Dante who died there in 1321. In The Divine Comedy *the prophet Muhammed is consigned to the ninth pit of hell, where he languishes amongst traitors.*

NORWAY

Norway's Aschehoug rushes *Satanic Verses* to print

Speeding up the publication date by two-and-a-half months—and keeping it secret—Oslo-based Aschehoug became the third publisher to release Salman Rushdie's *The Satanic Verses*.

Originally scheduled for publication on July 1, the novel appeared instead on April 12 to avoid actions against it by groups opposed to its release. It was produced in secrecy and only a handful of people directly involved knew of the publication date, according to managing director William Nygaard.

Norway has a Muslim population of approximately 20,000. The Defense Council for Islam has protested the book's publication and intends to sue Aschehoug for libel and violation of the "blasphemy paragraph" in Norwegian law, Nygaard said. The council, however, has stressed repeatedly that it intends to keep protests within the confines of Norwegian law and has so far made no threats against the publisher.

Attempts at arson have been made on two bookshops in Oslo.

The police do not exclude the possibility that racist groups may be responsible. Muslim leaders have denied that members of their community were involved.

Nygaard said the novel "has met with enormous response from both the reading public and the media."

(*Publishers Weekly*, 5 May 1989)

EGYPT

Letter from Cairo
KARIM ALRAWI

The *mufti* of Egypt, Dr Tantawi, the country's grand sheikh and one of the most senior Muslim authorities in the Muslim world, reaffirmed last week, in reference to questions on the legitimacy of assassinating Salman Rushdie, that no Muslim can be killed without a full and fair trial.

'The court must ask for the writer to explain his intentions and not be limited by misreadings and misunderstandings,' he said. The *mufti* added that the accused, even if found guilty, can seek clemency and forgiveness.

Several other high-ranking religious authorities in Egypt have come out in support of this position. Even Sheikh Shaarawi, the Arab world's most prominent preacher, who claims not to have read a novel in 40 years, appears to endorse Dr Tantawi's stand.

Among the radical Islamic groups the attitude is very different. Their attitude is that the whole affair is a plot to discredit Islam, a trap into which the Iranians, in their haste, have fallen and from which they are now unable to extricate themselves without loss of face.

In Egypt, however, the fallout from *The Satanic Verses* will affect Mr Rushdie less than it is likely to affect other writers who have been struggling to get the country's censorship laws modified and eventually repealed. At the opening of the 21st Cairo International Book Fair last month, in a speech to a hall full of writers, Farouk Husni, Egpyt's Minister of Culture, argued for the need to limit the activities of the board of censors to religious works that may be blasphemous.

The minister's call was challenged by the main religious weekly, *Al-Noor*, which in virtually every issue for the last four months has kept up an attack on Naguib Mahfouz, Egypt's Nobel Prize laureate. Whether through cartoons depicting Mahfouz burning in hell or reports of attempts by Egyptian publishers and distributors to get the ban on his novel, *Gebalawi's Children*, lifted, *Al-Noor's* message is clear: Mahfouz is a blasphemer and must be punished.

The Egyptian press and news media have hardly reported any of the international controversy over *The Satanic Verses*. One significant reason for this is the government's reluctance to give the Islamic opposition an excuse to stir up feelings on a sensitive issue. So far the subject of blasphemy has been raised many more times in parliament in connection with the screening of the American film *The Last Temptation of Christ*, at the Cairo Film Festival in December, than it has over *The Satanic Verses*, Jesus being respected as a major prophet by Muslims.

The first warning signs that this may be changing came in the call by the Grand Sheikh of Al-Azhar University, the foremost religious institution in the country, for British Muslims to seek legal ways of banning the novel.

But what has caused much greater concern are reports by sources close to *Al-Noor* that there are plans to convene a conference at Mecca later this year at which both Naguib Mahfouz and Salman Rushdie will be denounced as blasphemers and possibly even apostates. . . .   (from *Guardian*, London, 3 March 1989)

'Khomeini is a terrorist'
NAGUIB MAHFOUZ
Der Spiegel *interviews the 77-year-old Egyptian writer who received the Nobel Prize for literature in 1988.*

Mr Mahfouz, why did Arab writers not protest as soon as Khomeini called for Salman Rushdie's death?
Protests are now taking place in the whole Islamic world.
But there are also literary figures who think it is right for Rushdie to be punished for his Satanic Verses.
Of course there are people who do not agree with the content of the book because they see in it an insult to the Prophet Mohammed.

But as far as I know, in this country no one has wished Rushdie's death.

Should Khomeini as a prominent Islamic Imam not have pronounced such a verdict?

Khomeini is a terrorist, who has precipitated millions of people towards destruction. Islam authorizes no one, not even spiritual leaders who meddle in politics, to impose a death sentence on other people.

Yet the old man in Iran has caused world-wide agitation and driven thousands of Muslims into the street.

Khomeini exploits the ignorance, the illiteracy of the masses. He displaces them into hysteria and misuses them to bring about acts that have nothing to do with Islam. Khomeini has already done more harm to Islam than many others in the history of our religion.

Yet he has become a factor to be reckoned with in the Islamic world, someone who can altogether poison the relations between Islamic and non-Islamic countries.

No. The Iranian phenomenon is not typical for the large majority of Islamic states. No country until now has copied Iran's theocratic system. If it weren't for ignorance and stupidity, we would pay no attention to Khomeini's agitation. . . .

Critics say that Al-Azhar University, the foremost institution of Sunni Islam, has prevented the publication of your book.

The Grand Sheikh of Al-Azhar University has clarified that the only way to take objection with Rushdie's book must be to work out a learned argument, in other words to reply with a book—that is the correct way, not with a death sentence.

The hardline Islamic weekly, *Noor* (Light), in Cairo, several weeks ago compared you to Rushdie. Does this trouble you?

No. In Egypt, unlike Iran, we work according to the law of the state, and not according to the opinion of a cleric.

Islamic fundamentalists say that human rights are the outcome of a Western system of thought and part of Western cultural imperialism. A well-known Egyptian lead article shocked readers with the sentence: 'The rights of Islam have precedence over human rights.'

Let's be clear: Human rights have nothing to do with what a critic calls 'cultural imperialism' or 'cultural invasion'. To be plain, I have no idea what some hotheads mean by this. When I take advantage of the cultural goods of others, I broaden my horizon, increase my knowledge. This is something positive. I take in what I like, build on it; I refuse what doesn't speak to me. . . .

Is Western parliamentary democracy, the multi-party system, capable of being integrated with Islam? Prominent Islamic thinkers don't think so.

Democracy is the best system humanity has. Of course democratic structures are compatible with our religion.

(from *Der Spiegel*, no. 9, 1989)

To the imams' arms

In the continuing and widening row over Mr Salman Rushdie and *The Satanic Verses*, where do Arab writers stand? The answer appears to be: on shifting ground. Mr Naguib Mahfouz, the Egyptian Nobel laureate and the most celebrated figure in contemporary Arabic literature, began by supporting Mr Rushdie, a stand to be expected from the man whose writings have been attacked in the same way and banned in his own country; but now he has changed his mind. Complaining that his pro-Rushdie words have been 'misinterpreted', he is publicly backing the Egyptian government's decision to ban *The Satanic Verses*. Although he does not support Ayatollah Khomeini's *fatwa*, he has found another *fatwa* he thinks reasonable, issued by the clergy of al-Azhar mosque, the keepers of Islamic orthodoxy in Egypt: *The Satanic Verses* should be considered as 'an insult to Islam and a threat to sectarian harmony', but Mr Rushdie should have been given a chance to repent before he was condemned, and should have been condemned only in a court of clergy.   (*Economist*, London, 11 March 1989)

Cairo chief denounces Khomeini

SMYAM BHATIA
Kom Al Ahmar

An Egyptian Cabinet Minister has insulted Ayatollah Khomeini and says that he disapproves of the Iranian leader's death sentence against the British author Salman Rushdie.

Only a day after Islamic foreign ministers meeting in Riyadh refused to endorse the Ayatollah's sentence, Egypt's interior minister, General Zaki Badr, denounced Khomeini as a 'dog' and a 'pig'. He also attacked Muslim fanatics within the country, accusing them of religious intolerance.

Badr is no ordinary Minister. His portfolio, which gives him charge of internal security, makes him one of the more important members of the Egyptian Cabinet. Comments about Khomeini will not go unnoticed.

Speaking to foreign reporters who were invited to join him for lunch at the Nile delta village of Kom Al Ahmar, Badr said: 'Khomeini is a dog, no that is too good for him. He is a pig.' Asked about the Rushdie affair, Badr replied: 'Of course the book is wrong, but to kill him—this is not the way.'

It is the first time that a Minister from an Islamic country has abused Khomeini in such an unequivocal way. Both the pig and the dog are considered unclean animals in Islam and the insult was so unusual that the reporters gathered around Badr had to consult their tape-recorders to make sure they had an accurate record.

Relations between Egypt and Iran have been frozen since the late President Sadat gave refuge to the exiled Shah of Iran. The bitterness deepened when Egypt sided with Iraq in the Gulf War.

Badr has a reputation for using intemperate language within the National People's Assembly, but his deliberate slight of Khomeini is a measure of the Egyptian government's frustration with Iran's refusal to conform to traditional rules of international behaviour. The Egyptian authorities are concerned that the Rushdie affair could mark the start of new efforts to export the Islamic revolution.

(*Observer*, London, 19 March 1989)

Nobel prizewinner threatened

Nobel Prize winning author Naguib Mahfouz has been threatened with death for supporting Salman Rushdie, reports the *Observer*.

The Egyptian author is apparently under attack for his book, *The Children of Gebelawi*, published in 1958 and proscribed by religious authorities. He says, however, that his real offence is that he defended Rushdie against the Ayatollah Khomeini. 'I said at the time that he was acting against the laws of the world and the laws of Islam.'   (*Bookseller*, London, 5 May 1989)

CANADA

*In North America, the Rushdie controversy did not receive a great
deal of attention until the fatwa was imposed by Ayatollah Khomeini on 14 February 1989. Although the affair soon grew most
vociferous in the US, the initial reaction of the Canadian government itself became, briefly, an issue.*

Canada blocks *The Satanic Verses*

Revenue Canada officials stopped further imports of *The Satanic
Verses* at the border yesterday pending a review of the book for
possible hate propaganda after a letter addressed to the Prime Minister from an Ottawa-based Moslem association was passed on to
them for action.

Linda Murphy, acting director of prohibited importations for Revenue Canada, said one of her five appraisers will read the novel to
determine whether it infringes on the hate propaganda provisions
in the Criminal Code of Canada. She said the letter was passed from
the PMO to Revenue Minister Otto Jelinek's office and on to her
department.

Coles Book Stores Ltd., one of Canada's largest booksellers, removed the book from its 198 stores across the country yesterday,
saying it was concerned about the safety of its 1,850 employees.

"The book is not available at any Coles store in the country. This
difficult decision was made in the interest of employees' safety,"
the Toronto-based company said in a statement.

Nigel Berrisford, vice-president of book marketing at W. H. Smith
Canada Ltd., said that his company ordered 1,200 books and that
most stores are sold out.

"The second we get more, we'll be putting them into the stores,"
he said.

W. H. Smith spokesman Bruce Reid said: While W. H. Smith
appreciates that this novel has caused offence to certain religious
groups, our company policy is to make available to our customers
books which they wish to purchase and which contravene no Canadian laws.

Revenue Canada reviews about 4,000 books and publications a

year for violations of the Criminal Code dealing mostly with hate propaganda, obscenity, and sedition.

"We've alerted our ports that if they see the book, it should be detained for review," said Sheila Batchelor, Revenue Canada assistant deputy minister. But she added that it is unlikely that it would constitute hate propaganda *per se.*

Ms Murphy said she cannot say whether it is hate propaganda until it has been reviewed by an appraiser.

Revenue Canada does not have the power to go to bookstores and strip books off the shelf to review them. It can only act against publications brought into the country.

No threat of any kind had been received by any Canadian mission and Iran has not protested against the importation or sale of the book in Canada, she said.

Ms Murphy rejected a suggestion that Revenue Canada was ordering the book's detention to appease the ayatollah. "That is inaccurate," she said. The only reason shipments of the book were not ordered detained before was that no complaint had been received by the prohibitions directorate.

(*Globe & Mail,* Toronto, 18 Feb. 1989)

The Rushdie Affair
Editorial

Many outrageous comments have been made in the wake of Iran's call for the murder of British author Salman Rushdie, but for sheer bloodymindedness it is hard to match the remarks of Iran's chargé d'affaires in London. Ayatollah Ruhollah Khomeini's command to faithful Moslems to kill Mr. Rushdie "does not imply any political gesture by Iran, nor does it imply any interference in internal affairs of your country," Akhoond Zadeh Basti said last week. ". . . If the purely religious-based opinion of a religious head is going to be interpreted politically, it is very unfortunate."

At the risk of taking Mr. Basti too seriously, what could be more political than calling for the assassination of a foreign national? It is the attempted extra-territorial application of Iran's capital sanction against blasphemy, without the inconvenience of a fair trial. It is a calculated assault on international law.

It took a few days for Western nations to get up to speed in their political response, but the members of the European Community have now agreed to recall their ambassadors and restrict the movements of Iranian diplomats on their soil. Britain will go further by withdrawing its embassy staff from Tehran. West German Foreign Minister Dietrich Genser said the EC's action was partly in solidarity with Britain, "but it is also a signal to assure the preservation of civilization and human values, the preservation of freedom of speech and expression."

Canada has balked at such forceful remonstrance; External Affairs Minister Joe Clark fretted that Canada should not overreact over a single issue. But Canada, no less than other countries, is vulnerable to the sort of mini-jihad Ayatollah Khomeini has launched. It is a Briton today; it might be a Canadian tomorrow, and not necessarily an author.

Meanwhile, the government came within centimetres of a nasty blunder last week. An Ottawa association complained to the Prime Minister's Office that the Rushdie book constituted hate literature; the PMO sent the letter to Revenue Canada, whose officials promptly said they would detain any further shipments at the border pending an examination of their contents. Oh, what solace that would have given the sworn enemies of Mr. Rushdie; fortunately, officials decided over the weekend that there was no question of the book being hate literature, and new shipments may enter at will.

The reaction of booksellers themselves has been mixed. It was sad to see Coles Book Stores Ltd. turn pale in the face of the Ayatollah's wrath and remove Mr. Rushdie's book *The Satanic Verses* from its 198 Canadian stores. Capitulation doesn't deter threats and acts of violence; it encourages them by showing that menace pays.

To its credit, W. H. Smith Canada Ltd. said it saw no reason to banish Mr. Rushdie's book from its shelves: "While W. H. Smith appreciates that this novel has caused offence to certain religious groups, our company policy is to make available to our customers books which they wish to purchase and which contravene no Canadian laws." (The book, we might note, has circulated freely in Canada since its publication last year.)

It may well be that international outrage at Iran's actions plays into the hands of hard-line Iranians, and that this whole crusade is a product of domestic Iranian politics; but no country that believes in international law can afford to let Mr. Rushdie and his allies stand alone in their ghastly predicament. The spiritual head of a nation has given religious adherents in other nations an exhortation to murder; if such practices are not bitterly challenged, who among us is safe? Even those who found *The Satanic Verses* offensive have a stake in finding the Ayatollah's incitement to murder many times more so.   (*Globe & Mail*, Toronto, 21 Feb. 1989)

UNITED STATES

Copies of The Satanic Verses *arrived in the United States in January, although the official publication date was set as 22 February. By the time of the Ayatollah's* fatwa, *the book had been on the best-seller lists for over a month.*

Following the fatwa, *the principal bookstore chains, Barnes & Noble, B. Dalton and Waldenbooks, as well as many independent bookshops, pulled* The Satanic Verses *from their shelves. Fear for employee's safety was paramount in the decision. Prior warning of the threat to the Pan-Am Flight 103 plane, which crashed in Lockerbie as a result of a terrorist bomb in December 1988, had been received but had not been circulated. This focussed attention on the need of employers to make relevant information available to staff and potential clients. 'We believed . . . that the tragic Pan-Am incident had created a precedent for our needing to inform our employees of the risks they face and involve them in decision making. The threats that were received could not just be ignored,' a high-ranking executive of the BDB Corporation stated.*

How Rushdie's publishers see the crisis
JOHN F. BAKER

An official at Viking Penguin, who asked not to be identified by name for security reasons, gave *PW* the following thoughts in the course of a hectic weekend:

On more printings: We'll continue to supply books as we have them and need them. We'll print new copies as needed but it's difficult at this stage because we don't know what's happening to all the unsold chain copies. And can we be sure that independent stores will continue to sell the book if they have it?

On the economies: Some commentators have taken the position that we're making a lot of money off this book. There's no way we'll ever make anything on it no matter how many copies we sell; we've had too much expense on security, all over the world. We didn't buy the book because we thought it was controversial, but because it was a distinguished work by a distinguished author whom we're proud to publish.

On the chains' reaction, particularly Waldenbooks: I think they were pre-emptively cautious. There were many steps that could have been taken consistent with a legitimate desire for the security of store staff. Surely a position could have been found somewhere between doing nothing and doing everything. Cutting off supplies altogether seems to go beyond what appeared necessary. Surely they could have allowed managers to decide on a local level whether or not, in view of their kind of clientele, there was any serious security risk, and proceed accordingly. The chains have a great deal of power and have to think carefully about how they use it. It's difficult for an independent to say the issues don't exist for him if a national chain with 1200 stores has decided not to sell the book. Bookstores are not just in the "product" business. They're in the business of ideas, which are precious, and there are obligations that go with that. If I thought there was a true risk I wouldn't say anything critical, but I doubt there is really any serious risk nationwide. And then Walden was followed by Dalton and Coles of Canada. It was unfortunate, because it gave the other side a signal that they were winning.

On other publishers' reactions: This isn't just a book only Viking Penguin wanted to publish. All the major houses read it and bid on it, and it could as easily have been one of them in this situation as us. Some other publishers have been very supportive, and there's talk of adding other publishers' names on the spine for future printings, but that would be something they would have to have approved by their parent corporations.

On the feeling of isolation: We don't want to focus simply on our trouble, as one publisher, but treat it as a horrible thing that is happening to all of us—something utterly outside normal publishing experience. But it's hardly a thing that one publishing company can handle all by itself. There's no way we can deal directly with the Ayatollah.

On government involvement: I think the strategy has been to try and do things behind the scenes at first: the softly, softly approach, to explain there was no intention to hurt or be offensive.

On the pressure: I don't know if Viking Penguin can stand this indefinitely. The pressures have been very great, and don't forget that, before the Ayatollah, the British side has been living with this since September.   (*Publishers Weekly*, 3 March 1989)

Rushdie's publisher assails 'censorship by terrorism'
EDWIN MCDOWELL

A spokesman for Viking Penguin yesterday condemned censorship by terrorism and intimidation, and he coupled his remarks with criticism of the major bookstore chains that have pulled *The Satanic Verses* from their shelves.

He also said the publishing house is reprinting the novel, by Salman Rushdie, which has sold out across much of the United States.

"Unlike the major retailers," said the spokesman, who asked that his name not be used for reasons of personal safety, "we have not pulled in our horns. We have never stopped publishing the book, and we are publishing it in relationship to changing demand, although demand is very difficult to gauge because of the action of the big retail chains."

The spokesman added, "Viking Penguin thought we had acquired, edited and published a literary book, and had no sense of the controversy that later emerged."

Eight other publishers bid for the book, he said, and they apparently also did not know of "the extra dimensions that would come to surround the book."

The spokesman continued: "That said, it is inconceivable to most of us in the West that a writer, and a distinguished writer at that, should not be able to express his ideas, and that publishers should not be permitted to publish them, booksellers not permitted to sell them, and that readers should be excluded from the marketplace of ideas. If the present tendency continues, the Ayatollah will have prevailed. This is not censorship with respect to the First Amendment, this is censorship by terrorism and intimidation."

Muslim groups have said the novel defames the Prophet Mohammed, and on Tuesday Ayatollah Ruhollah Khomeini of Iran issued a death threat against Mr. Rushdie. On Friday, the Iranian President indicated that the threat could be withdrawn if Mr. Rushdie issued an appropriate apology.

Yesterday Mr. Rushdie said he regretted the distress that his novel had caused to Muslims.

The Authors Guild and the National Writers Union demanded yesterday that President Bush publicly condemn the threats by Iran and warn that the United States will respond if any harm comes to an American citizen.

Describing the threats as a "unique and horrifying license to murder," the 6,500-member Authors Guild asked President Bush in a telegram to issue a "forceful statement" saying "this kind of monstrous behavior has no place in the international community."

The telegram asked Mr. Bush to state that any attempt to threaten or harm American citizens involved with the book "will be met by the full power of the American government." A White House spokesman said yesterday that the telegram had not been received.

Daniel J. Boorstin, the historian and former Librarian of Congress, called for the Government to take a strong position. "It says it's doing so much about terrorism," he said. "Now that Khomeini has proclaimed himself to be a terrorist, our Government should respond publicly in strongest terms."

Dr. Boorstin said that when *The Satanic Verses* becomes available again, "everybody should buy a copy, as an affirmation of the freedom of the press in America and our unwillingness to be held hostage in our own country."

The writers union demanded that the Government "provide whatever protection is necessary" for publishers, vendors and writers. It also announced that a demonstration will begin at 10 A.M. on Wednesday outside the Iranian Mission to the United States.

Alec Dubro, national president of the union, said the demonstrators will then picket outside the stores of the B. Dalton, Waldenbooks, and Barnes & Noble chains to protest the decision to pull the Rushdie novel from their shelves.

Meanwhile, bookstores throughout the United States reported heavy demand for the novel, which has been virtually sold out for the last several days.

The controversy has generated so much interest in the Islamic religion that the Strand Book Store, at 828 Broadway in Manhattan, has sold more than 250 copies of the Koran, the sacred book of Islam, compared with 10 to 15 copies in a normal week.

At the St. Marks Bookshop, at 13 St. Marks Place in Greenwich Village, which sold out its copies of *The Satanic Verses*, Robert Constant said: "The phone has been ringing off the hook. Almost everyone coming in the door wants a copy."

Carolyn Orifel, a saleswoman at Spring Street Books, at 169 Spring Street in Manhattan, said the store received 100 requests for the book on Friday. "The minute anyone says 'Do you have,' we say, 'No,'" she said. "People don't believe us. They think we're hiding it in the back and selling it from behind the counter."

(*New York Times*, 19 Feb. 1989)

On 21 February 1989, President Bush issued a statement in support of EEC Foreign Ministers.

Article 19, PEN and the Authors Guild sponsored a public reading of The Satanic Verses *on 22 February, its official publication day.*

The National Writers Union held a series of demonstrations outside selected bookshops and the Iranian Mission to the United Nations.

American writers denounce 'terrorism against an idea'

America's literary community lashed out yesterday in response to the death threats against Salman Rushdie, and the refusal of the country's three biggest book-sellers to keep *The Satanic Verses* on their shelves.

Norman Mailer, author of *The Naked and the Dead*, told a group of protesters that the Ayatollah Khomeini's death threat offered writers 'an opportunity to regain our faith in the power of words and our willingness to suffer for them'. He was speaking at a protest meeting in New York organised by a coalition of American PEN, the Author's Guild and Article 19, an international organisation which fights censorship of writers.

Ayatollah Khomeini was discovering 'that yes, maybe we are willing to suffer for our ideas. Maybe we're even willing ultimately to die for the idea that serious literature, in a world of dwindling certainties, is the absolute we must defend,' Mailer said.

The gathering was addressed by some of the country's best-known literary figures, including Susan Sontag, Joan Didion and E. L. Doctorow. Mailer seemed to capture the mood of the writers with his address, which focused on the author's right to freedom of expression however controversial the content of his or her work. He went on to castigate America's bookselling chains. . . .

Mailer said that the booksellers had overreacted to the threat of violence by Muslim fundamentalists. The chances of any employee being hurt for selling *The Satanic Verses* was 'more than 6,000 to one'.

However, like other American writers, he refrained from calling for a boycott of the booksellers. The three chains control more than a quarter of all book sales in America, and the writers fear their livelihood could be threatened by a boycott, even though many independent book sellers are continuing to sell the book. . . .

Until yesterday, prominent American writers seemed reluctant to discuss the controversy, and few agreed on what action should be taken in response to the fundamentalists' threats. However, the New York gathering brought the controversy into sharp focus for the first time in the United States. Writers' groups and individual authors directed most of their criticism yesterday at the US government, as well as the booksellers who had withdrawn the novel.

The Article 19 organisation issued a statement condemning the Bush administration's failure 'to condemn forthrightly and unequivocally the attempt to murder Salman Rushdie and his publishers'. It demanded the repudiation of Ayatollah Khomeini 'as an outlaw and enemy of all humankind'.

In an interview before yesterday's protest Tom Wolfe, author of the best-selling *Bonfire of the Vanities*, said it was a time for writers to close ranks, 'but not only writers; this is something of concern to everybody. It's a situation that could occur anywhere.' . . .

Abbie Hoffman, the author and 1960s protest leader, also participated in the demonstration outside the Iranian mission to the United Nations. 'This is a new form of terrorism,' he said. 'This is terrorism against an idea, and it's intolerable in the modern civilised world.' . . .   (from *Independent*, London, 23 Feb. 1989)

The Senate unanimously passed Resolution 72 declaring its commitment to 'protect the right of any person to write, publish, sell, buy and read books without fear of intimidation and violence.' The resolution condemns the Khomeini threat as 'state-sponsored terrorism,' expressing support for publishers and booksellers who 'have courageously printed, distributed, sold and displayed *The Satanic Verses.'* While expressing sensitivity to and respect for religious belief and practice and repudiating religious intolerance, the Senate resolution calls upon the President to 'take swift and proportionate action . . . in the event that violent acts should occur.'

(Communique from Association of American Publishers, 7 March 1989)

The Satanic Verses *went back on the book chains' shelves. Between December and March, Viking received some 30,000 letters of protest as well as 16 bomb threats.*

Statement by Attorney General Richard Thornburgh (2 March 1989)

The United States Department of Justice is committed to an all-out effort, using the full resources of the Federal Bureau of Investigation, to seek to prevent terroristic attacks on American publishers and booksellers and to vigorously prosecute anyone responsible for such acts.

There is no place in our society for threats against the exercise of First Amendment rights by American publishers, booksellers and the general public in connection with the book *The Satanic Verses* by Salman Rushdie.

The Ayatollah Khomeini may be able to control the selling of books in Iran, but in America we believe in the right of free speech and the free discussion of ideas.

Acting under the direction of President Bush and within the confines of our free and open society, the FBI will utilize its ongoing intelligence-gathering activities to aid in protecting against attacks on books stores and publishers. In addition the Bureau will vigorously investigate any such incidents, and the US attorney's offices will prosecute any on a priority basis.

President Bush has expressed his concern about this matter and has made it clear, as I have, that we must use every available resource to protect the right of free speech in the United States.

(Department of Justice)

Congress condemns threats

SENATOR PATRICK MOYNIHAN

Mr. President, this matter was on the Senate floor last week, and only a long meeting of the Committee on Armed Services prevented our adopting it.

It states in the most emphatic terms that the United States absolutely rejects the intellectual terrorism practiced by the Ayatollah Khomeini. He has called for the assassination of a Moslem-born author residing in Britain. He has also called for attacks upon, vengeance upon, and violence to the publishers of *Satanic Verses*, Viking Penguin in New York.

Let it be understood in the parts of the world from whence such threats emanate: We are not intimidated and the resources of civilization against its enemies are not exhausted.

It is important to note that this resolution is sponsored by the chairman and ranking member of the Committee on Foreign Relations and of course by our distinguished leaders, the majority leader and the Republican leader.

Mr. President, I have also to inform the Senate of something we had thought would not happen in our State of New York. Early this morning the office of the *Riverdale Press*, a highly respected weekly newspaper in New York City, was fire bombed and all but destroyed.

This was done in the aftermath of an editorial published by that newspaper: a thoughtful, moderate, but firm editorial defending the right to publish, to distribute and to sell. The editorial comment was entitled 'The Tyrant and His Chains,' and begins, 'How fragile civilization is; how easily, how merrily a book burns.'

Mr. President, as a statement of solidarity with the publishers of the *Riverdale Press*, I ask unanimous consent that this editorial be printed in the Record at this point.

There being no objection, the editorial was ordered to be printed in the Record as follows:

THE TYRANT AND HIS CHAINS

'How fragile civilization is; how easily, how merrily a book burns,' wrote Salman Rushdie when a group of English Moslems publicly burned copies of his novel, *The Satanic Verses*, in West Yorkshire last month.

The powers of reason and imagination are indeed the underpinnings of our civilization. To suppress a book or punish an idea is to express contempt for the people who read the book or consider the idea. In preferring the logic of the executioner to the logic of debate, the bookburners and the Ayatollah Khomeini display their distrust for the principle on which self-government rests, the wisdom and virtue of ordinary people.

SENATE RESOLUTION 72

Whereas, on February 14, 1989 Ayatollah Ruhollah Khomeini of the Islamic Republic of Iran called for the assassination of Salman Rushdie, author of *Satanic Verses*, and of the officers of Viking, the U.S. publisher of the book;

Whereas on February 21, 1989 President George Bush condemned Iran's threat against Mr. Rushdie and his publisher as 'deeply offensive to the norms of civilized behavior'; Now, therefore, be it

Resolved by the Senate. That in recognition of threats of violence made against the above mentioned author and publisher, the Senate—

(1) declares its commitment to protect the right of any person to write, publish, sell, buy and read books without fear of intimidation and violence;

(2) unequivocally condemns as state-sponsored terrorism, the threat of the government of Iran and Ayatollah Ruhollah Khomeini to assassinate citizens of other countries on foreign soil;

(3) expresses its support for the publishers and booksellers who have courageously printed, distributed, sold, and displayed *Satanic Verses* despite the threats they have received;

(4) applauds President Bush for his strongly worded statement of outrage against the Iranian government's actions and calls upon the President to continue to condemn publicly any and all threats made against the author and his publishers;

(5) commends the European Community member states for with-

drawing their diplomatic corps from Iran in response to the Ayatollah's death sentence;

(6) recognizes the sensitivity of religious beliefs and practices, respects all religions and the commitment of the religious to their faith, and repudiates religious intolerance and bigotry, and

(7) calls upon the President of the United States to take swift and proportionate action in consultation, as appropriate, with other interested governments, in the event that violent acts should occur.

SUSAN SONTAG
From testimony before the Subcommittee on International Terrorism, Senate Foreign Relations Committee, 8 March 1989.

. . . I cannot speak for all writers, and while I officially represent the 2,200 members of PEN American Center, I remind you that writers are a contrary and individualistic breed, not disposed to collective expression or given to unanimity on anything. Nevertheless, I cannot recall a time when PEN's members have been as concerned and as united on a public issue as they have been in recent days with respect to the death threat aimed at Salman Rushdie, and its ramifications for freedom of expression here in the United States.

. . . Distressed at the silence of the White House, I sent a letter to President Bush on Feb. 20 on behalf of the PEN membership, which read:

'We ask that you issue a public statement condemning the death threats made by the Ayatollah Khomeini against author Salman Rushdie and his publishers. These threats from Iran must have a vigorous and swift response. The attempt at censorship by terror, and the fear that it has engendered, strikes not only at writers, publishers and booksellers, but finally at libraries, schools, and the entire basis of the United States as a literate, free country. In this emergency, we respectfully request that you bring the office of the presidency to the support of our cherished American institutions that are in jeopardy and to declare your readiness to take the necessary steps to protect American citizens in the free and unintimidated exercise of their constitutional rights.'

The next day the President said that he would hold Iran responsible for any attacks 'against American interests'. We found this particularly maddening, since from the very beginning fundamental

American interests were at stake: our Constitutional rights to write, publish, sell, buy and read books free of intimidation. That they were already threatened was obvious from the widespread and quite understandable expressions of fear—fear for their physical safety— voiced by the employees of the publishing house, employees of bookstores, and some of the writers considering protesting the sentence of death passed on Mr. Rushdie and his publisher.

As the American writer Ralph Ellison noted recently, 'A death sentence is a rather harsh review.' And may I remind the committee that a death sentence was passed not only on Mr. Rushdie but on his publisher, the President of Viking Penguin, who is an American. (Mr. Rushdie's wife, Marianne Wiggins, who has been obliged to go into hiding with him to escape the suicide squads the Ayatollah claims to have dispatched to execute her husband, is an American.) It has been noted that this is the first time in the history of the century that the death penalty has been extended beyond the borders of a single country in defiance of the laws of other countries.

. . . The Ayatollah has not retracted his execution order—which I repeat, includes Mr. Rushdie's American publisher—and Salman Rushdie is still in hiding. His life will never be the same again.

Will other groups with other grudges be more inclined to threaten violence to achieve their goals? In an important sense, that did not work in the Rushdie case. While both Mr. Rushdie and his publishers apologized for hurt sensibilities, they retracted nothing, and the publisher proceeded with plans for a second printing. Later this week, the book will be available to the vast majority of Americans who wish to purchase it or borrow it from the library. For this we can thank many courageous publishers, writers and independent booksellers.

And yet there is considerable fear. Some 'chilling effect' seems inevitable. At least for a while, there is likely to be a great deal of self-censorship—certainly on matters relating to the Islamic religion, and probably on a host of other topics which can provoke strong, and potentially violent reaction. Most of these decisions— the book not written; the manuscript rejected; the book order not made, by individual or school or library—will be hidden from public view.

What can the United States Senate do to reduce the danger to American freedom of expression from such pressures? Terrorist threats to an independent, free, pluralistic national culture are now international and the response has to be, in part, a foreign policy response. We must stand up to Iran or any other country whose leaders have the ability to intimidate our citizens, curtail our taste for freedom, hijack our fundamental institutions. And please do what you can do to further the awareness—in yourselves, in the Executive Branch and in your constituents—that our integrity as a nation is as endangered by an attack on a writer as on an oil tanker.

... And a final word: the matter of Salman Rushdie has made him the world's best-known endangered writer, but he is far from the only one. In all too many parts of the world, to take up one's pen is to risk violence, most often from governments which treat criticism as treason. PEN works year-round to bring attention to the plight of these writers, and assisting them should be an imperative of US foreign policy.

American writers in support of Salman Rushdie

The following are extracts from statements made at the public meeting of 22 February 1989.

E. L. DOCTOROW

Usually in this century writers are killed by secular authorities. Hitler and Stalin habitually murdered writers who offended them, the Gang of Four went after the writers and poets of China, and of course, Latin American generals, to this moment, take turns outdoing each other in the peculiar sport. Iran itself under the rule of the detested Shah Palavi, who was installed in a coup staged and funded by the CIA, committed writers and other Islamic intellectuals to prison without trial and then routinely tortured and murdered them. In fact, such excesses of secular dictatorship led to the Iranian revolution under the leadership of the Ayatollah Khomeini. So, in this century at least, we in the West tend not to think of the killing of writers as a particularly religious thing to do.

Islam is a great worldwide faith. An outsider can imagine a writer's blasphemy against it is a profound sacrilege, and at the same time wonder why the blasphemer cannot be recovered for the faith under the instruction of the clergy. We have to wonder why the blasphemy must be the occasion for the writer's contract murder rather than his enlightenment by means of serene spiritual counsel that would lead him through his penitence and remorse to true piety and possibly redemption. Even if such a course were not possible, one thinks surely the mechanism of excommunication, the most extreme punishment in the language of religion, would be the preferred theological version of the death sentence without trial, which has been established in this century as the technique of the profane tyrannies.

The great religions endure by their magnanimity of embrace. This is part of their truth, their embrace of the wretched fallibility of each of us, so that we may hope to live in some state of worshipful reconciliation with our maker. To go with God, to apprehend what is sacred, to live in clear spiritual resolution, is the desire of every human being of whatever faith. It is even the desire of intellectuals, for whom intellectual life is a form of faith. The writer's skeptical mind and inquiring spirit is the soul given to discourse, wide-eyed and sometimes rude in its perceptions, examining all ideas and feelings no matter how contradictory and ambiguous. It is nevertheless as desperately intended a pilgrimage toward revelation as the true believer's.

Those who are religiously convinced must not make the mistake of thinking that the complex intellectual life of a writer is less worthy of God than their own, or that striving through whatever terrible terrains of the spirit to an earned humility is to be necessarily less obedient to him. The writer lives in a universe of language; his mind is a democracy of contentious voices, each claiming to be the truth, and he hears them all and gives voice to them all. He is a field for universal music. The writer, according to Ralph Waldo Emerson, believes that all that can be thought can be written. In his eyes a man is the faculty of reporting, and the universe is the possibility of being reported.

This truly is our faith. Who can say that God didn't intend for some of us to serve him in this way? Who can say the writer does not prostrate himself before God each and every day he rises to his work? Or else we all commit sacrilege, the basic sacrilege of intending to write when the sacred text of the Word of God is already written. The poet of rhapsody and celebrant of God's glory, the pious scholar, the exegete who combs the sacred text, is no less hellbound than the satirist, the ironist, and the skeptic. All our books should be destroyed, and all of us must go into hiding.

FRANCES FITZGERALD

. . . We cannot yet adequately understand the cultural shock that Western imperialism delivered to the Middle East and the Indian subcontinent in the nineteenth century. In the first place, it happened so slowly that the shock waves are still reverberating. In the second place, we Westerners, much as we would strive to make the translation, cannot because we do not feel those shock waves in our own bodies. It is only those who do who can describe it. Salman Rushdie is one of them. He is one of the translators. He speaks to the East and the West at once. But by virtue of his calling he lives in a danger zone—the zone of trouble at the borders of culture and identity.

In another age this trouble might be purely personal—a matter for the individual conscience. But it is now big trouble, international trouble. This is so because in recent years mass parties have formed in reaction to the cultural chaos the West has produced in Iran, Pakistan and elsewhere. The 'West' must now be in quotation marks, as it signifies so many things, and it includes so many 'Easterners'. All the same, it is a threat and an allure which seems both suffocating and invasive, a force which threatens the very roots of identity.

That is why these days some Muslims are interpreting the great tradition of Islam in the way they do. It is far from the only way it is being interpreted. To see the Ayatollah as the representative of Islam is like seeing the Grand Inquisitor as the representative of Christianity. . . .

CHRISTOPHER HITCHENS

Today is the birthday of George Washington. And to celebrate this day, one third of the book 'outlets'—a word that becomes unpleasingly suggestive by their action—of this country have refused to stock or sell a book because its author has been condemned to death for a bounty by 'an old, mad, blind, despised and dying king,' to borrow from Shelley's pithy encapsulation of the salient qualities of King George III.

As writers and *soi-disant* intellectuals, it is most often our job to stress complexity, to point out with care and attention that 'it's not as simple as that.' But there are also times when it is irresponsible not to stress the essential clarity and simplicity of a question. The almost boastful threat to murder not just a book but an author is one such time. Moments of this sort have a galvanizing effect on our standby phrases and our most cherished cliches. Heinrich Heine once said that where books are burned, men will be burned. Now we can see for ourselves the dead straight line that connects the two offenses. What began with book-burning has culminated in the incitement to murder.

I want to read just one sentence from page 93 of the English edition of *The Satanic Verses*.

> To turn insults into strengths, Whigs, Tories, Blacks all chose to wear with pride the names they were given in scorn; likewise our mountain-climbing, prophet-motivated solitary is to be—Mahound.

With unusual economy, this short passage performs two services. It shows that Salman Rushdie is perfectly 'sensitive' to the nuances of feeling that he is accused of ignoring. (And accused, I might add, by those whose definition of 'sensitivity' seems rather closely attuned to the needs of power and bigotry—two famously 'insensitive' phenomena.) Instead of pluralism and tolerance today, we are faced with a pluralism of the intolerant; an ecumenicism of the Philistines, that finds likeable reasons to defer to the mullahs and which comes in the oily phrases of a prince of the church of this city, and in hesitant, poltroonish noises from the man who styles himself the Leader of the Free World.

Let us also extend Rushdie's appropriation of charged and insulting words. Consider the words 'heretic', 'blasphemer' and 'martyr'. The first two originated as insults, in fact as highly literal 'condemnations.' But we have appropriated them over time, and by force—the paradoxical exertion of the force of repression as it was directed against freedom of conscience. To us, 'heretic' recalls the finer moments of Jan Hus, of Thomas More and Martin Luther, and is the ideal counterpoint to the sinister meanings of the word 'orthodox.' Then, 'blasphemer' has been ennobled by Socrates, Galileo, Kazantzakis, Joyce and countless others who could not be content with mere human authority even when it came sanctified by the claim of divine right. 'Martyr' is a word we still respect for its original sense, though we have learned to distrust excessive or promiscuous zeal for it, and though we insist that a real movement for freedom will suffer martyrs, not create them. These are the differences, historically determined, between ourselves and the fanatics.

Such differences in meaning are not ontological. They arise from the Enlightenment, which is an inheritance we do not have the right to betray. Having brought ruin and despair to his country and to the Iranian revolution in peace and war, Ayatollah Khomeini seeks to resist the spread of doubt and the possibility of a Reformation. He is a desperate man who has almost exhausted the toxic appeal of martyrdom and holy war. How depressing it is that just at the moment when there might be a synthesis between the Muslim world and Enlightenment ideas—which are by no means 'Western' property—we should see such nervousness about the upholding of these principles, in this country, even in their most elementary form.

What if it is said, jeeringly, that we risk nothing? Well, we risk a great deal by ceding even an inch of ground to the book-burners and the murderers. But, to abandon the defensive, why *should* we let Mr. Rushdie face this unprecedented trial alone? As readers and as critics, and in multifarious other ways, we are all directly complicit in the propagation of *The Satanic Verses*, and we are all in the debt of its author. I suggest a public declaration that until the menace of murder by contract has been lifted from our fellow writer and from his decent and brave publisher, all of us who believe in the life of the written word announce ourselves publicly as co-conspirators. They can't kill us all, and we may impress on many sincere believers who are worried about the blasphemous association of their faith with crime and repression that, any rumors to the contrary, *we too have unalterable beliefs.*

We have all often had to wonder what we would have done in the unjust lands and the unjust times. Well, now we have a chance, in a small way, to find out. It is now time, as a minimal gesture of solidarity, for all of us to don the Yellow Star, and to end the hateful isolation of our friend and colleague.

NORMAN MAILER

... By my limited comprehension of the Muslim religion, martyrdom is implicit in the faith. While all faiths sooner or later suggest that a true believer may have to be ready to die for the governing god, it is possible that the Muslims, of all religions, have always been the most dedicated to this stern test. Now, it seems as if the spiritual corruption of the twentieth century has entered Islam's ranks as well. For, any Muslim who succeeds in assassinating Salman Rushdie will be rewarded with the munificent sum of $5,000,000. This must be the largest hit contract in history. Islam, with all its mighty virtues and vices, equal at least to the virtues and vices of every other major religion, has now introduced a novel element into the history of theology. It has added the logic of the syndicate. One does not even have to belong to the family to collect. One has only to be the hit man. Of course, the novelist in me insists on thinking how I would hate to be that hit man trying to collect five million dollars. Now that the deed was done, I might be looked upon as an infidel. 'Oh, you see,' my Iranian paymaster might say, 'we really cannot afford the five million. We lost so many men in the war with Iraq. There are so many widows in need of alms, and we have our orphans, and our veterans who are now missing a limb. Tell you, kind killer, we think you might wish to make your charitable contribution.'

This is but a novelist's speculation. That is what we are here for—to speculate on human possibilities, to engage in those fantasies, cynicisms, satires, criticisms, and explorations of human vanity, desire, and courage, that the blank walls of the mighty corporations like to conceal from us. We are scribblers who try to explore what is left to look at in the interstices. Sometimes we make mistakes and injure innocent victims by our words. Sometimes we get lucky and make people with undue worldly power a bit uncomfortable for a short time. Usually, we spend our days injuring each other. We are, after all, a fragile resource, an endangered species. It is not untypical of the weak and endangered to chew each other up a little on the way down. But now the Ayatollah Khomeini has offered us an opportunity to regain our frail religion which happens to be faith in the power of words and our willingness to suffer for them. He awakens us to the great rage we feel when our liberty to say what we wish, wise or foolish, kind or cruel, well-advised or ill-advised, is endangered. We discover that, yes, maybe we are willing to suffer for our idea. Maybe we are even willing, ultimately, to die for the idea that serious literature, in a world of dwindling certainties and choked-up ecologies, is the absolute we must defend.

EDWARD W. SAID

In 1984 Salman Rushdie published a superb essay in *Granta* entitled 'Outside the Whale,' in which he showed that today's writer could not be inside the whale, insulated from history and politics. 'The modern world,' Rushdie says, 'lacks not only hiding places, but certainties.' These words have an ominously prophetic applicability to Salman Rushdie's situation today, not only because he has to be in hiding in order to save his life, but because he wrote a book that made 'a very devil of a racket' in challenging certainties, provoking anger and amazement.

Rushdie says:

'If writers leave the business of making pictures of the world to politicians, it will be one of history's great and most abject abdications.

'Outside the whale is the unceasing storm, the quarrel, the dialectic of history. Outside the whale there is a genuine need for political fiction, for books that draw new and better maps of reality, and make new languages with which we can understand the world. Outside the whale we see that we are all irradiated by history, we are radioactive with history and politics; we see that it can be as false to create a politics-free fictional universe as to create one in which nobody needs to work or eat or hate or love or sleep. Outside the whale it becomes necessary, and even exhilarating, to grapple with the special problems created by the incorporation of political material because politics is by turns farce and tragedy, sometimes . . . both at once. Outside the whale the writer is obliged to accept that he (or she) is part of the crowd, part of the ocean, part of the storm.'

The Satanic Verses is an astonishing and prodigiously inventive work of fiction. Yet it is like its author, in history, the world, the crowd and the storm. It is, in all sorts of ways, a deliberately transgressive work. It parallels and mimics the central Islamic narratives with bold, nose-thumbing, post-modern daring. And in so doing it demonstrates another side of its author's unbroken engagement with the politics and history of the contemporary scene. Salman Rushdie is after all the same distinguished writer and intellectual who has spoken out for immigrants', black and Palestinian rights, against imperialism and racism, as well as against censorship, and he has always unhesitatingly expressed willingness to take active political positions whenever his voice has been needed. I think what shocks Moslems in the novel is the book's knowing intimacy with the religious and cultural material it so comically and resourcefully plays with. There is also the further shock of seeing Islam portrayed irreverently and—although as a secularist I have difficulty in using this word—blasphemously by a Moslem who writes both in and for the West. The cultural context is horrifically and even ludicrously inhospitable to such transgressions.

Most Moslems think of the current situation between their community and Western civilization in singularly unhappy terms. How many Islamic writers, Moslems say, from Egypt, Iraq, Palestine, Pakistan or Senegal are published, much less known or read, in the West? And why is that ignorance there, if not for the disregard, indifference and fear with which things Islamic are considered here? Israel bans hundreds of books in occupied Palestine territories, and Palestinian writers are jailed without trial: where are the protesting voices of Western writers and intellectuals?

Islam is reduced to terrorism and fundamentalism and now, alas, is seen to be acting accordingly, in the ghastly violence prescribed by Ayatollah Khomeini. The fury increases as do the pieties and the vindictive righteousness. Above all, however, there rises the question that people from the Islamic world ask: Why must a Moslem, who could be defending and sympathetically interpreting us, now represent us so roughly, so expertly and so disrespectfully to an audience already primed to excoriate our traditions, reality, history, religion, language, and origin? Why, in other words, must a member of our culture join the legions of Orientalists in Orientalizing Islam so radically and unfairly?

To try to answer these questions is by no means to deny the anguish and seriousness in the questions. But it is, as a beginning, to say that although it contains many spheres, the contemporary world of men and women is one world; human history therefore has many divisions, many peculiarities, but it too is one. In this world Salman Rushdie, from the community of Islam, has written for the West about Islam. *The Satanic Verses* thus is a self-representation. But everyone should be able to read the novel, interpret it, understand, accept, or finally reject it. And, more to the point, it should be possible both to accept the brilliance of Rushdie's work and also to note its transgressive apostasy.

If this peculiar paradox is also an emblem of the fate of hybrids and immigrants, that fate too is part of this contemporary world. For the point is that there is no pure, unsullied, unmixed essence to which some of us can return, whether that essence is pure Islam, pure Christianity, pure Judaism or Easternism, Americanism, Westernism. Rushdie's work is not just *about* the mixture, it *is* that mixture itself. To stir Islamic narratives into a stream of heterogeneous narratives about actors, tricksters, prophets, devils, whores, heroes, heroines is therefore inevitable. Most of us are still unprepared to deal with such complicated mixtures, but, as Rushdie says in his essay, 'in this world without quiet corners, there can be no easy escapes from history, from hullabaloo, from terrible, unquiet fuss.'

But what those of us from the Moslem part of this world need to add is that we cannot accept the notion that democratic freedoms should be abrogated to protect Islam. No world culture or religion is really about such violence or such curtailments of fundamental rights. If we have accepted Rushdie's help in the past, we should now be ensuring his safety and his right to say what he has to say. To dispute with him, to engage with his work does not, cannot, be the same thing either as banning it or threatening him with violence and physical punishment.

LEON WIESELTIER

. . . One day the Muslim world may recall with admiration its late twentieth-century Anglo-Indian Voltaire.

We declare here today that Salman Rushdie is also one of our own, that we know him, that all our force, such as it is, is now at the service of his work and his life. But we, in the West, must not gloat. We must remember that Europe, too, was once a stifled, theocratic, feudal, crusading society, that burned books and burned people. It was blasphemy that made us free. Two cheers, today, for blasphemy.

In the West, we read More and Milton and Galileo and Spinoza and Locke and Voltaire and Jefferson and Mill and Mann and Tucholsky and Koestler and Sakharov a little smugly, because they won. Glibly we attach an historical inevitability to the triumph of their spirit. We recognize the persecution of Rushdie: the man of the word against the man of the Word, the power of the word against the power of powers. We know all about the debt that democracy owes to heresy. But we forget, sometimes, that it did not have to be so. We forget, sometimes, that freedom was also the fruit of tragedy.

Who is this man of God who has no mercy in his heart? But then let us be his match, and in the defense of Rushdie, in the defense of the imagination, in the defense of the mind, show no mercy ourselves. Let us be dogmatic about tolerance. For we, the lucky ones, have been taught, at this late date in the history of infamy, when even we needed the lesson, that democracy has its martyrs, too. I pray that Salman Rushdie does not become one of them.

STATEMENT FROM MARIANNE WIGGINS
Read by Susan Sontag

Today, on the publication day of *The Satanic Verses* in the United States, two writers are in hiding—one, to save his life; the other as a matter of her own free choice in an act of solidarity. Writers everywhere have been weighed and measured by an edict from Iran. We are a dangerous breed and always have been, because words outlive their authors, words can emanate from silence, words can find their way from hidden places. Only fear can stop a writer writing. Only fear can stop a book from being sold. Fear dies with the individual— the written word, which we celebrate officially today, is one unleashed, colossal, unrepentant, joyous, passionate, expansive and courageous monster. Rejoice in it.

STATEMENT FROM JAMES A. MICHENER
Read by Susan Sontag

The recent behavior of Muslim leaders throughout the world has been a painful embarrassment to me. Years ago I wrote a short essay, 'Islam, the Misunderstood Religion,' an ecumenical defense of that faith. The essay was widely reprinted and circulated throughout the Muslim world, making me a kind of champion of their beliefs.

In later years I lived in or visited extensively every Muslim nation except Saudi Arabia, from Indonesia westward to Spain, which had been Muslim for centuries. As result of these visits I came to know that world as intimately as an outsider could. I was awed by the strength, vitality and wide variation of Islam. It was a powerful force.

But the current calls for the assassination of foreigners whom the Muslim leadership does not like are a fearful error and a step back to the time of the Crusades. Three days ago in a shopping mall in Miami a friend of mine saw a fiery-eyed young man picketing a bookstore with a sign in Arabic. Fortunately my friend could read Arabic and the sign said: 'Assassinate the writer.'

I warn my Muslim friends that it is absolutely unacceptable for them to inject themselves into the international writing and publishing scene with their calls for assassination and it is equally unacceptable for us to surrender to such terrorist blackmail.

I speak not only as a fellow writer, but as an American citizen. Others like Norman Mailer and Susan Sontag will warn against the censorship perils in this case. I speak only to the Muslim leadership abroad and in this country: Do not persist in this folly. You make yourselves look ridiculous. You damage your reputation and that of your religion. You make sensible Americans ask: 'Have these men gone mad?' Accept Rushdie's regrets. Argue against the book in your own countries. But do not try to ban it in ours.

Words for Salman Rushdie

The following extracts are taken from an article in the New York Times Book Review, *12 March 1989.*

In a response to the crisis of Salman Rushdie, 28 distinguished writers born in 21 countries speak to him from their common land— the country of literature. For expressing their ideas publicly in the past many of these writers have suffered censorship, exile—forced or self-imposed—and imprisonment. Some have been politically active on behalf of the rights of writers under totalitarian regimes. Many are on the record here and in their own countries in support of Mr. Rushdie, the Indian-born British author of the novel "The Satanic Verses," who was still in hiding in England with a price on his head when The Book Review went to press. He has been accused by the Iranian revolutionary leader Ayatollah Ruhollah Khomeini of slandering Islam in his novel. The Ayatollah has called for his death.

MARIO VARGAS LLOSA
Peru

I've been thinking about you very much and what happened to you. I am in total solidarity with your book, and I would like to share with you this assault on rationalism, reason and freedom. Writers should unite forces in this most crucial moment in creative freedom. We thought this war was won a long time ago, but it wasn't. In the past, it was the Christian Inquisition, Fascism, Stalinism; now it's Muslim fundamentalism, and there will probably be others. The forces of fanaticism will always be there. The spirit of freedom will always be menaced by unrationality and intolerance, which are apparently deeply rooted in the human heart.

NIEN CHENG
Born in China, lives in the United States

You must be firm and brave, because in some ways your position is worse than being in prison. You cannot identify your enemy. In Communist China during the Cultural Revolution many people who were not locked up suffered more than I did. They were beaten more frequently than I was. In prison you only have to contend with guards; hysterical mobs are worse. Death threats were only hinted at to me, but my daughter was beaten to death by a mob, though they did not intend to kill her. I hope you can resume normal life in the near future.

CHINUA ACHEBE
Nigeria

What does one say? I think probably all I can say is: Don't despair. The world has become a very dangerous place, but it is our responsibility to keep fighting for the freedom of the human spirit. It's not just for writers that we must do this, but for everyone. If we secure this freedom, the whole world benefits.

ANITA DESAI
India

Silence, exile and cunning, yes. And courage.

JOSÉ DONOSO
Chile

The situation you are in is completely unfair, completely uncivilized. Stay in hiding until it blows over. This thing will blow over soon. After a while people will not remember the scandal, but if the book is good, they will remember the book. Let's hope all this is going to help writers band together against situations of this sort and reaffirm the fact that the word is more powerful than the sword.

ELIE WIESEL
Born in Rumania, lives in the United States

Any attack on you is directed at us all. Censorship in literature is the enemy of literature and death threats, addressed for whatever reason, if they succeed in silencing the author, would mean not only the end of literature but the end of civilization.

IRIS MURDOCH
Born in Ireland, lives in England

Wars end. The night will end.

CZESLAW MILOSZ
Born in Lithuania, lives in the United States

I have particular reasons to defend your rights, Mr. Rushdie. My books have been forbidden in many countries or have had whole passages censored out. I'm grateful to people who stood then by the principle of free expression, and I back you now in my turn.

UMBERTO ECO
Italy

Nobody can ignore your ordeal, for at least three reasons.

First (and once again), a man is being persecuted for having written a book.

Second, for the first time in the history of this century the death penalty is extended beyond the borders of a single country, in spite of the laws of other countries. Exile, the last resort of free men, does not work any longer.

Third, your potential killers are summoned through the media; ironically, any medium covering the event contributes to inform and mobilize new potential killers.

You deserve the full and passionate solidarity of any man of dignity, but I'm afraid this is too little. This story of a man alone against worldwide intolerance, and of a book alone against the craziness of the media, can become the story of many others. The bell tolls for all of us.

RALPH ELLISON
United States

Keep to your convictions.
Try to protect yourself.
A death sentence is a rather harsh review.

RUMER GODDEN
Born in India, lives in Britain

As someone who lived for so many years in India, I think you should have been more aware of what you were doing to offend Muslims, because they are exceedingly sensitive. Anything to do with their religion provokes a tremendous response, as it does with many committed Christians of the very orthodox type. Whatever you have done, probably you wrote it as a good story. I tremble for your safety.

ADAM MICHNIK
Poland

I am deeply distressed that once again a time has returned when it's possible publicly to call for murder. My distress is all the greater because the designated victim of the murder is a writer. A world in which a fanatic governing Iran can rent paid murderers all over the globe is a world in which no one is safe. Salman Rushdie was condemned to death and that's why it's every person's duty to give him shelter. We need to be on the side of the writer and against those who want to murder him. I'd like Salman Rushdie to know that my house is his house.

ROBERTSON DAVIES
Canada

Your suffering shows the world, in an extreme form, what every serious writer must face. To write truly is not to deal in entrenched ideas but to give voice to whatever we can raise from the depths of the human spirit, which is where the future lies, waiting for the call. To raise the future inevitably provokes the malignity of the past. We are sorry for your distress but we would not wish unsaid what you have written, for the task of all of us is to say what entrenched opinion considers unspeakable.

OCTAVIO PAZ
Mexico

We are seeing a disappearance of the modern values that came with the Enlightenment. These people who condemn you are living before the Enlightenment. We are facing a historical contradiction in our century.

I would say to you, remain firm. I defend the writer's right to be wrong.

BHARATI MUKHERJEE
Born in India, lives in the United States

I should like you, Salman, to know that we care more about your personal safety and about the preservation of your books and your message than we do about the chain bookstore owners' angst, which unfortunately has seized the media headlines. The religious establishment seems to have proved itself to be the source either of threat or of cowardice. I hope in spite of everything your next novel will be so scaldingly blasphemous that even liberals will cringe.

JOSEF SKVORECKY
Born in Czechoslovakia, lives in Canada

Meaning no harm, I, too, wrote a few sentences in my first novel that angered the mighty in my country. At that time, they only confiscated my book from bookstores and threatened my liberty, but although they did not threaten my life, perhaps I have at least some idea of what it is like. I pray that tolerance and respect for life prevail. I keep thinking of you.

THOMAS PYNCHON
United States

Our thanks to you and to Marianne Wiggins, for recalling those of us who write to our duty as heretics, for reminding us again that power is as much our sworn enemy as unreason, for making us all look braver, wiser, more useful than we often think we are. We pray for your continuing good health, safety and lightness of spirit.

GEORGE KONRAD
Hungary

I will be speaking in Budapest on behalf of both you and Vaclav Havel [the dissident Czechoslovak playwright who was jailed in February for taking part in a protest in Prague]. I believe your causes are linked. It is absolutely irrelevant what was in your novel because a novel cannot be the object of any moral or legal judgment. It is an elementary question of the freedom of writing and I believe we writers have to share the responsibility you took, and we do support the publication of your work.

THOMAS KENEALLY
Australia

I remember the day you and Bruce Chatwin were setting off together from Adelaide to visit Alice Springs in central Australia. Now Bruce is dead and you are under a tyrant's sentence of death. All I can say is what I heard a number of authors crying in the streets of New York recently during a demonstration in favor of your right to free expression. "I am Rushdie." We all are.

MARGARET ATWOOD
Canada

You're the one in trouble; tell *us* what we can do to best support you. It's all too easy to pop off the handle and say what is on my mind without reflecting on your position. We feel deeply the horror of your position. And remember: You are worth a great deal more to the Ayatollah alive than dead, because dead you are no longer something to be waved around.

(from *New York Times Book Review*, 12 March 1989)

Within the American Muslim community, meanwhile, other voices were being raised, asking for greater sensitivity and respect for sacred beliefs while also rejecting violence and affirming freedom of thought and expression.

Statement of position on Salman Rushdie's *Satanic Verses*

We wish to share the following points in regard to the recent controversy over Salman Rushdie's book *The Satanic Verses*:

1. By depicting Islam, Prophet Muhammad, peace be upon him, his family, his Companions, his teachings, and the Angels, in a malicious, slanderous, highly defamatory manner, and by making obscene and derogatory references specifically to the Prophet's wives, Rushdie has grievously offended and violated the sanctity of the Muslim community. What makes it more painful is the fact that the author's blatant assault on Islam and the Prophet, besides being clearly unnecessary for his literary purposes, is in reckless disregard of the historical truths and heartfelt beliefs of the one billion-member Muslim community, and deliberately so.

2. We reaffirm our commitment to the freedom of thought and expression guaranteed to all people in this country, and which is at the same time a cherished Islamic value. However, it should also be pointed out that it is highly imprudent and inconsiderate for an individual to completely ignore the religious sensitivities of his fellows in humanity while exercising his freedoms. An individual's rights are undoubtedly guaranteed by the state, but it is the spirit

of harmony, goodwill and mutual respect among the members of society that ensures the full and balanced enjoyment and responsible exercise of those rights by all. The ideal of freedom of expression should not be a refuge for slander with the intent to do malice, nor blatant lies, nor defamatory ridicule. The publishers and book sellers of America, as well as the media, have a responsibility to maintain an acceptable standard of fairness that should exclude works of slander and bigotry.

3. Beyond the issue of freedom of expression, the media and publishing industry have traditionally exercised a sophisticated self-restraint in the interest of social order and harmony, as well as in consideration of moral and ethical norms and the ethno-racial and religious sensitivities of society. Muslims would like the media and publishing industry to accord them the same rights and consideration which have generally been extended to other ethnic, racial, and religious minorities threatened by stereotypical portrayal, innuendo, and false characterization. It is regrettable that Viking Penguin, Inc., the publishers of *The Satanic Verses* in the U.S., has shown complete insensitivity to our concerns and has declined even to receive a representative delegation of the Muslim American community. It must have become clear to them by now that this book has hurt the feelings of hundreds of millions of Muslims throughout the world. We believe that a public apology is only appropriate and conducive to harmony and good will.

4. The purpose of our peaceful expression of dismay with the contents of Rushdie's *Satanic Verses* is to register the depth of our feelings against the author's flagrantly slanderous references to the Prophet and his family; to correct errors and misconceptions about Islam that are likely to be taken as facts by the readers of his book; to impress upon publishers that they should have exercised better judgement in selecting and printing a book which has injured one-fifth of humanity; and to encourage the dissemination of accurate information about Islam, in North America and elsewhere.

5. Muslim Americans are grateful for statements issued by Cardinal O'Connor of New York, the Archbishop of Canterbury, and the Lord Chief Rabbi of the United Kingdom in condemning this book. We urge the communities of faith in North America to add their voices of condemnation to ours in the face of such assault on belief in God, religious consciousness, divine revelation, and the

person of the Prophet Abraham, the patriarch of Islam, Christianity and Judaism.

6. Despite our strong feelings about the contents of this hate-inspiring book, Islam does not condone violence or the incitement to violence directed against its author and those associated with its publication. Equally, we cannot condone the highly incendiary remarks of those who have suggested that violence be taken against Muslims at large.

7. Muslim Americans recognize those individuals in the news media who extended themselves to bring a balance of opinion and commentary to the American public throughout this affair. We anxiously await the day this attitude will become generalized throughout the fourth estate.

8. It is only sensible and in harmony with the American tradition of fairness and tolerance for publishers and booksellers in the United States to refuse to broker hate against Islam and Muslims—or any other religion or people, for that matter—and to voluntarily withdraw this slanderous work from their shelves. We condemn the threat or use of violence to assure such withdrawal. It is, however, most inappropriate and in bad taste for American and European novelists to taunt Muslims on both continents and throughout the world with public readings constituting a frontal attack on Islam and its revered principal figures.

9. Muslim Americans affirm their belief in and commitment to the One True Universal God of all humanity; and affirm their utmost respect for all the Prophets and Messengers—including Noah, Abraham, Moses, Jesus, and Muhammad (may the peace and blessings of God be upon them all); and affirm their commitment to human equality and brotherhood. For all this is vital to the moral-social order, and a light unto humanity.

In the words of God as revealed to the Prophet Muhammad in the Quran, "Say, My Lord has forbidden indecencies, whether open or veiled, and sin and violence, and that you associate with God that for which he sent down no authority, and that you say concerning God what you know not" (7:33).

"O mankind! We have created you male and female, and appointed you peoples and tribes, that you may know one another. Surely the noblest among you in the sight of God is the most God-fearing of you" (49:13).   (Islamic Society of North America)

True message of Mohammed is peace not revenge

DR. H. MORSI

To the Editor:

There is no doubt that the book *The Satanic Verses*, by Salman Rushdie slanders Prophet Mohammed in particular and the religion of Islam in general.

However, it is a mistake for the Casper Star-Tribune and the wire services to say that Moslems feel that the book contains blasphemies against Mohammed. One can only blaspheme against God. Mohammed was a human messenger of God and not a deity to be worshipped by Moslems.

While all Moslems are angry and hurt by the publication of this book, a vast majority of these Muslims disagree with the excessive reaction especially called for by the Ayatollah Khomeini to execute the author.

Violence and murder are forbidden by the religion of Islam. As a matter of fact, such actions are considered to be un-Islamic as the very definition of the word Islam is: Peace, Purity, Acceptance, and Commitment.

The actions being taken today by Khomeini and his followers are far more appropriate to and reminiscent of the Dark Ages when the Spanish Inquisition was operating in the name of Christianity and burning people at the stake.

As a religion, Islam calls for the complete acceptance of God's laws (and murder is certainly against them). As a way of life, the true messenger of Islam is the attainment of peace, both inner and outer peace, by the submission of oneself to the will of the one and only God.

One might wonder how Mohammed himself would have treated the author of such a book? History tells us that for his own sake, he never even lifted his finger against anyone. When someone asked him to curse his enemies and persecutors, he replied, "I have not been sent to curse, but as a mercy to mankind."

When he returned to Mecca after years of forced exile, he freely forgave his enemies who had spared no effort to annihilate him, his followers, and the religion of Islam. "This day there is no reproof against you." This was his practical example of the maxim "Love your enemies."

Maybe those who are calling for the head of Rushdie and giving Islam a bad name, should look a little harder into the exemplary life and tolerance of Mohammed.

• *The author is Director of the Islamic Cultural Center of Chicago.*

(*Casper Star-Tribune*, 1 March 1989)

V

Reflections ⟨~

At the Institute of Contemporary Arts in London on 19 March a conference took place on the issues placed on the cultural agenda by The Satanic Verses. *The Nigerian novelist Ben Okri, the British novelist Maggie Gee, and writer and Channel 4 Commissioning Editor for Minorities Farrukh Dhondy took part in the opening session, chaired by Alan Yentob, Controller BBC2. This session reflected on Truth and Fiction. Malise Ruthven, author of* Islam in the World *and professor of religious studies, Marina Warner, novelist and author of a book on Joan of Arc, and Sara Maitland, novelist and theologian, then discussed Writing and Religion. What follows is an edited version of their comments.*

TRUTH AND FICTION

ALAN YENTOB

I am pleased to see that this looks like the benign sort of meeting that one expects to find at the ICA, which is not what we've seen, distressingly, in the streets of this country in recent weeks. This, I hope, will be the beginning of what needs to be a long dialogue and also a healing process between the Muslim community in this country and writers and artists, and not simply a continuation of confrontation.

Huge questions have been opened. The astonishing chasm which exists between the secular and sacred worlds couldn't have been manifested in a more distressing and extraordinary way than in the events of the last few weeks. The spark which ignited this fire is a serious and ambitious work of imaginative fiction. I think it's very important to say this, because looking at some of the correspondence in the pages of our newspapers, one would imagine that this book was written simply as a provocative act and that it has no serious purpose. This is a book on which the author, Salman Rushdie, worked with dedication and commitment for five years, well before talk of advances or prizes or publishers' rights or the intervention of the Ayatollah Khomeini. It's also important to note that Rushdie is a man who has always seen himself as part of two worlds and has always spoken eloquently on behalf of the immigrant culture which he feels is an important part of the community of interest in this country.

Of course, the peculiar resonance of Salman Rushdie's work is precisely that it explores the gap between cultures and that it embraces many of the vivid forms of storytelling which embellish the literature of today. The modern novel as a European form comes out of the Enlightenment. Rushdie is part of that tradition, but also part of the oral tradition that exists within India and Pakistan. Questions of the relations between truth and fiction have their place in both traditions, but perhaps with a very different gloss. It is that we shall explore first of all today.

BEN OKRI

... Writers are amongst other things the dream mechanism of the human race. Fiction affects us the way dreams affect us. They share the same insubstantiality. They both have the capacity to alter reality. Dreams may be purer because they are not composed of words, but when fiction has entered into us, it no longer exists as words either. We can control our fictions to some extent, but we cannot control the effects that they have on the world and we can't wholly control our dreams.

Sometimes at night we dream blasphemous and scandalous things: we dream murders and transformations; we sometimes even dream truths. There is no single way of interpreting dreams that is acceptable to all human beings. And writers create one book which sometimes becomes a hundred different books in the minds of those who read it. Sometimes we dream strange things that make us wonder if there isn't a subversive self, an irrepressible mischievous spirit in us that delights in showing just how false are the shapes, the boundaries and the rules of our lives; showing us just how unstable is this thing we call 'human beings' and how we can't entirely get away with legislating and restricting the behaviour and the freedom of the mysterious human frame. It may be that sometimes our dreams disgust us so much that we want to restrain the impish freedom of this faculty. . . .

In Salman Rushdie's novel, a character dreamt of a blasphemy, while another character anticipated some of the events which have already broken out into reality. There are no longer any stable frontiers between the imagination and the world. In terms of the facts of the world or of the recent months, the products of our imagination are lagging far behind. If reality is a war of different dreams, then our fiction should be the battleground.

It is in this light that one can begin to understand something of the shift in the terrain of *The Satanic Verses.* While I cannot swear that it entirely succeeds in unifying its diverse themes, I can say that it is a crowded text which refuses to be read from a single angle. It refuses a single way of reading the world. It is a text of changing surfaces. It opens with an act of terrorism and ends with a reconciliation. Within a single fact, there are many dreams which spawned it and within each dream, there are a hundred narratives. The novel is an amalgam of related shadow worlds, suppressed worlds. It has no centre as such: rather it has linked circles and so its internal core is made up of marginal conditions—immigration, metamorphosis under pressure, the image of black people as devils reclaimed. So that Saladin Chamcha becomes the metaphor used to describe people like him. He sprouts horns and develops hooves during his travel from his homeland to England. Somewhere between there and here, he was dehumanised and became his visible metaphor. And it is he who turns out to be something of an angel. His opposite, who develops a halo, unleashes the most evil in the novel. . . .

In a discussion we once had, I remember telling Rushdie that as a writer I felt that I needed protection. He disagreed. But these are strange times; many things stifle our dreams. We may be getting smaller. We should beware of turning into rhinoceri. If we are too silent we are in danger of passing a death sentence on the imagination. We are all witnesses. Writers are only dangerous when they tell lies. The human race is not yet free. We need to protect one another because authors might increasingly become an endangered species. But that is over-statement.

There will always be those who dare to dream. For literature dies not with the fear of imprisonment or the smell of death, but when writers stop dreaming and stop telling the truth. When love is all there is that is worth living for and when love is connected to writing and to justice, writers themselves tend to become fundamentalists. But their fundamentalism embraces all humanity in compassion and equity.

MAGGIE GEE

Most of the factors in the Rushdie affair are unique, a traffic accident between religious passion and political expediency. However, it's also true that novels are intrinsically likely to get into trouble. What's so problematic about the novel form?

First, it's very modern, the only major literary form to have arisen post-printing. Historically novels have tended to become popular when absolute authority in church and state is breaking down and when individuals are becoming more mobile and aware of their own specific identities and beliefs. Because the public fictions no longer fit, individuals invent their own private fictions, alternative worlds. This can be seen as a god-like act, inherently blasphemous.

The novel is bold. Its writers were the first to dispense with the appeal to 'authority', *auctoritas*, the stock of traditional narrative matter on which earlier story-tellers based their work. When novelists say 'This is new, I made it up', they are taking a great risk, for they are saying in effect that everything within these pages is their fault.

In Iran the novel is only 60–70 years old; but even in Europe, where it is five times older, it's still young enough to disturb readers with its potent, puzzling mixture of central invention and circumstantially detailed exterior. Why else are novelists so often asked which characters in a novel are themselves? Why else do so many readers assume that if any scene in a novel is particularly vivid, it must have really happened?

Readers do want to know just what is literally true in a novel and what is offered as dream or fantasy. This may be a naive reaction but it is in no way a foolish one, since the need to be told the truth by others is a cornerstone of cooperative living. Novelists have to work out page by page the precise relationship their work bears to the real outside world about which readers hold such passionate beliefs. Questions of tact may arise here.

The paradox is that most novelists would probably say that when they are inventing a fiction they are better able to tell the truth in its fullest and widest sense than at any other time. They may find truths about the future as well as the present; they can tell truth through play and fantasy and dream as well as in linear statement.

Literary fiction has come to be of special interest to 20th-century academics with the growing recognition that all other types of discourse—scientific, historical, religious, political—are fictions too. In one sense literary fiction is a model for the others, but in a much more important sense it challenges them. Of its nature (individualistic, eccentric, exploratory) the novel sets itself against public fictions. Unsurprising, then, if those who are protected by public fictions turn savagely on the novelist who dares to undermine them. In that sense all serious novelists are subversive, and we must all be ready to stand shoulder to shoulder with Salman Rushdie.

However, the final irony is that it isn't actually Rushdie's novel which has caused this furore, but cruder, smaller fictions *about* his novel, propagated by powerful elites. Thus has his creation fallen back into the hands of the very same public fictions that the novel has from its origins challenged.

FARRUKH DHONDY

To me, this debate, these occurrences are important, because they begin to define the kind of writer one wants to be. And as you define what kind of writer you want to be, it assists you to know what you think. And when you begin to know what you think, you define the kind of civilisation to which you want to belong.

We're talking about a book here which deservedly goes into Booker lists, wins prizes, because it firmly belongs to a progressive tradition of European writing. It then gives rise to the most massive national and international fight that has been caused since the Magna Carta; and to the most desperate and fearful threat ever laid on the life of an innocent man trying to do, quite brilliantly, what he conceives of as his metier, something he cannot avoid doing: being a writer.

It also gives rise to some massive ironies. Salman Rushdie attacks the Government and now the Government has to protect him, simply because it is the Government of Britain. The multi-cultural aspect of the book sympathises with people who might be thought of as the Bradford Muslims; it defends them against the ravages of a racist society. And it is they who have set off the controversy. The regime of Benazir Bhutto, the first democratic regime in Pakistan for ten years, had to ban the book as its first tactical act of survival and had then to order its police to shoot down demonstrators who were using *The Satanic Verses* to challenge all liberality.

Perhaps the cruellest irony of all is that all these forces have been unleashed by people on all sides who have never read the book and are battling over it. . . .

It seems to me that writers who have come from an ex-colonial tradition and straddle two different worlds have by this affair been given a very clear diktat. We must now choose between different sorts of writing, different forms of being. The first one—and I grew up with it in India—is the 'onward Christian, revolutionary, Islamic soldiers' school of writing; the school of Soviet realism, the writers of hymns to a revolution that is not closely observed, but desired. To an extent even multi-culturalism, though it has not dared to say it, is a form of that.

One is offered another choice. In the years in which I conceived the ambition to write, the best writer to emerge from the ex-colonial world was undoubtedly V. S. Naipaul. Coming from Trinidad, Naipaul has made it his business to trot around the world and use his imagination to explore the world without any flights of fantasy. In a deeply felt obituary for his brother, he writes:

'There is a way currently in vogue of writing about degraded and corrupt countries. This is the way of fantasy and extravagance. It dodges all the issues; it is safe. I find the way empty, morally and intellectually.'

Whatever else one may think of that judgement (and it certainly had Márquez and perhaps Rushdie in mind), Naipaul is wrong in one respect. Such writing is certainly not 'safe'.

Despite the danger then, the one clear message of the affair is that one has constantly to choose as a writer between supporting an ideology and telling the imaginative truth. Part of that telling is, of course, to find the truth, know it, grasp it, for the moment before it slithers away again.

WRITERS AND RELIGION

ANON.

The relationship between writers and religion raises at least three very broad questions. The first concerns the contradictory interaction of religion and literature themselves. Much of the greatest art in Western and other civilisations has been produced through a degree of religious inspiration: this is true of architecture, music, painting, sculpture and writing. In English literature one has only to think of the metaphysical poets. At the same time, reaction against religion, and satire upon it, has, equally, been the basis for much literary and cinematic work: from Joyce to Buñuel. Within the literature of the Islamic world there is, equally, a long tradition of critical, anti-clerical, hedonistic literature: it is not for nothing that Khomeini has tried to stamp out not only Western cultural influences, but much within Persian culture. Hebrew and Yiddish literature has much to offer in this vein as well.

The second broad theme raised is that of cultural universalism versus relativism: how far it is legitimate and possible to assess and react to the religious practices of others on the basis of general principles, whether or not these are of Western generation, and how far we must accept the right of each nation or religion to define its own morality. Sentencing someone to death for insulting a prophet strikes many in the West as unacceptable. Others consider this reaction 'ethnocentric'. The question is raised by many other practices in the contemporary world: China and Saudi Arabia obviously regard public executions as legitimate in the late twentieth century. We tend not to. Many of those who defend Rushdie's right to speak also call for 'understanding' and 'tolerance' for the hurt Muslims say they feel: it is not always easy to reconcile these positions, or to decide where tolerance becomes appeasement.

The third large issue that arises is that of 'blasphemy' itself, hardly the concept that most people imagined they would be discussing at the ICA at the end of the 1980s. Taking the example of Raymond Williams's *Keywords*, it may be worth seeing how this word developed. In origin it is not a religious concept: Greek *blapto* (to harm) + *pheme* (speech) simply means to defame or insult. It has, however, acquired two further meanings: to insult the divine, and to insult the sacred. The Greek New Testament uses the word in two senses—of insulting God and of insulting a person. Yet these multiple meanings only raise further questions: is it insulting of God to say there is more than one God, or that there is only one, or that God is a woman, or a black, or does not exist at all? The term 'sacred' also allows of imprecision: some nations apply it to their territory, flag, monarchy. The Muslim and Judaic traditions also have concepts of 'blasphemy', but these, too, contain multiple meanings. Islamic *kufr*, the term applied by Khomeini to Salman Rushdie, covers 'atheism', 'insult to god', 'heresy' and, the key in this case, 'apostasy'.

It is the issue of 'apostasy', i.e. breaking with the faith and setting such an example to others, which underlines much of the furore over *The Satanic Verses*: but it also brings out the historic continuity within 'blasphemy' controversies. All of the major trials in Western civilisation have been about blasphemy: Socrates, Christ, Galileo, Spinoza. Yet in each case these people were also charged with sedition and corrupting the young. In the history of blasphemy within the Christian tradition, it is clear that the issue has come up at moments of great social and political tensions: in the breakdown of the Middle Ages and later crises. The height of blasphemy trials in the UK was in the late seventeenth century, when a new religious orthodoxy was being imposed. The condemnation of Rushdie by Khomeini also reflects a pervasive crisis within the Iranian revolution, and the Islamic world more generally. It is part of a crisis of legitimacy within Islam, and it is perhaps in that conflict, one that runs between members of the Islamic world rather than between Islam on the one side and Western secular civilisation on the other, that the ultimate verdict on the controversy over *The Satanic Verses* will be given. The question, in the words of the novel itself, is not whether it has strengthened belief or unbelief, but whether it has contributed to making doubt more possible.

MALISE RUTHVEN

In 1959 when the Egyptian newspaper *Al Ahram* serialised *The Children of Gebelawi* by the Nobel Prize winner, Naguib Mahfouz, devout Muslims led by their preachers and prayer-leaders took to the streets in protest, demanding that the novel be banned. Mahfouz's sin had been to suggest—in a highly allegorical manner—that the God of Adam, Moses, Jesus and Muhammad, who seemed to wreak such havoc and destruction in the world, might be 'dead'. Although the editor of *Al Ahram*, Mohammed Heikal, was able to complete the serialisation, thanks to his friendship with President Gamal Abdul Nasser, it was not until 1967 that the book became available, in a somewhat expurgated version. Three decades earlier an equally eminent Egyptian writer, Taha Hussein, was forced to resign his teaching post at Cairo University: the crime for which he had earned the ire of the faithful was a work of literary criticism that cast doubt on the authenticity of some of the pre-Islamic poets. These poets are the source for the rules of grammar and syntax used in Quranic exegesis: it was feared that to cast doubt upon them would be to call parts of the divine text itself into question.

To an observer of modern Islam the row over *The Satanic Verses* therefore has the air of *déjà vu*, though few would have anticipated its virulence or the way it would escalate into an international crisis. At first sight the notoriety the novel has acquired might seem strange: as a work of fiction *The Satanic Verses* is a good deal less subversive of Islamic orthodoxy than other more scholarly works published in Britain, such as John Wansburgh's *Quranic Studies* or *Hagarism* by Patricia Crone and Michael Cook, which question the canonized version of Islamic origins. In the Genet-like sequence in the imaginary city of Jahiliya (the scene which has caused most offence to orthodox Muslims), a fictional Indian film star suffering a schizophrenic breakdown in which he supposes himself to be the Archangel Gabriel dreams of a brothel where prostitutes take on the roles of the Prophet Mahound's wives. While the scene might seem deliberately offensive to the pious, who revere the Mothers of the Believers almost as much as the Prophet himself, the author could hardly have gone further in distancing it from any pretensions to historical realism. At the same time Rushdie is familiar enough with the early Muslim annalists to know just where to stick the knife into orthodoxy: in one of the dream episodes in *The Satanic Verses* Salman the Persian mis-transcribes a portion of the Holy Quran: the story is based on the historic account by the annalist Al Tabari, who records that one of the Prophet Muhammad's scribes, Abdullah ibn Sa'd, lost his faith after a deliberate mistake in his transcription of the divine text went unnoticed by the Prophet. Similar use is made of the famous episode of the satanic verses itself, in which Satan is supposed to have introduced verses into the Prophet's mind permitting a modified version of polytheism, in order to placate the citizens of Mecca. The story is recorded by Al Tabari and other early sources regarded by Muslims as unimpeachable. A scholarly-minded Muslim moving from faith towards scepticism is likely to seize on these and similar stories retold by Rushdie, which undermine the orthodox position that the Quran was 'dictated' by God without human editing. Exegetical commentary was limited to elucidating the meaning of the text, not, as in higher criticism, to establishing its authenticity. The same applied, *a fortiori* to the Messenger: paradoxically, the fact that the Prophet Muhammad was not officially venerated as a Divine Person (at least in the Sunni tradition) protected his personhood from religious scrutineers.

Muslim readers, particularly those whose knowledge of the book is confined to the offending passages, do not read *The Satanic Verses* with minds conditioned by occidental literary conventions. The novel is a recent implant in the Muslim world. The form itself comes close to blasphemy in the sense that it creates an alternative reality to that established by the Creator. In a society where most people are illiterate or semi-literate, reading and writing are public acts. The verb in Arabic for 'to read' also means 'to recite' and is pregnant with religious meanings: the command 'Read/recite! in the Name of thy Lord' are the very first words God is supposed to have addressed to the Prophet Muhammad: the word 'Quran' itself refers to Muhammad's reading or recitation of the divine word. In Muslim countries private speech between individuals is much freer than what is written: print—which was only introduced in the late nineteenth century—has largely been restricted to the public realm. The idea of a personal encounter between reader and writer, central to modern understandings of fiction, seems not to have been grafted beyond a relatively small Westernized élite.

As Maggie Gee explained earlier, the novel—as distinct from the story which elaborates hallowed themes—tends to appear at a time when religious authority is in decline and empirical philosophy in the ascendant. To this I should add that the Enlightenment, of which this process was part, was not simply a matter of confrontation between sacred and secular realms. There was also a transformation that took place within the realm of the sacred itself. In the eigh-

teenth and nineteenth centuries theologians like Friedrich Schleier-
macher (1768–1834) began to analyse the biblical texts using the
historical methodology known as 'higher criticism'. For nearly two
centuries Western Christians have had to come to terms with the
idea that what is in the Bible is not the word of God as such, but
rather a record of what human beings thought God was telling them.
Once scholarly doubt had been cast on the claimed divine author-
ship of the various books of the Old and New Testaments, the stage
was set for confining Christianity to the space it now occupies
within the spheres of private belief and personal faith. The adjustment enabled Christianity to survive, albeit in a reduced sphere
within a secular pluralist West. Though liberal theology still faces
a fundamentalist backlash, particularly in the United States, its he-
gemony in the mainline churches is not yet seriously challenged.

The situation in the Islamic world has been very different. Here
under the aegis of reforming autocrats or colonial governments the
purview of Islamic law, which derives from the Quran and the *had-
iths* or Traditions of the Prophet, was severely restricted; but Islamic
religious establishments never abandoned their insistence that Islam should govern every aspect of the life of the community and
the individual. Legal reforms were imposed from outside: attempts
to reform Islamic theology and law by reference to modern scholarly
criteria met with determined resistance from the *ulema*, the qualified interpreters of the sacred text. The scholarly work that could
lead to a modernisation of Islamic theology is largely being carried
out by academics—including some Muslims—working in Western
institutions.

Not surprisingly, the religious establishments in Iran and elsewhere feel deeply threatened by modern scholarship. In reporting
Khomeini's *fatwa* (legal ruling) condemning Salman Rushdie as an
apostate, Tehran Radio reported Khomeini's view that Rushdie's
book was 'the result of years of effort by American, European and
Zionist so-called experts on Islam gathering in international semi-
nars and conferences on the religion with the aim of finding the best
way to insult and undermine Islam's highest values and traditions'.

This response is not confined to a small group of religious profes-
sionals. The problem is that, like it or not, Muslims in Britain and
abroad are responding to *The Satanic Verses* as an assault on their
collective cultural identity, an identity rooted in the sacred my-

thology surrounding the Prophet Muhammad and the Quran. An attack on this sacred mythology, even in the context of fiction, is perceived as an attack, not just on ideas, but on an identity whose very base is the sacred text of the Quran and the sacred personhood of the Prophet. The necessary process of religious adjustment, whereby the focus of commitment shifts from the public arena to the realm of the subjective, is happening for Islam in the West, rather than for Islam within the Muslim world. The Islamic world has not been allowed to establish its own pace, its own agenda. Both have been forced upon it from outside, by the power of the West and the force of international markets.

Once one tries to read the novel through Muslim eyes one begins to grasp the nature of this response. Whereas Christians have learned to cope with rationalist attacks on their faith by philosophers, novelists or secular forces by recourse to a kind of stoicism rooted in private faith and virtue—on the model of Christian in *Pilgrim's Progress*—Muslims tend to respond collectively to perceived attacks on those things they hold sacred, including attacks from within. It is difficult for the present to see the way forward: a cultural impasse has been reached, and in Britain relations between the Muslim and host communities have been set back, possibly by a decade or more. One gross inequality revealed by the Rushdie affair is the fact that the blasphemy laws protect the Church of England but no other religious community: to abolish them would at least put all religions in Britain on an even footing. Beyond that we need to develop a culture in which freedom of expression is more strongly rooted and legally protected. During a recent visit to the United States I was impressed by the fact that though different religious sects attack each others' doctrines publicly—often in terms that would be regarded as blasphemous—all do so under the protection of the First Amendment, which equally guarantees freedom of religion and freedom of speech. A Bill of Rights containing similar provisions might, in the course of time, help persuade Muslim citizens that there is in fact a world of difference between an assault on their religion, and a work of art which addresses itself to the intimacies of private experience.

MARINA WARNER

As I'm incompetent in the history of Islam, I'll try to shed some light on the current tragic crisis from my reading of Christian history. It seems to me that there are aspects of this predicament—the personal predicament of Salman Rushdie, the national predicament of the entire community of the UK, and the international predicament—that can be illuminated from the history of repression by the Catholic Church. Farrukh Dhondy used a striking phrase this morning, 'When the word is important, the guardians of the word become important.' What one sees when one looks at the history of the Inquisition and its struggles with theologians is a struggle for control of the word, a struggle for excluding outsiders from guardianship. The first woman, for instance, to die for a book, Marguerite Porete—who was burned at the stake in Paris in 1310 wrote nothing more inflammatory than a lay guide to prayer. But it was in French, and so accessible to all, and she was a woman—she could not be allowed control of the word and its interpretation, like a priest.

Rushdie is hardly the writer of devotional aids, of course. He falls into another category of writer who got into trouble with the Church—the satirists: Rabelais, Voltaire, Erasmus, and, of a different persuasion, but no less preoccupied with religious questions, Jonathan Swift. Rushdie blends many narrative styles—including Eastern oral story-telling. But among the Western traditions he has adapted, one that has had a dominating influence on *The Satanic Verses* as well as *Midnight's Children* is the moral satire: he belongs in the lineage of *Candide, Gulliver's Travels, Gargantua and Pantagruel,* and *In Praise of Folly.* As Erasmus wrote, 'How unjust it is to allow every other walk of life its relaxations but none at all to learning, especially when trifling may lead to something more serious. Jokes can be handled in such a way that any reader who is not altogether lacking in discernment can sense something far more rewarding . . .'

Erasmus got into trouble; Rushdie's jokes have indeed led to something more serious. The two issues that it seems to me from the Press have excited the outrage among the Moslem community here are the scene in the brothel, where the whores take the names of the Prophet's wives, and the fundamental narrative device of the novel, that the satanic verses themselves were interpolated by the Devil, and so impugn the authenticity of the Koran as the word of God.

The first issue has come up twice today already—that the insult Rushdie has committed is an insult against the purity of women. A man this morning declared that he felt as strongly as if Rushdie had sullied his wife or his daughter; then again, Malise Ruthven described an enlightened and learned Moslem colleague, who had offered Salman shelter in his home on a point of principle, but who nevertheless declared that the novel had so grievously violated his beliefs, it was 'as if Rushdie had raped his own daughter'. Characterising the offence in the language of sexual outrage connects with the repressions of Catholicism, because the history of the Church's authority is very often bound up with the proclamation of the necessary purity of women, and especially with the virginity of Mary, the mother of God. Her body is a mirror of the Church's strength and inviolability. And just as Catholic women are asked to emulate Mary, so, I feel, every Moslem woman, especially the Prophet's wives, personifies the integrity of the faith and the community of people who hold that faith. There's an identity between popes who exalt Mary and extend the power of the Church in despotic ways, like Pius IX, who proclaimed the Immaculate Conception a dogma in 1854 and went on to declare the infallibility of the Pope. Both pronouncements were countermoves in a struggle against the rising influence of socialism in Europe. The present Pope, who has summoned liberation theologians to Rome to explain themselves, and disciplined and silenced them and others, is a Pope of retrenchment, unlike John 23rd, a Pope of reform, who refrained from heroic exaltation of Mary and dramatic exhortations to women's chastity. John Paul II is entirely dedicated to the Virgin Mary—his personal motto is Totus Tuus, All Thine, and he has of course spoken out often about the importance of tradition in women's roles. As the Black Virgin of the Holy Mountain of Jasna Gora, Mary embodies Poland; her impregnable purity comes to symbolise the Polish people as a culture, as an embattled nation.

The offence Rushdie has perpetrated against the women of the Prophet can be understood in this light: it's an offence against the identity of the religion and the people who follow it under pressure from outside—Western—influences. The return of the veil in Islam, and among pockets of Moslem families in Britain too, represents a retrenchment against the yielding of boundaries, against slippage of distinctions, against assimilation. Just as Catholic women are exhorted to follow Mary's example, so Moslem women are perceived to be the keepers of the religion's own integrity: they become the visible actors of the word's power.

The consequences for women themselves aren't considered at all—they are the vehicles of theology, not autonomous, or even semi-autonomous agents—and this is a religion which not only practises purdah, but also clitorectomy. Rushdie indeed struck home in a taboo area, because the sexuality of women, such as he evokes, does not belong to them, but to the guardians of the word. The control of women is crucial to the control of the word; they are historically bound together.

The second point that seems to have distressed people is the idea that the Devil managed to interpolate verses into the Koran. Erasmus came into conflict with the Church because he found that the original canonical translations of the New Testament had not been accurate. He wrote—and his words seem pertinent to the present controversy—that analysis of a text does not necessarily dethrone the text: 'Surely there can be no danger that the world will immediately abandon Christ, if someone happens to hear that a passage has been found in the Holy Scriptures which has been corrupted by an ignorant or drowsy copyist, or wrongly rendered by some translator . . .' Of course Salman Rushdie never cast himself in any way as a learned commentator on the authenticity of the Koran, in the Erasmian sense, but the crisis has given his levity, his satire, a new, momentous seriousness, and its lessons should be built on, to make an appeal to moderate thinkers within Islam, who are able to entertain the possibility of historicist and textual analysis of the Koran, and to open a way for women within the religion that offers them the strengths of community but frees them from its oppressions. Is this impossible?

I was reading recently Elaine Pagels's book *Adam, Eve and the Serpent*, and she shows how Augustine's authoritarian pessimism only came to dominate Christian thought after a protracted struggle with the humane, tolerant and subtle wisdom of Julian of Eclanum. Julian didn't believe that sex was the hereditary taint of original sin, but an aspect of humanity that could lead to good. Augustine's darker view suited the emerging temporal and centralised power of the new Church because wickedness justifies repressive discipline, human sinfulness necessitates recourse to the authorities who can mitigate it.

The plea I would make today is to do everything we can to give access to the other voices within our community, the voices as it were of Julian of Eclanum, of moderation and understanding, against the language of intolerance and despotism and terror. Then perhaps—but it's a big perhaps—we can arrive at something helpful, rather than totally destructive as we are experiencing at the present.

ON CENSORSHIP

Article 19 of the International Covenant on Civil and Political Rights

1. Everyone shall have the right to hold opinions without interference.

2. Everyone shall have the right to freedom of expression; this right shall include freedom to seek, receive and impart information and ideas of all kinds, regardless of frontiers, either orally, in writing or in print, in the form of art, or through any other media of his choice.

3. The exercise of the rights provided for in paragraph 2 of this article carries with it special duties and responsibilities. It may therefore be subject to certain restrictions, but these shall only be such as are provided by law and are necessary:

a. For respect of the rights or reputations of others;

b. For the protection of national security or of public order (*ordre public*), or of public health or morals.

Censorship's 'final solution'
NADINE GORDIMER

Riots, book-burning, the demand that a work shall be banned worldwide, publishers boycotted, the threatened toppling of a prime minister, five dead—has ever a book been the pretext for such a frenzy of righteous barbarism?

Reviled, sentenced to death by a religious authority, a price offered for his head, forced to flee his home and live under police guard—has ever a writer been persecuted as Salman Rushdie has?

Victor Hugo, Flaubert, D. H. Lawrence and others may have suffered public opprobrium or exile. Milan Kundera may have been forbidden to write, and forced to earn a living cleaning windows. In

Stalin's Soviet Union writers were banished to the Gulag. In South Africa, some writers have been forbidden to publish. Even in the most repressive regimes, none—however they had offended public morals or political orthodoxy—was condemned to Rushdie's double death: his book to be expunged from world literature for ever, his life to be forfeited.

And this bloodthirsty baying comes from a pack of millions, not one fraction of which has even read the book. That is clear from the simplistic reduction in which it is arraigned as being literally 'about' the Prophet Mohammed—and nothing else.

Anyone who actually has read what I regard as a brilliant novel, knows that dominant among its themes is that of displacement.

Rushdie describes the process which brought imperialists to adjust themselves among the populations they conquered, and in our age brings people from those populations to reconcile the dichotomy.

The method being used by the Moslem leaders and communities against Salman Rushdie is quite literally a murderous refinement of the unchanging principle of censorship, which was and is and always will be to harness the word to the tyrant's chariot.

The tyrant may be a dictator, a regime, or a form of moral or religious bigotry. For me, the Rushdie affair has revealed how any of these agents of censorship can advance, in collusion, the tyrannical cause against freedom of expression.

I am no stranger to censorship, living in South Africa. At various times three of my own books have been banned, and for several years now the press and media here have been grimly restricted under successive States of Emergency imposed to stifle opposition to apartheid.

Yet it was an ugly revelation to find—in my country where the Government outlaws freedom of expression, where all who use the written word are fighting against the Publications Control Board and its ancillary laws, where individual Moslems have a proud and brave record in the liberation movements—that local Moslem extremists rose in fanatical response to a proposed visit by Salman Rushdie last November.

He had been invited to speak on censorship at a book week dedicated to that theme. The story is one that has become familiar: rabble-rousing meetings outside mosques, threats not only to Rushdie but to those, including members of the Congress of South African Writers, involved in the invitation.

And all of this, of course, by people who had not read the book. I know, because I had the only copy in the country, a proof sent to me by his American publisher.

No matter; it was easy for the Moslem extremists to get the book banned, at once, in absentia. A word to the Publications Control Board (no doubt) from some member of the Moslem community with influence in the House of Delegates (that is the segregated 'house' of Indian collaborators in our apartheid tricameral parliament that excludes Africans) and it was done.

We writers had the alternative of risking Salman Rushdie's life for our principles of freedom of expression or cancelling the visit. Now, with five dead in Pakistan, it can be seen that we made the only possible choice. But through religious thuggery the State gained an ally in repression of the word here.

I admit I have no religious sensibilities, of any faith, to be offended by a work of fiction. But I accept and respect that others have. Numerous books, plays, films, have appeared in which Jesus Christ and the virgin Mary and even God himself have been satirised, fictionally divested of divinity, and act as imperfect mortals.

But the Christian faith remains unshaken. Surely Islam cannot be threatened by the fantasy of a single novel? Satan has taken a hand, all right, in the affair of *The Satanic Verses*. I can't believe that anyone's divinity could sanction what is now being done to a writer. Religious fanaticism has discovered censorship's Final Solution for that great enemy of darkness, the word.

I write that with a shudder.

• *Nadine Gordimer, South Africa's most distinguished novelist, has been writing for many years in the face of many forms of censorship and repression.*

(*Evening Standard*, London, 3 March 1989)

The British Government has made several interventions over the publication of memoirs by former intelligence personnel. The Spycatcher case was one of these. The letter that follows concerns another controversy that coincided with the Rushdie affair.

Dear Sir,

So the Government *can* ban a book if it wants to. As the with-drawal of *Codebreaker Extraordinary* shows (9 March), where there is a will there is a way.

Clearly, protecting Churchill's reputation (and this country from embarrassment) figures high on Mrs Thatcher's agenda. She chose to ignore sincere requests from the Muslim community when she was asked to intervene in the Rushdie affair last October. Since then, she has righteously proclaimed that 'freedom of expression' is a cornerstone of our free democracy—unless you are an old man writing your memoirs, that is.

I am looking forward to a full-page advert, signed by the world's literary élite, condemning this outrageous attack on personal liberties.

> Yours faithfully,
> IBRAHIM B. HEWITT
> The Islamic Organisation for Media Monitoring
> London, N7.
> 9 March

> (*Independent*, London, 13 March 1989)

Paying due regard to our beliefs
From the Chief Rabbi

Sir, The appalling Rushdie affair has released, like Newton's Law, equal and opposite forces of elemental magnitude. It has incited religious passions on the one hand and freedom crusades on the other on a scale and of an intensity probably unmatched in modern times.

In a search for legislative controls to defuse the current super-tensions and to promote inter-religious co-existence, it has been suggested that the existing laws of blasphemy be extended beyond their strictly Christian confines. Some Christian and Muslim leaders have supported this idea. But I believe the solution lies elsewhere.

When the Chairman of the Islamic Society for the Promotion of Religious Tolerance in the UK asked me last October to support the protest against the publication of *The Satanic Verses*, I readily agreed, and he was informed that I deprecate not only the falsification of established historical records but the offence caused to the religious convictions and susceptibilities of countless citizens. In a civilised society we should generate respect for other people's religious beliefs and not tolerate a form of denigration and ridicule which can only breed resentment to the point of hatred and strife.

While I fully share the worldwide outrage at the murderous threat against the book's author, publishers and distributors, I stand by my view that the book should not have been published for the reasons I gave, now reinforced by subsequent events which have already cost many lives and may yet erupt into more sinister national and international upheavals.

In my view Jews should not seek an extension of the blasphemy laws. In any event, the Jewish definition of blasphemy is confined to 'cursing God' and does not include an affront to any prophet (not even Moses, in our case). Living in a predominantly Christian society, with an established Church, we should be quite content to leave the legislation on blasphemy as it stands, enshrining the national respect for the majority faith.

What should concern us are not *religious* offences but *socially* intolerable conduct calculated or likely to incite revulsion or violence, by holding up religious beliefs to scurrilous contempt, or by encouraging murder.

Both Mr Rushdie and the Ayatollah have abused freedom of speech, the one by provocatively offending the genuine faith of many millions of devout believers and the other by a public call to murder, compounded by offering a rich material reward for an ostensibly spiritual deed. It should be illegal to allow either provocation to be published or broadcast.

We already have legislation proscribing by common consent many excesses in the freedom of expression, precious as this is. There are laws not only on blasphemy, but on pornography, libel, incitement of race hatred, subversion, and breaches of national security. There may be arguments on the precise definition of these offences, but the principle is universally accepted.

Likewise there should be widespread agreement on prohibiting the publication of anything likely to inflame, through obscene defamation, the feelings or beliefs of any section of society, or liable to provoke public disorder and violence. It must obviously be left to public and parliamentary debate to determine where the lines of what is illegal are to be drawn.

If Britain were to pioneer such legislation, other nations would no doubt follow suit, perhaps even leading to an international agreement among all civilised peoples to protect the supreme values of innocent human life and freedom by outlawing the amplification of words which, as experience has now shown, by poisoning the atmosphere can be as lethal a threat to mankind as any physical pollution.

Yours sincerely
JAKOBOVITS,
Office of the Chief Rabbi,
Adler House,
Tavistock Square, SW1.
2 March

(*Times*, London, 9 March 1989)

Restraining freedom

SIR—Your thought-provoking leading article (Mar. 4) on *The Satanic Verses* has hit the nail on the head. The real issue in the present controversy is the right to freedom of expression, an issue larger than Mr Rushdie's book.

The Moslem community in Liverpool has tried throughout the controversy to examine whether there can be any freedom without restraints. We have always maintained that we value the right to freedom of expression as much as anyone else, but we object to its misuse.

No freedom can be absolute and, in a democratic society, the individual, whether a writer, an artist or an ordinary man in the street, must voluntarily restrain his freedom to stay within the universally accepted bounds of civilised conduct. If he does not, then he is asking for restrictions to be imposed on him.

Some argue that writers and artists are a special category and must enjoy unrestricted freedom of expression. This notion must be challenged. No one who has read the book can deny that Mr Rushdie has transgressed all boundaries of decency and propriety in *The Sa-*

tanic Verses and for that he must be condemned. Yet, as you rightly
say, we must defend his life at all costs.

M. AKBAR ALI
Liverpool

(Daily Telegraph, London, 9 March 1989)

A dangerous opportunist

ROALD DAHL

SIR—With all that has been written and spoken about the Rushdie affair, I have not yet heard any non-Muslim voices raised in
criticism of the writer himself. On the contrary, he appears to be
regarded as some sort of a hero, certainly among his fellow writers
and the Society of Authors, of which I am a member. To my mind,
he is a dangerous opportunist.

Clearly he has profound knowledge of the Muslim religion and
its people and he must have been totally aware of the deep and
violent feelings his book would stir up among devout Muslims. In
other words he knew exactly what he was doing and he cannot plead
otherwise.

This kind of sensationalism does indeed get an indifferent book
on to the top of the bestseller list (*Spycatcher* is another example),
but to my mind it is a cheap way of doing it. It also puts a severe
strain on the very proper principle that the writer has an absolute
right to say what he likes.

In a civilised world we all have a moral obligation to apply a
modicum of censorship to our own work in order to reinforce this
principle of free speech.

Yours faithfully,
ROALD DAHL,
Gipsy House,
Great Missenden,
Buckinghamshire.
27 February

(Times, London, 28 Feb. 1989)

Understanding the place of literature in society

Dear Sir,

Literature, propaganda, argument and dogma may all enjoy the right of freedom of expression, but it does not follow that any one of them is the equivalent of the other. The tenet of freedom of expression has been repeatedly and rightly adduced in the defence of *The Satanic Verses*, but there is a danger of its being applied in an indiscriminate fashion, which may, in the long run, weaken respect for a principle of immeasurable importance. Logic is as valuable as freedom of expression: the taking of offence does not mean that the book is about nothing else than the causing of offence.

In one sense, the battle for freedom of expression has been lost, since, while the book's critics are able to exercise freedom of expression, whether through meetings, public demonstrations or statements in the media, Salman Rushdie, who does not exist just in his book, is not. He has been coerced into silence and non-association.

In another sense, the very reiteration of the principle by the book's defenders risks suggesting that the book is no more than a vehicle for the expression of certain statements, arguments and assertions—which is what its enemies paint it to be.

A work of literature is *more* than free expression. It is creative expression, which does not argue, state or assert, so much as make. A novel exists, *lives* in the minds of its readers, as no statement or assertion can; which perhaps explains the response to the book's extreme opponents who have so terribly invoked death and, in so doing, confused the book with its author. These are literally vital matters; and the defence of the book as literature should not be regarded as some feeble, minor plea. The work of Jonathan Swift no doubt offended many in its time but now has a treasured place in our literary heritage, not to say in the history of free expression. The playwright Vaclav Havel, recently imprisoned in Czechoslovakia, is no doubt regarded by the authorities as a worthless troublemaker, but is championed in the Western press and by some brave fellow countrymen as a distinguished man of letters.

Sir Geoffrey Howe may hold his own view of Salman Rushdie's novel, but his recent sweeping assertion that 'we' (arrogating the whole nation) find the book offensive reveals what little respect the Government has for the place of literature in society, and smacks of an attempt to discredit a reputation while defending the man. It is such a sinister generalisation that it is one of the functions of literature to challenge.

Propaganda is an instrument of power; art is an instrument of life. Whatever else *The Satanic Verses* is or does, it has life: energy, invention, colour, animation, intelligence, humour, questions, doubts, passion, quickness: life. There may be many arguing over the book who have not read it; but let those who have read it, whatever their view, acknowledge first that the book breathes what all human beings share, and let them argue from there.

Yours faithfully,
GRAHAM SWIFT
London, SW18.

(Independent, London, 7 March 1989)

The following is an edited transcript of a lecture delivered at Cornell University, 1 March 1989. A fuller essay, based on this lecture, was subsequently published in pamphlet form by the Committee of Muslim Scholars and Leaders of America.

The moral dilemma of Salman Rushdie's *Satanic Verses*
DR ALI A. MAZRUI

Now, the theme before us concerns the writer and the worshipper. Well, judging from the introduction you have had, I am myself placed between believer in Islam on one side and believer in the open society on the other. I am torn between being a writer and being a worshipper. . . .

Let me just begin with comparative censorship, partly because I myself have been a victim of it. There has been a lot of self-righteous indignation in the West among professional academics, among writers. Now, to some extent, this indignation is justified for those who take those positions regardless of what is being attacked. But there are a lot of people who are much more selective in their belief in the open society.

In Britain, elaborate efforts have been made by the Government to discourage journalists interviewing so-called Northern Ireland terrorists. The British have a category of censorship concerning Northern Ireland. In parts of the United Kingdom, you can quote a so-called militant of the Irish Republican Army, but you may not broadcast his own voice on the radio. You may have the words, but not his voice, and you may certainly not show them on the television screen.

Sinn Fein, as a political arm of the Irish Republican Army, is subject to severe censorship restrictions when it is speaking precisely as a political party in Northern Ireland. . . .

The bid by the Thatcher administration to stop the publication of the book by Peter Wright called *Spycatcher* when I was in New Zealand the year before last, that was the big issue of discussion then. It was, of course, before Rushdie. And who was demanding that this book be not published? Not the Ayatollah Khomeini but Maggie in London.

So, basically, they have issues that they regard as important and sensitive, on which they seek to impose censorship.

Now, Locksley Edmondson mentioned my television series. Program 3 of my television series is called New Gods. It starts with the bust of Karl Marx. And you hear my voice saying:

'Religion is the sigh of the oppressed creature, and the soul of soulless conditions. So said Karl Marx. . . . '

And I had originally gone on to say, 'the last of the Great Jewish Prophets'. British viewers did hear that, Australian viewers heard that, viewers in Finland heard that, viewers in Nigeria heard that, viewers in Jordan heard that, viewers in Israel watching Jordanian television heard that 'the last of the Great Jewish Prophets'. Viewers in the United States did not. It was censored.

You can compare the degree of offence of Mahound in Rushdie's book with the remark which says, 'Karl Marx was the last of the Great Jewish Prophets.' And the difference is between heaven and earth. Nor was my statement intended to be remotely derogatory, since I am an admirer (a) of Karl Marx, and (b) of Jewish intellectual contribution to world history. But this society regarded that that would risk offending Jews. . . .

I have bundles of press clippings connected with the series across the nation. I haven't seen a single journalist say, 'Why was Ali Mazrui's phrase censored?' Not a single journalist regarded it as a violation of my freedom of expression. Not a single one. Those who asked me the questions about it, not one of them regarded it as legitimate to criticize PBS for having subjected me to the deletion of a phrase thought likely to offend Jewish sensibilities. And I am sure, large numbers of those same journalists regard it as outrageous

that anyone should want *The Satanic Verses* banned. Why? Because
freedom of expression is indivisible when it suits them. So, for the
comparative censorship and Western self-righteousness, those of
you who believe in it absolutely and would defend it even if it is
the Jewish faith or the Christian faith that are being attacked, I can
respect. Those who only work themselves up in indignation if it is
somebody else's symbols that are being attacked, I cannot respect.
That's high selectivity. It is a form of blasphemy, but blasphemy
against freedom and not against religion. . . .

Now, what we need to understand with regard to Muslims' reaction to this particular problem is the notion of cultural treason.
The Western world understands the concept of treason in relation
to the State. The Western world even understands capital punishment for treason against the State. . . .

The British have executed Irishmen on charges of treason while
they fight for Ireland under British subjugation. Perhaps the most
illustrious case in this century was Sir Roger Casement, who was
executed after attempting to involve the Germans in the liberation
of Ireland.

Now, in Islam, there is a concept which can be translated as
treason, not to the State but to the Ummah, to the religious community and to the faith. And capital punishment is often also the
supreme penalty. Salman Rushdie has been viewed by some as being
a traitor in that sense.

Again, the United States this century has also recognized treason
against the State sometimes as deserving capital punishment. That
definitely applied to Julius and Ethel Rosenberg, who were accused
of treason in the 1950s under the atmosphere of the McCarthy era,
and they were executed.

The American system seeks to defend the secular political order,
even to the extent of executing traitors. What the Ayatollah Khomeini raised as a possibility is the defense of a religious order, even
at the expense of the life of an individual.

Now, blasphemy. Again, it is true that the sister religions of Islam
have modified their positions. But don't forget, it is relatively recent.
First, the Mosaic Law does decree death by stoning as the penalty
for the blasphemer. The Mosaic Law, even in Israel, is no longer
enforced.

Scottish Law in Britain, until the eighteenth century, similarly made blasphemy a capital offense. In Britain, today, blasphemy is an offense, though not a capital offense. Today, it is still both a statutory offense and a common law offense.

And British newspapers, on February 20th 1989, were debating the issue because the definition of blasphemy was limited to blasphemy against Christianity. So the Law in England did not allow for blasphemy against the religion of a minority, that is, the Muslims in Britain. Now in the United States, individual States have had laws against blasphemy.

And then, treason. In English Law, treason today—and those of you who are legal experts will correct me if I am wrong—still includes violating the king's consorts sexually. That is treason. Or, violating the eldest unmarried daughter, as well as the wife of the eldest son and heir. All those are parts of the package of treason, under English Law still, as far as I can make out, intact in the books. Treason, therefore, includes polluting the royal blood line, or obscuring it. This is quite apart from treason being defined as giving aid and comfort to the King's enemies.

US Law on treason defines treason more narrowly in terms of war and military defense. But, if the Rosenbergs' case in the 1950s is anything to go by, it does include this defense of the political system against the rival system of communism. So, instead of religion in the old sense, you have a secular style of ideological preference, for which the United States is armed to defend even at the expense of the human species.

For what, after all, does nuclear armament, in defense of liberal democracy, mean? It means that, rather than give up this particular secular ideological system, the country is prepared not just to assassinate an individual, not just to enact a revolution nearby, but even to risk the annihilation of the human race. Again, it's a toss up between the secular political order and the religious one.

As for the tendency to see blasphemy as a form of treason. Well, it of course originated in societies which did not make so sharp a distinction between church and state. It originated in societies where the political order was also sacred. And then comes Salman Rushdie and he immediately reactivates precisely the sort of issues embodied in that merger of blasphemy and treason.

The Prophet Muhammad (SAS) dictated the Koran some of the time. Muslims believe this was the direct word of God coming to him not just by inspiration but as if he was the Messenger, in a literal sense uttering words formulated by God. He dictated some of the time, in a way very similar to what John Milton did. Milton dictated *Paradise Lost* because he was blind: Muhammad (SAS) dictated the Koran because he could not himself write.

And so, Rushdie starts from there, and proceeds then to say, 'Well, was it inspired? Maybe a lot of changes took place.' So he has a fictional character who begins to change the dictation, initially with small alterations. If the Prophet (SAS) said 'All Knowing', he might change it to 'All Seeing', for example. And then the scribe begins to get more confident: maybe you can change things more fundamentally. And goes on like that. And so, gradually, then, it becomes obvious, according to the character, that the words were not divinely inspired. Now, in a way, this goes to the very bottom of the heart of the Muslims' interpretation of ultimate law in society. It undermines some of the essential legitimacy.

Secular countries take an oath in defense of the constitution. The Koran, in this case, is the equivalent of the constitution. And this particular writer seems to have launched an attack against it. What is more, he has done it in a manner which is not to reform Islam from within, but to be lionized by critics of Islam, and sometimes by enemies of Islam. And he has also done it in a manner which earns him a lot of money.

When I was in Pakistan, in November 1988, this book was already being discussed. I was very intrigued by the analogy, which was being made by Pakistanis in the circles in which I moved. They said: 'It's as if Rushdie had composed a brilliant poem about the private parts of his parents, and then gone to the market place to recite that poem to the applause of strangers, who invariably laughed at the jokes he cracks about his parents' genitalia, and he's taking money for doing it.'

At the time, I hadn't really gone into the book, and I wondered whether it was fair or not. Now, at least I understand where the Pakistanis were coming from—that this is an invasion of one's ancestry—almost as basic as the private parts of one's parents; and that, to go around making fun of it to the cheer of the enemies of the faith, and be paid $850,000 before publication is like composing that poem for the market place. Hence, they are wondering what is his motive, what could make anybody act like that. . . .

I have mentioned that I don't myself believe in capital punishment for either form of treason. I don't believe in capital punishment for murder, for that matter. But what was new about the Ayatollah Khomeini's death sentence, perhaps, was not the idea of murder by remote control: it was the openness with which he incited it. It was worthy of Agatha Christie's title *A Murder Is Announced.*

If Western countries want to kill somebody in some other country, it becomes part of a covert operation, not an announcement on the radio. The Central Intelligence Agency, or MI5, may take the initiative; the Israelis may fly all the way to Tunis and kill somebody in his bedroom, and then deny it. Just deny it. In the case of the Israelis, everybody knows how they did it, and even then they didn't deny it too vigorously. You just send somebody to go all the way to Tunis. By the time you get there it's 2.15; he is probably sleeping. If there are guards kill them first, and then go for your man.

The Westerners murder by remote control. They do it, but they do it through covert and spying operations. And, for entertainment, they do James Bond films, 007, who is an exaggeration of what is done from time to time in any case, including easy killing. Or, it can be *Mission Impossible,* for American viewers, emphasizing the principle of deniability: 'Jim should you or your associates ever be caught, the Secretary will totally disavow any link with you. This tape will self-destruct in five seconds. Good luck, Jim.'

As for attempted assassination by bombing, there seems little doubt that the Reagan administration wanted to kill Qaddafi from the air, in the course of the bombing in 1986. They went specifically for what they thought was his residence in a bid to make sure the man was well and truly eliminated. They succeeded in killing other people, but Qaddafi is still around. Unfortunately, they also killed an adopted child of his. I hope nobody regarded that as a consolation prize.

In the 1960s the Americans conspired to attempt to kill Fidel Castro, and there is a whole school of thought which says the Americans paid with the assassination of John F. Kennedy as being linked to that. In other words: murder by remote control. There is a style of doing it. Is the Ayatollah just opening a whole new tactic? It is not more immoral, the way it was done, it is just bad taste. He announces it on the radio instead of sending his spy to do it for him.

And then, Ronald Reagan says, 'You can run but you cannot hide.' Ronald Reagan was declaring that the sovereignty of other countries was no asylum for enemies of America. You can run but you cannot hide. He was declaring the whole world as fair play for American movement. The United States skyjacked an Egyptian civilian airplane in international air space, and took it to Italy in violation of Italian air space, because they had somebody there that they accused of terrorist involvement.

And the dual way in which the West contrives to catch suspects, of terrorism or of spying or other things, is either by direct kidnapping or by enticing the victim beyond a particular country's territorial waters. So, you observe the formalities of international law, you encourage the person you want to deal with, to come: come on let's go, I've got this motor boat. Really? Yes, let's go. And then, once they are well and truly outside of territorial waters, you kidnap them. Maybe sometimes you don't even do that.

And the Israelis probably did not do that with Mordechai Vanunu, the nuclear technician, who gave material to a British newspaper about Israel's nuclear program. He was a traitor in Israel's eye, because he provided information and photographs for such articles for a British newspaper. It is not for the Soviet Union, or anything as dastardly as that, but for a British newspaper in September 1986. He was also, at the same time, guilty of cultural treason—he changed religions, and became a Christian. Again, the Israeli secret service arranged it. Here is a woman, Cindy. Vanunu was a young man. You know we are all vulnerable, the flesh is weak. So Cindy goes, passes as an American student, and says, well, we can even go to Rome. There is a flat, an apartment there, we could have a good time there, and my sister is not there. So, poor, misguided Vanunu goes to Rome with Cindy. Then, in the apartment he is overwhelmed, probably by use of some gas, then taken outside territorial waters, and then taken to his realm. The traitor captured. Given a secret trial. The Israelis, fortunately, don't kill people, except when they are really bad Nazis. But normally they don't observe capital punishment, they are ahead of most societies in the world on that issue. And, Vanunu gets sentenced to eighteen years in jail, after secret trials for his treason both to his Jewishness and to his Israeli loyalties.

Now, if the Iranians had been as sophisticated as the Israelis, they would have enticed Salman Rushdie to international waters. I

think it is very unlikely that Rushdie would fall for the sex ploy in
Rome, in the Mediterranean; but, he might have been persuaded for
other reasons, maybe intellectual—and then they could kidnap him.
So, if word leaked out that a British citizen was being tried in Teh-
ran, the Iranians could either add the charge of espionage against
Mr Rushdie, or charge him with incitement to violence.

And then, incitement more directly. In sentencing Rushdie to
death in absentia, the Ayatollah Khomeini was, rightly, inciting
violence against the citizen of another country. And yet, Mr Rushdie
is still alive. While twenty other Indians in the subcontinent in
which he was born are dead. Who did the inciting? Who incited
whom? Did Mr Rushdie really fail to see that what he had written
was the sort of stuff which would provoke violent demonstrations
in the Indian sub-continent, or did he not care? . . .

The West is quite used to direct forms of incitement or to con-
trived forms of incitement. The West is also used to destabilisation
by remote control. But Mr Rushdie should have known better. The
United States could destabilise Salvador Allende's Chile, and have
the incitement confirmed by President Ford and Secretary Kissinger.
Iran's first revolution of this century, the Nationalist Revolution
and under Muhammad Mosaddeq in the 1950s, was sabotaged by
the Central Intelligence Agency of the United States, with its own
brand of inciting. Both South Africa and Israel have been guilty of
inciting problems in other countries.

The Indian Government's ban of *Satanic Verses* has been supported by an impressive range of Indian intellectuals. A letter to the
Indian Post was signed by a number of Sikhs, Hindus, as well as
Muslims. Was India's ban of the book a case of building a repressive
society, as Mr Rushdie accused Rajiv Gandhi of? *The Times of India*
has the following answer:

'No, dear Rushdie, we do not wish to build a repressive India. On
the contrary, we are doing our best to build a liberal India, where
we can all breathe freely. But in order to build such an India, we
have to preserve the India that exists. That may not be a pretty India,
but it's the only India we have.'

In Black Africa, if it were possible to compartmentalize, I could
risk publishing *The Satanic Verses* in a country like Senegal, although the country is 80% Muslim. But its publication in Nigeria
would be a major risk, though the country is only 50% Muslim.

The serialization of such a book in a Christian-owned newspaper in Nigeria could precipitate riots, and deaths in the streets of Lagos are possible.

The Satanic Verses could be one of the most divisive books in world politics since Hitler's *Mein Kampf*. Of course, Hitler's book was anti-Jewish, while *The Satanic Verses* is interpreted as anti-Muslim. Hitler had political aspirations, while Rushdie's ambitions are literary and financial. But fundamentally, the two books are works of alienation, and divisive in intent and impact. If I had been grown-up at the time of the publication of *Mein Kampf* and the Jews were burning it, I would join them in the burning. . . .

But the Ayatollah is still wrong in the death sentence. When all is said and done, Islam began with the act of reading; it is the very first verse of the Koran. It says, 'Read'. That is 'Iqra', read, from the very beginning. And it tells the Prophet (SAS), that reading is how God teaches:

'Read in the name of your God. Who creates, creates man from a clot. Read, for your Lord is most gracious. It is He Who teaches by means of the pen, and teaches man what he doesn't know. Now, man may act as arrogantly and consider himself self-sufficient. Yet to your Lord will you return'.

So, this is a religion born out of the imperative, 'read'. It is the very first contact between the Messenger (SAS) and God. That should have been taken into account by the Ayatollah. Lifting the death sentence, but keeping the curse, if he must. Keeping the spiritual penalty, but lifting the physical threat.

Mr Rushdie may have turned his back against a religion which pronounced the first imperative, 'Read'. But, having now read Mr Rushdie, let us leave him to the judgment of Heaven.

• *Ali Mazrui is Albert Schweitzer Professor in the Humanities, State University of New York at Binghamton, and was writer and host of the BBC/PBS television series,* The Africans: A Triple Heritage.

Lessons of the Rushdie affair
WILLIAM PFAFF

Salman Rushdie should actually be pleased with himself. He has done what most writers dream of doing but fail to accomplish. He has made himself be taken seriously.

There are inconveniences to being taken seriously. They include the possibility of being murdered for what one says. Should a writer, an intellectual, not be prepared to die for what he believes? One would think it a remarkable tribute to Mr. Rushdie that "a billion Moslems"—so the Iranian government claims—refuse to brush aside his writings as unimportant and want to kill him.

It has been the constant effort of the writers and artists in this century to shock the bourgeoisie, the established powers. This was easy enough at the start of the modern movement, at the end of the 19th Century and beginning of the 20th, but today the modern movement in the arts has itself become an establishment, with the bourgeoisie its largest audience and its sponsor as well.

The effort to shock has become an increasingly calculated one, as it has become increasingly futile. Much that is written today to shock is deeply conformist. It is fashionable writing. It expresses no radical alienation from established society; verbal radicalism has become the accepted course toward establishing oneself.

A genuine aesthetic or moral revolutionary should hardly expect the police to protect him. Political revolutionaries—the people of the Red Brigades, terrorists and subversives in Latin American and Middle East—take for granted that they may be killed for their convictions.

Salman Rushdie has truly outraged the Islamic society from which he himself comes. We have, in the West, become so accustomed to indifference or complicity on the part of the writer's audience that it is a radical discovery to find that words wound, and that there are people who can be driven to fury by words, potentially to murder, because a writer mocks, or seems to mock, their deep convictions.

A factor in our shock is that it is difficult to think of principles we in the West believe in deeply enough to want to kill someone who mocks them. Religion? Hardly. Political values—such as liberty of expression? What a laugh. The first reaction of American and British booksellers to Iran's denunciation of Mr. Rushdie's *Satanic Verses* was to run up the yellow flag, suppressing the book. Publishers in France and West Germany said they must think again about issuing *Satanic Verses*. Canadian customs blocked its import.

Mr. Rushdie himself issued a statement saying that he really had not meant to hurt anyone's feelings and that this affair has reminded him that "we must be conscious of the sensibilities of others." If he was not serious about outraging the sensibilities of others, why did he write the book?

The press reaction, in Britain above all, has been one of delectation in the horror of it all. Poor Mr. Rushdie will be tracked all his life by fanatics, the papers say. "Death squads" even now make their way toward London. The author will have to be under police guard forever. He will have to have plastic surgery.

Actually, one suspects that Mr. Rushdie's ordeal will come to an end before too many months have passed. It would not be prudent for him to make public appearances just now, or sign his books in the bookstores—those still willing to sell his book. Were I he, I would spend the next few months on a Caribbean beach or a South African vacation, or go to the Club Med in Tahiti. I would change apartments and would not in the future list myself in the phone book. I might even grow a mustache. I don't think that I would bother to have my face reconstructed. It is painful and my friends might be confused.

Time passes, and even ayatollahs and their followers, like newspapers and their readers, find new sensations to occupy their attention. The threat to Mr. Rushdie is an episode in the power struggle in Iran, and when that struggle is over *Satanic Verses* will lose its interest. It may even be remaindered. Mr. Rushdie can then come out of hiding.

The affair is important for teaching facts people find uncomfortable: Ideas do count, and they may carry with them serious costs. They are dangerous. A writer has to take responsibility for what he writes. Does Mr. Rushdie take seriously what he wrote? Do the booksellers and publishers of America and western Europe believe in books and free ideas? Are principles to be defended when they prove inconvenient? Is religion a serious matter? The answer thus far given in North America and Western Europe to all these questions seems to have been no.

(*Los Angeles Times*, 23 Feb. 1989)

ON ISLAM

AZIZ AL-AZMEH

Like all religions, Islam is neither above nor beyond history. For 1400 years, it has taken a bewildering variety of forms, each of which has proclaimed itself the most authentic. Without this protean quality, no religion can become universal or span a diversity of times, places, societies and cultures and be the religion of medieval Kurdish tribesmen, 18th century Moroccan peasants, Cairo scholars, Malaysian traders, Saudi monarchs and Iranian revolutionaries.

This elementary fact seems to be fast receding from the public consciousness with the spectacle of self-appointed inquisitors, judges and executioners in the name of a definitive Islamic monolith. In the name of this monolith, we are witnessing the fostering of a deliberate archaicism, the call for the restoration of a putative utopia.

In this utopia, nothing protrudes over the surface of uniformity in ritual, obscurantism, piety, or interpretation of the Koran. Nothing disturbs the authority of the elders, nor the seclusion and subordination of women reduced, in the prurient imagination, to causes for temptation or saved by relegation to motherhood.

Not unnaturally, this call for the absolute introversion of the single voice can only thrive on adversity. It must generate tokens of evil, and can only conceive difference in terms of triumph or annihilation. Salman Rushdie has found himself caught up in the midst of this fantastical frenzy, and has become a token by means of which the authors and purveyors of this particular brand of recent Islam can project their demonology, and foist upon the various Muslim communities in this country a uniformity that has no justification in their histories or traditions.

Muslims generally, including British Muslims, belong to many nationalities, cultures, classes, and are divided, like everybody else, by different and contradictory ideological and political directions. The denial of this great diversity of Islamic traditions and of the reality of history does not convince the observer that a monolithic Islam is forming a society according to a pre-established model, but rather confirms the fact that religions do not constitute societies or histories but are rather constituted by them.

(from *Guardian*, London, 17 Feb. 1989)

CHARLES PAUL FREUND

. . . If one grants Mr Rushdie and his criticism status within an Islamic tradition, it is possible to see him as the first significant— or at least the loudest—voice of this sort to emerge from the Islamic community in a very long time. The fact that he himself makes no religious claims and is anything but a religious figure is beside the point. What is important is his heretical novel; it speaks for any nascent rationalist tendencies in the Islamic community.

It would make good historical sense if a rationalist Islam were beginning to re-emerge. The reasons are the same ones that shaped Islamic rationalism when the faith began: When Islam's powerful armies conquered a series of peoples from Egypt to Spain 1,300 years ago, learned Moslems discovered how interesting those peoples and cultures were. That contact affected their thinking about their own faith, and ultimately influenced the shape and direction of Islam itself.

Several hundred years later, the Islamic world turned inward. Between its withdrawal from Spain and the landing of Napoleon in Egypt, there was little cultural contact between it and the West. Even after Napoleon, it was the West that was the interloper in the Moslem world; the Moslem reflex was to seek self-protection from cultural and spiritual contamination.

Today, unprecedented numbers of immigrant Moslem communities exist among rationalist westerners. The urge to assimilate culturally within a few generations will be powerful, as will the urge to find some accommodation to surrounding Western values. If hybrid forms of Islam emerge, it shouldn't surprise anybody. The role of a Salman Rushdie in such a process should be self-evident; it is certainly evident to his fundamental Moslem critics.

The important question for Mr Rushdie is whether it is as evident to his potential allies: some Moslems, in the Moslem world or the Western, have developed an outlook—rationalist, assimilationist, rejectionist—in some way similar to his.

The first time around for rationalistic Islam coincided with one of history's most extraordinary golden ages. Moslems from Baghdad to Córdoba developed mixed communities far more tolerant and advanced than most in Christian Europe. They were responsible for important achievements in architecture, medicine, mathematics, chemistry, philosophy, astronomy and more. They helped develop the idea of the university, and built libraries. They helped prepare Europe for the Renaissance—and then changed their minds about their relationship to the world, and turned their backs on many of their achievements. . . .

(from *International Herald Tribune*, 21 Feb. 1989)

The Islamic world: going too far

JOHN ALLEMANG

In the West, writers win prizes for going too far. Taking risks, daring to say the unsayable, is what makes creative artists like Salman Rushdie a breed apart.

But in the world of Islam, as Mr. Rushdie now knows to his peril, things are different.

"One of the most grievous sins in Islam," said Mahmoud Ayoub, a professor of Islamic studies at Temple University in Philadelphia, "is to create discord in the community." With his provocative—or, to use an outmoded word that still applies in the Islamic world, blasphemous—novel, *The Satanic Verses*, Mr. Rushdie has sown seeds of discord among Moslems. And for this, as the West looks on aghast at the strength of the reaction and appalled at the lack of respect for freedom of expression, Mr. Rushdie has been condemned. To die.

Islam at heart is a religion of the entire community, a pervasive system for living that considers the integrity of society to be of supreme importance. As a lapsed Moslem, even one who entered Rugby school in England at the age of 13, Mr. Rushdie knew that whatever he gave would go well beyond the intelligentsia. And to Moslems, at least, there is no question that the book is calculated to offend.

The novel's title, which refers to spurious verses received by the Prophet Mohammed from the Devil, stops Moslems short. The name Mahound, which Mr. Rushdie uses for the Mohammed-like prophet in his book, also gives offence, since Mahound is a Satanic figure. The rules of religion in *The Satanic Verses* seem preoccupied with such trivialities as urinating and farting and what part of the body can be scratched. The names of Mohammed's wives, women who are accorded reverance by the Moslem community, are given to prostitutes in the book.

"That's just going too far," Prof. Ayoub said. "I think the man is writing to offend. There's no evidence in the book that he is caught in uncertainty and doubt. He's not questioning his faith, he just wants to attract attention."

The standard response from critics and commentators in the West is that the novel, if it has been read at all by the thousands of demonstrators in Islamabad and Tehran, has been misunderstood. The references to Mohammed are fictional, isolated in a dream sequence, not to be taken seriously. If the references are to be taken seriously, then it is as thoughtful and carefully crafted insights, not as random abuse. And if you Moslems are still going to get worked up over a few pages of prize-winning prose, at least behave like gentleman. "Those offended have every right to denounce and picket but not to threaten and intimidate," pronounced an editorial writer in *The New York Times.*

But this definition of the right to protest is just one more way in which Westerners would impose their values on the Islamic world. The model in everyone's mind, of course, is Martin Scorsese's film *The Last Temptation of Christ.* It too was found thought-provoking by the critics and offensive by the religious. Apart from a bomb in a Paris cinema that left one man dead, however, the anguished protesters confined themselves to picketing and denunciation from a safe distance. Freedom of expression won out, as we have been taught that it always should and would.

The laws of religion, insofar as there is any unanimity among the religious in this pluralistic society, cannot become the laws of the state. Anyone who strives to knit the two together need only be reminded of that telling and characteristic verse from the Bible: "Render therefore unto Caesar the things which are Caesar's and unto God the things that are God's."

And there lies the important difference. Our more or less Christian post-Reformation, post-Enlightenment, post-modern melange champions a world-weary tolerance. Rage threatens social stability.

But the Islamic world does not work in the same way. The outrage displayed by Moslems in Pakistan and Iran to the outside world is a sign of cohesion, as the religion of Islam unites to face the faithless.

For Willard Oxtoby, professor of religious studies at the University of Toronto, the crucial differences can be traced to the origins of the two faiths. "Christianity spent its first three centuries as the religion of a minority," he said, "whereas Islam from its very beginning was both the spiritual and the political structure of a total community. This means that the kind of separation we make between sacred and secular does not always work in traditional Islam. It also means that the criticism of religious ideas is more directly seen as an attack on the community than a similar criticism by modernists in the West."

In a way, Mr. Rushdie's book was perceived as the last straw in the West's insensitive and uninformed treatment of the Islamic world. "The Moslem world behaves in this way because it sees itself as being in a state of siege," said Khalid Sayeed, a professor of political science at Queen's University in Kingston, Ontario. "Moslems are convinced that they are singled out for this kind of persecution."

The unfailing and uncritical support which the secularizing shah of Iran enjoyed from the West over the years might in itself justify anti-Western, anti-modern sentiment. But that is not to say (although Western analysts are implying it) that the religious complaints are insincere. Politicians opposed to Prime Minister Benazir Bhutto may be orchestrating demonstrations in Pakistan, Iran's Ayatollah Khomaini as defender of the faith just might be looking for a rallying point after the end of the war with Iraq, but *The Satanic Verses* remains offensive to Moslems.

The ayatollah, after all, is the ruler of a theocracy. He has a doctorate in canon law, which might appear a strange qualification for the White House or 10 Downing St. but which serves the premodern Islamic state of Iran admirably. The traditional Islamic law that governs Iran is essentially medieval, and under that law blasphemy is a capital crime.

In the West, Salman Rushdie is a typical intellectual who has shed the somewhat embarrassing trappings of his faith but continues to be interested in the contradictions of a sometimes cruel and arbitrary religion. But as far as a Moslem is concerned he is an apostate, which is itself a grave offence. And because religion embraces all decision-making in a traditional Moslem society, it becomes impossible to treat the writer's critical comments as anything other than an attack on the foundations of society.

"A disaffected writer like Rushdie," Prof. Oxtoby said, "is seen more as a traitor than simply as a person who lost his faith."

The strength of the reaction to *The Satanic Verses* took the West by surprise. But there have been precedents in the protests, generally ignored, against the movies *Ishtar* and *Mohammed, Messenger of God,* and over the fictionalized portrayal of an execution in the Saudi royal family, *Death of A Princess.*

That dramatization on British television in 1980 incited Saudi Arabia to press the protest well beyond the Islamic world. The ambassador in London was recalled, King Khaled shelved a state visit to Britain, the British ambassador was expelled and there was persuasive talk of cutting off oil supplies. Finally the British caved in and apologized.

People were incredulous that the Saudis would mount a case beyond their borders over their cruel laws and that an apology, however insincere, would be made in the home of free speech.

The cycle is repeating itself. The incomprehension at those strange Moslems is about to be replaced by disdain for the Western governments and businesses (bookstores among them) that will surely cave in.

But should we be so surprised? There are, after all, numerous parallels in our own society of outrage fomented by ideas. Start with the genetic theories of Philippe Rushton, if you like, and go back to Edward Banfield, whose views on race made many universities compromise their principles on free speech. Consider Nikos Kazantzakis, the Greek author of *The Last Temptation of Christ*, who was denounced by the Greek Orthodox Church and remains in death an object of hatred. And look, above all, at the hatred of anti-Semitism which has become ingrained in Western thinking, even if it compromises free speech. For Moslems there is inconsistency here.

"If I were to tell you," Prof. Sayeed said, "that I had a dream in which Hitler appeared and said he had been maligned, that he didn't kill the Jews, and then I wrote about this in lyrical prose, are you going to say to me that this is a work of art and should be judged by different standards?"

For some Moslems, Salman Rushdie is guilty not merely of writing hate literature but of inhumanity to people whose lives are miserable enough without mockery from the West.

(*Globe & Mail*, Toronto, 18 Feb. 1989)

A Muslim tells Salman Rushdie he did wrong

S. NOMANUL HAQ

Cambridge Massachusetts—Dear Salman Rushdie: A few years ago, when I read your *Midnight's Children*, I was overwhelmed. It was not the exuberance of your narrative and stylistic craft, nor the threads of your rich imagination woven with such effective intellectual control that engulfed me. Rather it was your formidable grasp of history and, through that, of the psyche of a complex culture in all its variations that formed the substratum of your tale.

And yet is is this question of your knowledge of history that I shall raise in connection with your seriously and alarmingly controversial *The Satanic Verses.*

Let me say at once that I do not hold you as an artist, not as a historian or a psychologist—nor as a theologian. But at the same time you do make use of what are facts of history and psychology, giving them your own distinct treatment.

No writer, you will agree, writes in a historical vacuum. But then, a responsible artist does not, without powerful grounds, mutilate history, Nor, unless there exists a mammoth justification, does he disregard the sensibilities and sensitivities of his own milieu, especially when it forms both the subject matter and the bulk of his or her audience.

Strangely, what I am saying is something that I learned from none other than yourself. You might recall your telling criticism of Sir Richard Attenborough's celebrated film *Gandhi.* You enraged Sir Richard, but in the controversy I remained your passionate supporter.

You censured the film for disregarding or minimizing certain important historical facts. And you said that in a work of an artistic nature, one cannot say everything, that there has to be a choice—but that there has to be a rationale of choice. One selects not to mislead but to make the story more meaningful. Ironically, this has precisely been your lapse in *The Satanic Verses.*

Most of your Western readers are unable to gauge the acuteness of your blow to the very core of the Indian subcontinental culture. They cannot estimate the seriousness of the injury because they do not know the history of the aggrieved.

You do know it and therefore one feels that you foresaw, at least to some extent, the consequences.

There is in your book, for example, the phantasmagoria of your own namesake Salman's corruption of the revealed word by his erroneous rendering of the words Mahound.

Here the veil is too thin to cover the identity of Mahound: He can be understood in no other way than as a caricature of the Moslem Prophet. You do know that Islam is consistently, acutely and uniquely sensitive to its scripture. Ordinarily, Arabic is written without short vowels, but no copy of the Koran today is vowelless: Moslems insist that it should and can be read only in one way. The Moslem view is that even incorrectly reading the Koran is a cardinal sin. The Koran is neither read nor recited in translation for the very reason that translation might introduce alteration.

This matter is deadly serious, and to make it a subject of insensitive fantasy is equally serious.

There is a further issue that your Western reader does not sense: that your corrupt Salman is the namesake not only of you in your book but of a historical personage who was a Persian companion of the Prophet, a companion who has been accorded a particularly elevated status by the Shiites. Given the militancy of the Shiites, when you made Salman the polluter of the revelation, you knew that you were planting your hand in the cluster of bees!

Your response to the uproar has been wavering and inconsistent, and your defense has the odor of self-righteousness. You say that people who have not read your book have no right to criticize it. But do you really think that reading the book will drastically alter their opinions? Then you talk about freedom of expression. Free speech is a tricky issue and cannot be taken too literally.

What do you think the response of black Americans would be if you were to mock Martin Luther King Jr.? Or the reaction of the Jewish community if you eulogized Hitler? Or the anger of a pious Hindu if you were to present a graphic description of the slaughtering of a cow?

And to say that the Moslem world has demonstrated a total lack of dignity and tolerance is to utter a historical irrelevance. The Moslem nations have not gone through the turmoils of the Enlightenment and they have seen no scientific revolution; their sensibilities are different. Often, a peaceful demonstration is not their way, and we cannot change them overnight. The best thing is to avoid hitting their most sensitive chords. And, Mr Rushdie, you knew that.

As for your waverings, you started out by expressing regret over the fact that you did not write even a more controversial book. You accused the leaders of the angry demonstrations in Islamabad of exploiting a religious slogan for secular and political ends. They may have done so, but what about the innocent and ignorant people who died in the violence? You expressed no sympathy for them. And now you issue a three-sentence statement that, at best, has the semblance of regret. Quite honestly, Mr Rushdie, your heart does not beat in this statement, your expression is glaringly perfunctory.

I am saddened that a bounty has been placed on your head and that a great writer like you, rather than presenting himself to the public, is in hiding. You have elicited the rage of entire nations. This is a pity. But, Mr Rushdie, you have cut them and they are bleeding: Do something quickly to heal the wound.

• *The writer, a Muslim, is a tutor in the history of science at Harvard University.*

(*International Herald Tribune*, 24 Feb. 1989)

A dissenting voice for whom Rushdie speaks
Karachi

Sir—Salman Rushdie speaks for me in *The Satanic Verses*, and mine is a voice that has not yet found expression in newspaper columns. It is the voice of those who are born Muslims but wish to recant in adulthood, yet are not permitted to do so on pain of death.

Someone who does not live in an Islamic society cannot imagine the sanctions, both self-imposed and external, that militate against expressing religious disbelief. 'I don't believe in God' is an impossible public utterance even among family and friends. Muslims hate Rushdie not so much for his irreverence as for his doubt; for his questioning 'divine inspiration'; for his humanisation of the Prophet, who had of late begun to acquire divine characteristics.

In the *Dar-ul Islam* (Realm of Islam) we may not debate such issues even in the privacy of our own homes. We may talk of 'progressive', 'enlightened', interpretations of Islam and curse the mullahs for their orthodox fundamentalism, but we may *never* question the veracity, rationality, justice or moral rightness of basic beliefs. And if we dare to recant, then it is the religious obligation of the faithful to execute us.

So we hold our tongues, those of us who doubt. Call it cowardice or hypocrisy, tact or appeasement, we bury our heads in the sand and wish it all away. But it comes home to us in our children, whose intellectual and spiritual straitjacketing begins early in the Realm of Islam.

Then, along comes Rushdie and speaks for us. Tells the world that we exist—that we are not simply a mere fabrication of some Jewish conspiracy. He ends our isolation. He ends it and simultaneously deepens it; frees us only to imprison us anew. Today it is impossible to speak of Islam in anything but the most hallowed and sacrosanct terms. Holier-than-thou attitudes are being affected everywhere. The book is reviled, the execution of the author demanded even by those who might otherwise have been credited with being fairly civilised. I have not met a single critic who has actually read the book.

The agony of dissent which finds no support is unbearable. Rushdie in his wretched predicament is comforted by the support of the international community of writers and intellectuals, peers and politicians—and his readers. But for secularists like myself, imprisoned in the theocratic dungeon that is a Muslim nation today, the isolation is total. I weep for my daughter, just four-and-a-half years old, already being taught to recite the affirmation of faith and learning religious dogma by rote at school. I want to tell her what *I* believe but don't want her to be the victim of ridicule by her peers—or worse, should she repeat such heresy publicly.

• *The name of the author of this letter was withheld by* The Observer *upon request.*

(*Observer*, London, 12 March 1989)

Context for the Ayatollah's decree: The religious and political in Islam
ABDULAZIZ A. SACHEDINA

Ayatollah Ruhollah Khomeini pronounced a sentence of death on Salman Rushdie, the author of *The Satanic Verses*. To understand his action, we need to know more about the context in which the ayatollah operates.

There is an interdependency between the religious and the political in the laws that govern the status of an apostate in the Moslem community. Importantly, political considerations surrounding the question of sedition have dominated the harsh treatment of apostates in Islamic law.

Let us consider what Islamic law regards an act of apostasy to be: an act of disbelieving after having believed. It is rejection of Islam by word, deed or omission.

Rejection of Islam by word means to deny God's existence and other doctrines of Islamic faith, including any part of the Koran or its main tenets, such as prayer and almsgiving. Rejection of Islam by deed means acting contrary to its teachings. Rejection by omission means refraining from performance of an act required by the Koran.

It is the duty of a Moslem state to assess the level of discord created by a declaration of an apostasy and lay down the appropriate punishment for it: There is no text in the Koran to support the death penalty for apostasy per se. However, the Koran speaks of rebellion as punishable by the severest penalties (5:33–34). Rebellion against an Islamic public order constitutes a general state of lawlessness.

The death penalty for the crime of apostasy is derived from the tradition attributed to the prophet Mohammed: "Whoever changes his religion, kill him." It is also sanctioned by precedents set by the early successors of the prophet.

There were two presuppositions at work when the laws of apostasy in Islam were systematized. The first is the existence of an Islamic public order embodying the divine will. Following from that, the act of apostasy was regarded as an act of sedition that had caused discord and had threatened the unity of Islamic community.

The demand for a society incorporating the spirit of Islam gives rise to an important tension in connection with the idea of religious liberty. On the one hand, religious belief in the Koran is beyond the reach of human coercion. In fact, to punish or constrain people because of their religious beliefs is, it would seem, simply to distract them from the voluntary basis of true religious belief and practice. To believe out of fear of punishment is not authentic belief at all.

On the other hand, the Koran appears to say that of creating a desirable political community, one that conforms with the wishes of God, is to constrain, by force if necessary, those who, as the Koran puts it, "take up arms" or "exhibit enmity" against God.

The consequence of this, as it has traditionally been understood, is that certain forms of religious expression and practice—particularly public denunciation or rejection of the fundamental teachings of Islamic faith—are to be regarded as a threat to the public security of the community. Such hostile religious acts must be treated with

the same severity as other. more clearly moral, threats to the security of the community, such as rebellion, theft, highway robbery
and the like.

The context for Ayatollah Khomeini's verdict is provided by the
early political experience of the Moslem community following Mohammed's death in A.D. 632. At that time, some Arab tribes had
renounced Islam and had refused to pay the taxes imposed on them
by the Islamic order. The Islamic authority saw this act of rebellion
as a breach of contract between the tribes and the Islamic government. As such, the act was interpreted as tantamount to the aban-
donment of faith and hence subject to severest punishment.

Islamic sources describing this episode reveal the tension among
the Moslem leaders regarding the use of force in matters of faith.
Could Moslem authority force people to believe in God?

The solution to this question depended on the way faith was to
be interpreted in Islam. Faith in Islam came to be understood both
as a personal witness and as a sense of loyalty to the Islamic public
order under the rightly guided Moslem head of state. In its personal
sense, religious faith was beyond the jurisdiction of any human
agency—who could enforce it?—but in its socio-political dimension, it came under the jurisdicton of Islamic power.

The early battles of Moslem forces against the apostatizing tribes
were, consequently, treated as cases of breach of contract between
Moslem power and the community members who had fallen short
of their obligations to the social over.

In light of the above, where does Salman Rushdie stand? Mr.
Rushdie has declared that he is not a practicing Moslem (and he is
not alone in this!). He claims to be a sort of a Moslem mystic who
abhors the formalism of Islamic faith, as is clear in his *Satanic
Verses*. Such a mystical attitude is not unusual in the Islamic community (witness the Sufi movement in Islam). On the basis of his
own description of his personal religion, it is hard to say that he has
become an apostate by word.

As to whether *The Satanic Verses* is a seditious blasphemy
against Islam and its founder, two issues need to be clarified. First
is the author's claim to vindicate his work, namely, that it is merely
fiction. Second is the ayatollah's assertion that the book has a hostile agenda to undermine the confidence of the Moslem community

in their faith and that the Western world has conspired for that very reason in the publication of this work.

In his book, Mr. Rushdie appropriates episodes from Islamic religious history, sometimes substituting fictional names for real ones and leaving enough circumstantial evidence to connect the fictitious to the actual history of the religion. To call this "fiction" is not wholly convincing to any Moslem, whether "fundamentalist" or otherwise. The novel then, can be classified as seditious blasphemy against Islam and regarded as an act of apostasy of deed committed by Mr. Rushdie.

However, Ayatollah Khomeini has to shoulder the burden of proof—proof of both a religious and a political violation. He must show not only that Mr. Rushdie has violated "the right of God" by blasphemous writing, but that he has violated the "rights of humankind"—the right of the Moslem community to be free from disruption.

The ayatollah has not, however, established that the community has suffered a serious disturbance, that the novel sewed the seeds of sedition among Moslems. Traditional Islamic sources took for granted the limitless, international "sphere of Islam" under the caliphs, the Moslem heads of state. But can this be the necessary context for the modern international order, based on the concept of sovereign nation-state, to execute the ayatollah's judgment on Mr. Rushdie's apostasy?   (*Baltimore Sun*, 26 Feb. 1989)

Islam and literature
FADIA A. FAQIR

As a Jordanian novelist writing in English whose work has been boycotted by Muslim fundamentalists, I would like to echo the sentiments expressed by Malise Ruthven (*November 25–December 1, 1988*). The conflict between literature and Islam predates the resignation of Taha Hussein in the 1930s: the bitter conflict started when the Archangel Gabriel dictated to Muhammad the following verse of the Quran: 'As for poets, the erring follow them. Hast thou not seen how they stray in every valley. And how they say that which they do not.'

Poets of the pre-Islamic era occupied a prominent position in society; their poetry was written in gold and hung on the walls of holy temples. The Quran presented itself as the final and supreme text, causing an unresolved crisis. To continue his writing career, Hassan Ibn-Thabit (Muhammad's poet laureate) switched to writing eulogies which glorified Islam. After Muhammad, most of the powerful pre-Islamic poetry only survived as *samizdat* literature. Since then, in most Islamic countries, writing has never been respected and is considered by strict Muslims as an act of subversion.

When Salman Rushdie's novel *The Satanic Verses* was being considered for the Booker Prize, and Tahar Ben-Jallon's *La Nuit sacrée* was awarded the Prix Goncourt, the London-based Muslim newspaper questioned the integrity of the members of the Booker and Goncourt committees. It accused the West of embracing the writings of Jallon, Rushdie, Naipaul and many others, not because of the literary merits or the aesthetic values of their texts, but because they criticized Islam and presented a tarnished image of Muslims. The columnist continued his assault by saying, 'For Muslim writers, the shortest cut to a literary prize is turning against himself and his religion.'

In the twenty-four Arab countries, systems, whether Islamic or secular, always bend to the wind of Islamic fundamentalism. Usually, intellectuals and writers are the first to suffer the fickleness of the systems. Hence the banning of *The Satanic Verses* in India, Saudi Arabia and Egypt. In most Arab countries Hanan El Sheik's novels, Nawal El-Saadawi's writings and the poetry of Muthler El-Nawab and Mahmoud Darwish are banned.

The main problem that faces the Muslim intellectual is that Muslim individuals never read the texts under debate but accept the value-judgement of their Imams and Ulamas. Consequently discussion with Muslims will be fruitless. How many Muslims have read *The Satanic Verses* or the works of Lévi-Strauss? How many Muslims have read Nawal El-Saadawi and discussed her writing with their religious leaders? The Jordanian novelist Zulickheh Abu-Risheh's *In the Cell*, a novel based on her experience of being married to one of the Muslim Brethren, is being attacked from the pulpit as the most serious threat to Islam. In the pages of local daily newspapers, Zulickheh was personally abused and reminded that women should not step out of line. At the height of the debate, her book was still not available in bookshops.

I experienced similar problems when my novel *Nisanit* was published by Penguin earlier this year. After counting the times a reviewer of the novel mentioned Lenin, Giap, Guevara, many Muslim fundamentalists accused me of promoting communism and decided to boycott the novel. When I told some of them that the novel does not promote any ideology, and in fact questions the whole notion of ideology, I got no response. Their ears hear only the preaching of the Imam, and some of the Muslim Brethren are ordered by their leaders not to engage in discussion with non-believers.

Writers living in Arab countries have attempted to resolve the dilemma in different ways. Some writers end up going to Friday Prayers in the mosque to ward off the anger of Muslim fundamentalist pseudo-critics. A group of men accused Suhair El-Tell, a Jordanian journalist and novelist, of promiscuity for using a phallic image. She took them to court and after a long, bitter struggle won the case. Others, like Nawal El-Saadawi, the Egyptian sociologist and novelist, were forced to tone down their criticism of Islam. In December 1987, Nawal El-Saadawi, addressing an audience, most of whom were veiled Muslim Brethren women, said, 'I am neither a communist nor a socialist.' Intimidated by the presence of the fundamentalists, she qualified her statements, compromising her position and undermining everything she argued for in her writing. Most of the sixty-six Arab intellectuals blacklisted recently by a Saudi Islamic group who announced the holy jihad on Modernism live either in London or Paris. Is exile the only answer to the resurgence of Islam?

• *Fadia Faqir lectures in the School of English and American Studies at the University of East Anglia.*

(*Times Literary Supplement*, London, 6–12 Jan. 1989)

The case for religious fundamentalism

SHABBIR AKHTAR

'We must be careful', writes W. L. Webb in the *Guardian* (February 19), 'not to reduce the Rushdie affair . . . to a simple neo-Victorian opposition between our light and their darkness.' Yet isn't that precisely how the issue has been interpreted by each and every Western writer, including so-called Islamic writers patronised by the establishment? For there can be no doubt concerning the media's endorsement of an operative veto on any exploration of the intellectual grounds for fundamentalist options in religion. Most journalists visiting a remote northern city called Bradford were visibly surprised to meet devout Muhammadan chaps who spoke English and even read books now and again.

The surprise is significant. The prevalent image of Islam as an anti-intellectualist creed is one of the many ironies and paradoxes generated by the Rushdie episode. Islam is, in fact, a literary faith par excellence based as it is on a document revered as an 'intellectual miracle' of reason and speech.

The Koran can claim the unique privilege of being the direct inspiration for a major world civilisation founded on a religiously sanctioned respect for literacy and scholarship. That Rushdie should choose to be a *literary* terrorist is itself a fitting tribute to the intelligent earnestness of Islam as a faith of the pen.

That *The Satanic Verses* is blasphemous should be, for the Muslim conscience, uncontroversial. There has been much talk, by confused Muslims and their anti-Islamic mentors, of the complexity of Islamic tradition, of the variety of proper responses to Rushdie's work. Given that the Koran is the book which defines the authentically Muslim outlook, there is no choice in the matter. Anyone who fails to be offended by Rushdie's book *ipso facto* ceases to be a Muslim.

Rushdie's attack on the authoritative integrity of a fallible Koran is part of a larger indictment of Islam as a faith which routinely and regularly confuses good with evil, divine with diabolic imperative. With respect to a faith that uniquely continues to distinguish itself for its totally uncompromising distinction between right and wrong, such an indictment is at once ridiculously ironic and radically offensive.

Having read *The Satanic Verses* twice, I am completely convinced that it is an inferior piece of literature whose popularity in the West invites one to look in the region of motives. Even on a sympathetic reading, Rushdie's book is an incoherent fantasy which will cater to an undiscerning appetite reinforcing misconceptions already entrenched in the Western mind.

Nor can Rushdie flatter himself with the conceit that he has properly indulged the sceptical temper let alone discovered the historical Muhammad. Rushdie is not ploughing a virgin field: sceptics there have been and always will be. What matters is the quality and integrity of their doubts.

A Job-like scepticism, reverent and sincere, is found in many Islamic thinkers and novelists, all the way from al-Ghazzali to Muhammad Iqbal and Najib Mahfuz. Within Rushdie's unprincipled prose, one looks in vain for the penetrating critique of a Mahfuz implying tragically that occasional divine tuition via messengership (in the Islamic style) does not suffice, human perversity being inveterate as it is. *Satanic Verses* falls short of the only real metaphysical achievement of an anti-religious genius, namely that even good and evil are (as Nietzsche would say) prejudices, albeit God's prejudices.

Even so, why all this fuss over an admittedly offensive book? Many writers often condescendingly imply that Muslims should become as tolerant as modern Christians. After all, the Christian faith has not been undermined. But the truth is, of course, too obviously the other way. The continual blasphemies against the Christian faith have totally undermined it. Any faith which compromises its internal temper of militant wrath is destined for the dustbin of history, for it can no longer preserve its faithful heritage in the face of the corrosive influences.

The fact that post-Enlightenment Christians tolerate blasphemy is a matter for shame, not for pride. It is true, of course, that God can defend himself. But a believer must vindicate the reputation of God and his spokesmen against the militant calumnies of evil. Only then can he truly confess the faith. For faith is as faith does.

In this matter, the Koran is bound to have the last word: God does not guide a people who sell his signs for a paltry price. Small wonder that the Christian clergy is failing to preserve and transmit the faithful heritage.

It is fashionable for Western writers to pretend to be suspicious of all apologias and enthusiasms. Yet aren't we all apologists for one belief or another? Nor will it do to pretend—as some might neatly think—'But truth needs no apology.' For that would only be so in a world in which truth were both manifest and men were honest. In the contemporary universe, truth is extremely hard to come by and, even when attained, there is no shortage of those professionally engaged in obscuring it.

The Rushdie affair is, in the last analysis, certainly about fanat-

icism on behalf of God. Immediately we must be cautious. For fanaticism is not the monopoly of the Muslim fundamentalists.
Indeed fanaticism is often merely other folk's passion. Nations can
be fanatical about trivial matters (such as religion and morality).
Could it be, then, that we can all live with some prejudices but not
with others?

It is unwise for us, in a multiracial society, to allow our idolatry
of art to obscure issues of social and political concern. Even sup-
posing, for the sake of a case, that Rushdie's novel is a literary
achievement, defending its publication at all costs is as unjustified
as threats to its author's life. Appeals to 'matters of principle' and
'historically hard-won liberties' are not convincing when placed in
the context of double or even triple moral standards. After this affair,
Muslims have reason to think the Crusades are not over yet. For
given the passions it has aroused, one wonders whether or not there
is some truth in the old Muslim accusation that there is still a
Western conspiracy, in a weak sense of the term, against Islam.
Whatever may be the truth on that score, the next time there are
gas chambers in Europe, there is no doubt concerning who'll be
inside them.

With the approach of Ramadan, faith will move mountains. Faith
needs to move mountains. Those Muslims who find it intolerable
to live in a United Kingdom contaminated with the Rushdie virus
need to seriously consider the Islamic alternatives of emigration
(hijrah) to the House of Islam or a declaration of holy war (jehad)
on the House of Rejection. The latter may well seem a kind of hasty
militancy that is out of the question, though, with God on one's
side, one is never in the minority. And England, like all else, belongs
to God. As for hijrah, the current British Government would no
doubt be happy to assist. But non-Muslims would do well to remember that the last time there was a hijrah, a unified Muslim
enterprise of faith and power spread with phenomenal speed in the
fastest permanent conquest of recorded military history.

What stays with us are myriad variations on an influential slogan
about power and powerlessness, all equally trivial, all equally true
or equally false depending on one's mood. The pen is mightier than
the sword; the sword is mightier than the pen; the pen is useless
without the sword; the pen is mightiest with the sword. It has taken
Islam to remind us that faith should be mightier than both.

• *Dr Shabbir Akhtar is a member of Bradford's Council for Mosques.*

(*Guardian*, London, 27 Feb. 1989)

Historical Rushdie

MICHAEL FOOT

If people are now being killed in Salman Rushdie's native Bombay because of his book, is it not time to cry halt, time for Rushdie and his publishers to call the whole thing off, recall copies and promise never to commit the same offence again?

To which the short, and the long, answer must be: the killings are not attributable to Rushdie's book; not a single sentence within it incites people to kill or offers excuse for the killers.

On the contrary, the reason for the killing is to be found in the religion of the killers or those who have incited them to kill, or in the measures of the police who felt required to take protective action against the peril of even more widespread killings, inspired by the same religious appeal or provocation.

And please don't tell us, for a start, that the ideas of such religious-inspired killing becoming more extensive is a fanciful excuse. It is nothing of the sort. It has been happening before our eyes, over the past seven or eight years, on a large, nearly-unprecedented scale, without a murmur of objection from those who claim to be outraged by Rushdie.

The killings in the Iran-Iraq war have been so huge that they are literally incalculable, and they have had the added indecency on the Iranian side that tens of thousands of boys have been sent to their deaths with keys of paradise around their necks. How many others have been killed in Iran itself, without this happy consolation, no one knows, and few people seem to care except the brave Iranian dissidents who have long warned us about the scale of the Ayatollah Khomeini horror. For them—and for us, maybe—it is a threat on the Hitler dimension. But for the moment I'm concerned about the numbers and wantonness of the killings. It would be a strange world which drew the contrasted conclusion that the trouble comes from Rushdie and not at all from Khomeini.

Most Muslims throughout the world, and most especially, we might say, those settled in this country, have every interest and duty to say how strongly and unshakably they oppose the Ayatollah and all his works, both his death threats beyond his frontiers and his murderous methods at home. Many have done so without hesitation or equivocation. When the horror has passed, they will deserve the highest credit—as did the trade unionists, Socialists and Jews who resisted Hitler in the back streets of Berlin and Munich when Chamberlain and Co. were still engaged in their appeasement act. These are truly the best spokesmen of their Muslim cause.

But these voices are drowned or at least subdued by others. I quote from Dr Shabbir Akhtar of Bradford's Council of Mosques (Agenda, February 27) who doubtless approved the shameful book burning in that city. 'Any faith which compromises its internal temper of militant wrath is destined for the dustbin of history, for it can no longer preserve its faithful heritage in face of the corrosive influences.' Dr Akhtar professes a fundamentalist, absolute religious allegiance which would permit no argument with Rushdie. He or at least his book must be destroyed.

However, Dr Akhtar's case gives us the opportunity to introduce Christianity and all its kindred intolerances into the debate. 'Many writers,' he continues, 'often condescendingly imply that Muslims should become as tolerant as modern Christians. After all, the Christian faith has not been undermined. But the truth is, of course, too obviously, all the other way. The continual blasphemies against the Christian faith have totally undermined it.' Indeed, there is a measure of twisted sense in the Doctor's analysis: the survival of Christianity has been due in part to its newfound mildness, its tolerance of other creeds, an ending or at least a mitigation of the old rivalries, say, between Protestant and Catholic. Once those contests led to unending killings too.

For Dr Akhtar's benefit, and indeed for the general enlightenment of mankind, we might put the case the other way round. Once upon a time there was little to choose between Christian and Muslim, or between Catholic or Protestant, in what Dr Akhtar now calls an 'internal temper of militant wrath' or the preserving of 'the faithful heritage'. Each side could be indiscriminate killers, and they did it in the name of religion.

How the world in general, and Western Europe in particular, escaped from this predicament, this seemingly endless confrontation, is one of the real miracles of western civilisation, and it was certainly not the work of the fundamentalists on either side. It was done by those who dared to deny the absolute authority of their respective gods; the sceptics, the doubters, the mockers even, the men like Montaigne who saw where the endless bloodletting would lead, and how each side must be ready to abjure absolute victory.

The great persisting threat to our world derives from this pursuit of absolute victory. Once it was Hitler's creed, and once it was Stalin's, and once it was called the Dulles doctrine, and once it came near to being adopted by a President Reagan launching fundamentalist anathemas against the evil empire. It is too soon to say that all these perils have passed, but on the intercontinental stage they have been miraculously reduced, with mankind to breathe again— as they did when the crusaders and their enemies became exhausted by their mad expeditions or when Catholic and Protestant reached their 16th-century compromise.

How strident or absurd or indeed wicked were the fundamentalist voices of those times, the Khomeinis and the Akhtars, who denounced any move towards détente or rapprochement as blasphemy or treachery or godlessness. How much wiser and braver were the Montaignes, the Jonathan Swifts, the Voltaires, the Salman Rushdies who knew that if such insanities were to be stopped, they must be mocked in the name of a common human decency with a claim to take precedence over any religion.

Montaigne's books were put on the Papal Index; Swift was accused, on the highest regal or ecclesiastical authority, of defaming all religions; many of Voltaire's volumes were actually burnt.

So Salman Rushdie keeps good company. He is a great artist, even if, like Swift or Voltaire himself, he does not possess all the virtues too. But no shield against religious intolerance off the leash can always prevail, as Voltaire himself explained in his epitaph on the Saint Zapata:

'He isolated truth from falsehood and separated religion from fanaticism. He taught and practised virtue. He was gentle, benevolent and modest, and was roasted at Valladolid in the year of grace, 1631.'

• *Michael Foot is a Labour MP and was chairman of the Booker Prize judges in 1988.*

(*Guardian*, London, 10 March 1989)

Khomeini exploits furor over 'Verses'

ANTONY T. SULLIVAN

Ayatollah Khomeini's pronouncement of a sentence of death against British expatriate author Salman Rushdie for writing *The Satanic Verses* was inspired more by political and geostrategic considerations than by those of religion.

Indeed, had Rushdie not existed, the Ayatollah would probably have had to invent him. When Rushdie's scandalous book was published in England in September 1988, Khomeini said nothing. It was not until riots erupted in Pakistan five months later that he decided to act.

By appropriating understandable Muslim outrage against Rushdie to his own pragmatic purposes, Khomeini has reset the Iranian Revolution on a path of uncompromising extremism. As a result, terrorism may increase, and the predicament of foreign hostages in Lebanon will likely worsen. Surely, Arab Sunni regimes will confront increasing restiveness from Shiite Muslims within their borders.

Khomeini has exploited the furor over Rushdie's book to undermine those Iranians who have advocated an opening to the West. *The Satanic Verses* now serves a purpose similar to that once served by the American hostages in Iran in 1979 and 1980, and by the Iran-Iraq war: It is one important engine that drives the vehicle of radical Islamic fundamentalism. Deftly, the aged Ayatollah has seized upon Rushdie's book to impose his own script on Iran's future.

It is unfortunate that Khomeini's reprehensible advocacy of killing Rushdie has focused public discussion in the West on the issue of free speech rather than on the substantive question of the book's content. To comprehend Islamic anger at what Rushdie has written, one must understand how all Muslims have traditionally been represented in Western literature and popular culture.

Take, for example, Dante Alighieri's *Divine Comedy*. In the *Inferno*, the great medieval Italian poet employs his most scatological language to portray the prophet Mohammed. Placing Mohammed in one of the lower reaches of hell as a notorious fomenter of discord, Dante describes him as:

"split from his chin to the mouth with which man farts.
between his legs all his red guts hung. . . .

and the shriveled sac that passes s—— to the bung. . . .
See how [Mohammed] is mangled and split open!"

Dante's obvious delight at the Prophet's condition reflects the
spirit that once sent Christian crusaders to war on Islam. And
Dante's observations are not irrelevant historical curiosities. Recently the mayor of Ravenna, Italy, received a threat that Dante's
tomb would be dynamited unless the mayor disavowed Dante's
commentary on Mohammed.

Similar descriptions of Mohammed and Islam abound in Western
literature of the last 700 years. Today, Muslims are offended by the
Western media's frequent association of Islam with violence, intolerance, and backwardness. This tendency is especially upsetting to
the rapidly growing community of six million Muslims in the
United States. Tragically, Salman Rushdie's deplorable book has
made even more difficult Western understanding of Islam's high
culture and its traditional commitment to toleration and to religious
and political pluralism.

Make no mistake: *The Satanic Verses* is offensive in the highest
degree. Echoing Dante, Rushdie resurrects the term Mahound, the
medieval Christian name for Mohammed, which centuries ago was
employed to denounce the Prophet as a dangerous schismatic at
best, and a hound of hell at worst. Mohammed's wives, revered by
Muslims as the "mothers of all believers," are portrayed as prostitutes in a brothel. Rushdie depicts Archangel Gabriel and the
Prophet himself as unstable homosexuals: "Gibreel [Gabriel] and the
Prophet are wrestling, both naked, rolling over and over in the cave
. . . and let me tell you he's getting in *everywhere*, his tongue in my
ear. . . ." Perhaps most objectionable of all is Rushdie's suggestion
that the Koran is a human creation partially inspired by the Devil.

This sort of trash has the same effect on Muslims that a book
eulogizing Hitler would have on Jews. Were any such eulogy to
appear, one suspects that the Western advocates of untrammeled
free speech would be somewhat less eager to man the barricades
than they have proved themselves in the case of *The Satanic Verses*.

Happily, awareness is growing of the real character of Rushdie's
book. The official Vatican newspaper has denounced it as blasphemous. Interestingly, England's chief rabbi has also denounced Rushdie, and prominent Israeli Rabbi Avraham Shapira is attempting to

prevent publication of the book in Israel because of its offense to religious sensibilities.

Meanwhile, numerous Muslim voices have decried Khomeini's exploitation of the affair. Distinguished authorities on Islamic law at the Islamic Studies in New Delhi and at Al Azhar University in Cairo have rejected Khomeini's death sentence. Saudi Arabia has committed its prestige to oppose any endorsement of Khomeini by the 46-member Islamic Conference Organization. The Islamic Society of North America has condemned any violence against Rushdie or the publishers or distributors of his book.

In the end, one would do well to ponder recent comments by Bernard Lewis, Princeton's distinguished scholar of Islam. "We can only commiserate with our browbeaten Muslim friends and colleagues," Lewis writes, "and lament the growing tendency of the non-Muslim world to perceive and portray the Muslim as a tyrant at home, a terrorist abroad and a bigot in both. This false and libelous picture of one of the great religions of the world . . . is a major tragedy of our time."

(*Detroit News*, 24 March 1989)

ON UNDERSTANDING AND TOLERATION

Rushdie's book is an insult
JIMMY CARTER

In preparation for the Middle East negotiations that led up to Camp David and the Israeli-Egyptian peace treaty, I tried to learn as much as possible about the Moslem faith.

Anwar el-Sadat, Menachem Begin and I had several talks about our common religious beliefs, and Sadat emphasized the reverence that Moslems have for Jesus and the Old Testament Prophets. Although Begin rarely commented himself, there is little doubt that these expressions of good will helped us find common ground in political matters.

Later, when American hostages were held in Iran, I learned more about the fundamentalist beliefs that separated many Iranians from most other Moslems.

Although more difficult to comprehend, their seemingly radical statements and actions are obviously sincere. The melding of fervent religious faith and patriotism during the long war with Iraq has created an environment that has contributed to the furor caused by Salman Rushdie's book, *The Satanic Verses.*

A negative response among Christians resulted from Martin Scorsese's film, *The Last Temptation of Christ.* Although most of us were willing to honor First Amendment rights and let the fantasy be shown, the sacrilegious scenes were still distressing to me and many others who share my faith. There is little doubt that the movie producers and Scorsese, a professed Christian, anticipated adverse public reactions and capitalized on them.

The Satanic Verses goes much further in vilifying the Prophet Mohammed and defaming the Holy Koran. The author, a well-versed analyst of Moslem beliefs, must have anticipated a horrified reaction throughout the Islamic world.

The death sentence proclaimed by Ayatollah Ruhollah Khomeini, however, was an abhorrent response, surely surprising even to Rushdie. It is our duty to condemn the threat of murder, to protect the author's life and to honor Western rights of publication and distribution.

At the same time, we should be sensitive to the concern and anger that prevails even among the more moderate Moslems.

Ayatollah Khomeini's offer of paradise to Rushdie's assassin has caused writers and public officials in Western nations to become almost exclusively preoccupied with the author's rights.

While Rushdie's First Amendment freedoms are important, we have tended to promote him and his book with little acknowledgment that it is a direct insult to those millions of Moslems whose sacred beliefs have been violated and are suffering in restrained silence the added embarrassment of the Ayatollah's irresponsibility.

This is the kind of intercultural wound that is difficult to heal. Western leaders should make it clear that in protecting Rushdie's life and civil rights, there is no endorsement of an insult to the sacred beliefs of our Moslem friends.

To sever diplomatic relations with Iran over this altercation is an overreaction that could be quite costly in future years. Tactful public statements and private discussions could still defuse this explosive situation.

We must remember that Iranian and other fundamentalists are

not the only Moslems involved. Around the world there are millions
of others who are waiting for a thoughtful and constructive response
to their concerns.   (*New York Times*, 5 March 1989)

Women against fundamentalism

*On Thursday 9 March a meeting of women called by Southall Black
Sisters and Southall women's section of the Labour Party issued
the following statement:*

As a group of women of many religions and none, we would like
to express our solidarity with Salman Rushdie. Women's voices have
been largely silent in the debate where battle lines have been drawn
between liberalism and fundamentalism. Often it's been assumed
that the views of vocal community leaders are our views and their
demands our demands.

We regret this absolutely. We have struggled for many years in
this country and across the world to express ourselves as we choose
within and outside our communities.

We will not be dictated to by fundamentalists. Our lives will not
be defined by community leaders.

We will take up our right to determine our own destinies, not
limited by religion, culture or nationality.

We believe that religious worship is an individual matter and that
the state should not foster one religion above any other.

We call on the government to abolish the outdated blasphemy
law and to defend, without reservation, freedom of speech.

Some of the women of the world have spoken. More will.

The Rushdie riddle

LETTY COTTIN POGREBIN

Last winter—after the Ayatollah Khomeini ordered Salman
Rushdie's assassination and *The Satanic Verses* was taken off sale
in the United States by two big retail chains—a group of writers
met secretly with Muslim leaders to try and defuse the situation.

"Our side" included Frances Fitzgerald, J. Anthony Lukas, Norman Mailer, Robert Massie, myself and the executive directors of

the two major writers' organizations, Helen Stephenson, The Authors Guild, and Karen Kennerly, PEN.

"Their side" was represented by Shaik Moizal Matin, a prominent businessman and physicist, Sayd Z. Sayeed, chair of the American Muslim Action Committee, and seven other Islamic religious and political leaders. The declared agenda was to search for common ground and to keep peace between American Muslims and the secular community. The hidden agenda was persuasion.

We talked for seven hours. Our side was willing to make some accommodation to "their side" as long as they understood that the First Amendment is our religion. We serve freedom of expression as devoutly as any believer worships his or her faith. And regardless of what we might think of Rushdie's novel as literature, we would, in Voltaire's words, defend to the death his right to publish.

"Their side" was willing to respect "our side" as long as we understood that *The Satanic Verses* was utter blasphemy, detestable, repugnant, an unspeakable offense to all that Muslims hold sacred. What's more, they insisted, it was within their freedom of expression to demand that we join their call for the withdrawal of Rushdie's book from the stores.

In other words, neither side understood the other at all.

As each group heatedly restated its position, I found myself seesawing oddly. I seemed to speak from one perspective and listen from another. My writer-self defended "our side" with conviction, but my shadow selves kept hearing "their side" and feeling it with a raw empathy that sprang from my own struggles to be understood. These shadows—my woman-self and my Jewish-self—know what it is like to have one's group grievances trivialized and dismissed. The writer couldn't listen but the shadows heard and understood.

A vast cultural chasm separated me from the nine male Muslims, several of whom wouldn't even shake my hand because I am a woman. However, I made the leap of empathy precisely because my woman-self heard an ironic feminist echo in the Muslim cry for validation. To many feminists, pornography is the equivalent of blasphemy. Just as it hurt Muslims to see writers rush to defend *The Satanic Verses*, it hurt many women to see the enthusiasm with which prominent authors supported Hustler magazine against a lawsuit by Jerry Falwell.

Defending the rights of pornographers tests feminist civil libertarians almost to the breaking point. Yet we accept the necessity to stand guard at the top of censorship's slippery slope lest the rest of us slide into peril. I know that my free expression might strike a fundamentalist Christian as pornography. I recognize that unless the First Amendment protects Larry Flynt, it may someday fail to protect feminists and Jews and others who espouse minority positions. However, what feminists wanted in the Hustler case is what I think the Muslims wanted here: acknowledgment of the pain inflicted by a particular form of expression upon the target of that expression.

My Jewish-self remembered when the American Civil Liberties Union defended the Nazis' right to demonstrate in Skokie, Illinois. Many Jews felt that constitutional principle was being distorted to justify anti-Semitic hate-mongering. The ACLU explained that they had to defend the worst forms of speech in order to build a wall around all speech, but they made sure America knew that they did not morally support everyone they were legally bound to defend.

My woman-self wanted that same distinction established in the Hustler situation. I wanted the writers to pause in their paean to the Bill of Rights and say that, law aside, they knew what it must feel like to be systematically humiliated and dehumanized in the name of sexual pleasure. With that paradigm in mind, I understood the Muslims' plea. I understood that there are times when human dignity seems at least as important as legal principle.

Although "our side" and "their side" came to an ideological impasse, we were able to agree on one thing: the repudiation of violence. We called a joint press conference to announce that agreement but also to benefit the Muslims who had failed in their previous attempts to attract media attention. (Norman Mailer pulled the crowd but Shaik Matin got half the time.) Since then, most writers— have prefaced their pro-Rushdie statements with a declaration of respect for Muslim beliefs.

Our dialogue did not change my position on the Rushdie case but it reminded me that ideology is never strictly intellectual. Its roots run deep into dark crevices of contradiction where the personal complicates the political. While the mind clings to reason, the heart can offer something beyond logic to make peace with its enemies. In other words, the writer behaves better with her shadows at her heels.   (*Ms. Magazine*, July/Aug. 1989)

Words apart

CARLOS FUENTES

Mikhail Bakhtin was, probably, the greatest theorist of the novel in our century. His life, in a way, is as exemplary as his books. Shunted off to remote areas of the Soviet Union by the minions of Stalinism for his unorthodox ideas, Bakhtin could not profit from rehabilitation when it came under Brezhnev, simply because he had never been accused of anything. A victim of faceless intolerance, his political nemesis was Stalin, but his literary symbol was Kafka.

His case was and is not unique. I have thought a lot about Bakhtin while thinking about Salman Rushdie during these past few weeks. Rushdie's work perfectly fits the Bakhtinian contention that ours is an age of competitive languages. The novel is the privileged arena where languages in conflict can meet, bringing together, in tension and dialogue, not only opposing characters, but also different historical ages, social levels, civilisation and other, dawning realities of human life. In the novel, realities that are normally separated can meet, establishing a dialogic encounter, a meeting with the other.

This is no gratuitous exercise. It reveals a number of things. The first is that, in dialogue, no one is absolutely right; neither speaker holds an absolute truth or, indeed, has an absolute hold over history. Myself and the other, as well as the history that both of us are making, still are not. Both are unfinished and so can only continue to be. By its very nature, the novel indicates that we are becoming. There is no final solution. There is no last word.

This is what Milan Kundera means when he proposes that the novel is a constant redefinition of men and women as problems, never as sealed, concluded truths. But this is precisely what the Ayatollahs of this world cannot suffer. For the Ayatollahs reality is dogmatically defined once and for all in a sacred text. But a sacred text is, by definition, a completed and exclusive text. You can add nothing to it. It does not converse with anyone. It is its own loudspeaker. It offers perfect refuge for the insecure who then, having the protection of a dogmatic text over their heads, proceed to excommunicate those whose security lies in search for the truth. I remember Luis Buñuel constantly saying: 'I would give my life for a man who is looking for the truth. But I would gladly kill a man who thinks that he has found the truth.'

This Buñuelian, surrealist sally is now being dramatically acted out in reversal. An author who is looking for the truth, has been condemned to death by a priestly hierarchy, whose deep insecurity is disguised by their pretension to holding the truth. The Ayatollahs, nevertheless, have done a great service to literature, if not to Islam. They have debased and caricatured their own faith. But they have shifted the wandering attention of the world to the power of words, literature and the imagination, in ways totally unforeseen in their philosophy.

For the intolerance of the Ayatollahs not only sheds light on Salman Rushdie and his uses of the literary imagination. By making this imagination so dangerous that it deserves capital punishment, the sectarians have made people everywhere wonder what it is that literature can say that can be so powerful and, indeed, so dangerous.

In a deservedly famous commentary, Philip Roth once distinguished between reactions to literature East and West. In totalitarian regimes, Roth said, everything matters and nothing goes. In the liberal democracies, nothing matters and everything goes. Suddenly, *The Satanic Verses* have pushed the 'nothing goes' of intolerance right out into the public squares of indifference. Suddenly, we all realise that everything matters, whether it goes or not.

I do not truly believe that there is a single intelligent writer in either Europe, both Americas, Africa, Asia or Down Under, who does not feel threatened by the possibilities so melodramatically opened by the Ayatollah's crusade against the freedom of the imagination. It can't happen here? You can bet your bottom dollar, peso, franc or pound that it can.

Saying the same thing as Roth, Italo Calvino once wrote that when politics pays too much attention to literature, this is a bad sign, mostly for literature. But, he added, it is also a bad sign when politics doesn't want to hear the word 'literature' mentioned. It means that the society has become afraid of any use of language that calls into question the certitudes it holds about itself.

I have always conceived the novel (at least those I try to write) as a crossroads between the individual and the collective destinies of men and women. Both tentative, both unfinished, but both only sayable and minimally understandable if it is previously said and understood that, in fiction, truth is the search for truth, nothing is pre-established and knowledge is only what both of us—reader and writer—can imagine.

There is no other way to freely and fruitfully explore the possibilities of our unfinished humanity. No other way to refuse the death of the past, making it present through memory. No other way of effectively giving life to the future, through the manifestation of our desire.

That these essential activities of the human spirit should be denied in the name of a blind yet omniscient, paralytical yet actively homicidal dogmatism is both a farce and a crime in itself. Salman Rushdie has done the true religious spirit a service by brilliantly imagining the tensions and compliments that it establishes with the secular spirit. Humour, certainly, cannot be absent, since there is no contemporary language that can utter itself without a sense of the diversification of that same language. When we all understood everything, the epic was possible. But not fiction. The novel is born from the very fact that we do not understand one another any longer, because unitary, orthodox language has broken down. Quixote and Sancho, the Shandy brothers, Mr and Mrs Karenin: their novels are the comedy (or the drama) of their misunderstandings. Impose a unitary language: you kill the novel, but you also kill the society.

I hope that everyone, after what has happened to Salman Rushdie and *The Satanic Verses*, now understands this. Fiction is not a joke. It is but an expression of the cultural, personal and spiritual diversity of mankind.

Fiction is a harbinger of a multipolar and multicultural world, where no single philosophy, no single belief, no single solution, can shunt aside the extreme wealth of mankind's cultural heritage. Our future depends on the enlarged freedom for the multiracial and the polycultural to express itself in a world of shifting, decaying and emerging power centres.

Salman Rushdie has given form to a dilemma previously embodied, at diverse levels, in the West, by the novels of Hernarus, Mauriac and Camus, as well as the films of Bergman, Fellini and Buñuel. And that is: Can the religious mentality thrive outside of religious dogma and hierarchy? These are questions essential to any ideas of freedom. But the burdens of freedom, as Dostoyevsky's Grand Inquisitor well knew, can be heavier than the chains of liberty. 'Long live my chains!' exclaimed the Spanish patriots painted by Goya as their revolutionary liberators, the Napoleonic troops, mowed them down. And, in another direction, Georg Büchner proclaimed, in *Danton's Death*, that since God no longer existed, mankind was now responsible for its own destiny and could not shift the blame any more.

The modern age, by liberating both the freedom for good and the freedom for evil, has placed upon us all the obligation to relativise both. Absolute good is called polyanna. Absolute evil is called Hitler. Relative good is called Simone Weil. Relative evil is called de Sade. But the name of relativity is no longer virtue; it is value. Bad literature stays at the level of virtue; it pits good guys against bad boys. Good literature rises to the level of values in conflict with one another. This is what Salman Rushdie has done in all of his novels.

That he has dramatised the conflict within Islam does not, however, exempt the rest of us, within the Judeo-Christian tradition, from looking at our own sources of intolerance or at our own limits when our own symbols are set into conflictive motion. Artists have been silenced or 'disappeared' in Latin America for not spouting the official truth of our local, mostly military, Ayatollahs. Jean-Luc Godard in Europe and Martin Scorsese in the United States have been attacked for seriously exploring in the Catholic faith what Rushdie is exploring in the Islamic faith, that is, the combinations, the possibilities, the ghosts beyond the dogmas. A number of Jewish writers and comedians have poked fun at Judaism. What are the limits? What if a Jewish writer imagined Anne Frank as a young whore? What if a Catholic writer depicted Joseph, the jealous philicide, as the true betrayer of Christ?

The alarming thing about Salman Rushdie's experience in intolerance is that it has revealed a seething alliance of commercial cowardice and fundamentalist intolerance surrounding the self-proclaimed island of rationality in any given society. Sects coexist with commercialism in Georgia and Guatemala. Allow these two factors—booksellers and publishers succumbing to terrorist threats, and zealots of all faiths discovering their sectarian brotherhood, be it Muslim, Christian or Jewish—and the margins of freedom in our world will quickly and frighteningly shrink.

The defence of Salman Rushdie is a defence of ourselves. It is a matter of pride to say that Rushdie has given us all a better reason

to understand and protect the profession of letters at the highest
level of creativity, imagination, intelligence and social responsibility.   (*Guardian*, London, 24 Feb. 1989)

Salman Rushdie's insensitivity
CHRISTOPHER S. TAYLOR

Salman Rushdie, the Indian-born British subject whose book *The
Satanic Verses* is causing such furor, is a man who straddles two
worlds, one predominantly traditional and religious, the other
largely modern and secular. He exists in a marginal realm, one that
is neither fully part of the world he has left, nor completely of that
he has adopted.

The brilliance of Salman Rushdie as a writer is that he can so
eloquently capture and articulate the personal frustrations generated
by a contemporary world which is still defined, in large part, by the
long and painful struggle between traditional and modern modes of
social existence.

The particular marginal space in the human experience from
which Salman Rushdie writes is a precarious place. It has served
him well as a source of inspiration, but it now threatens his very
life. The pronouncement of a death sentence on Rushdie by the
Ayatollah Khomeini, and all the current insistence in the West over
Rushdie's "right" to write whatever he wants, underscore exactly
how far apart two worlds can be.

We in the West believe deeply in the right of all people to think
freely and to express those thoughts freely. We understand this right
to be "endowed inalienably" by our "Creator." There is ultimately
no objective way to prove this assertion, we simply accept is as
something which we firmly believe. We should also recognize, however, that our belief in this right of free expression is held with no
more conviction or sincerity than those of who support the position
taken by the religious leaders of Iran.

Their understanding of rights is fundamentally different from our
own. Their reality is founded on acceptance of and absolute submission to the will of God, as it was received through divine revelation and elucidated through centuries of Islamic jurisprudence.
They do not feel compelled to acknowledge the validity of any
"right" not specifically conferred by God. Thus, Islamic law makes

no provision for freedom of expression, but it does for apostasy and blasphemy. Further, to believe in that law implies acceptance of the penalties prescribed for its violation.

Because there is no objective method of demonstrating conclusively that the Islamic perception of reality is ultimately more or less valid than our own, the inherent right we invoke must be recognized for what it is an ideal that we collectively cherish and believe in without universal acceptance from others or absolute, incontestable proof that we are correct. This implies that the "right" of free expression is finally meaningful only to the extent that we are able, and indeed willing, to protect it.

As a professional writer, Salman Rushdie knows intimately the importance and power of words. He knows both the good and the evil that words can arouse in the hearts and souls of men. His special circumstance, which makes him a part of two very different worlds, entails a special obligation to know and weigh the impact of his words in both of those worlds. The great potential of Rushdie is that precisely because he stands at the intersection of two worlds, one modern and secular and the other traditional and religious, he has much to offer both worlds in terms of a mutual understanding, or at least an acceptance of each other.

The tragedy of this book is that Salman Rushdie has driven his two worlds apart, not brought them closer together.

The trouble with his latest work arises from two chapters involving a series of dream sequences that have deeply offended the Muslim world. That the chapters in question refer to the Prophet Muhammad cannot seriously be disputed by anyone remotely familiar with the Islamic religious tradition. Rushdie's recent protests to the contrary are as disingenuous as they are self-serving.

The problem is less that Rushdie has expressed his own doubt about faith than it is the technique he has employed to articulate that doubt. This essentially involves an insulting depiction of the Prophet Muhammad, which can hardly be anything but deeply offensive to a true believer, even the most tolerant, educated, or Westernized among them. Rushdie cannot claim ignorance of the world he has so deeply offended. The fact that Rushdie has chosen to use the technique that he did raises serious issues of his responsibility and sensitivity as a writer. To communicate one's own doubt is one thing, but to do so by deliberately debasing and demeaning what others still cherish as sacred is to cross an altogether different line.

What has enraged millions of believing Muslims is the way Rushdie has chosen to articulate his doubt by insensitively degrading and devaluing what they continue to perceive as sacrosanct. The specific Muslim tradition of the life of Muhammad that Rushdie has chosen to parody is unfortunately just obscure and unfamiliar enough to his Western readers that most of them will never understand what he has done, or appreciate why it is so offensive to Muslims. At the same time, however, the life of the prophet is so familiar and sacred to devout Muslims that Rushdie's treatment of it cannot help but offend.

In light of this situation, is it not fair to ask how responsibly Rushdie has exercised the treasured right of free expression guaranteed him in the world he has adopted as his own? In questioning his own faith, was it truly necessary for him to depict the prophet of Islam as a lying, licentious misogynist and fraud? In searching for our own truths, how much must we destructively trample on and degrade the honest and simple faith of others? Why, at a time when the mutual understanding between the Islamic tradition that he was born into, and the Western secular tradition that he has adopted, is so clearly lacking, was it necessary to excite this type of anger, hate and confusion? Was it really so noble to exploit both the ignorant stereotypes which have for so long shaped Western misunderstanding of Islam, and of its Prophet, or the resulting insecurity that centuries of those twisted images have prompted in the Muslim world?

What exactly is to be gained from the further ignorant ridicule of the Muslim world, on the part of the Western audience that does not understand Islam, or the profound humiliation and resentment of the audience that believes very sincerely and deeply in Islam? When the discourse between our two traditions is already so strained and garbled, do we really need this provocative and inflammatory approach? Is the light it sheds worth the pain, and now blood, that it has cost? Rushdie is certainly not the first writer to explore the difficult issues of personal crisis of faith generated by the inner clash of tradition and modernity, but he may well be one of the most insensitive to probe that complex dimension of the human psyche.

It is unclear why someone whose reputation rests to such an extent on a personal awareness and understanding of the frustration often endured by people caught in the clash between a traditional and a modern world would deliberately engage in a project that could not have been more carefully designed to enrage and offend one of those two worlds, while not leaving either world ultimately more informed about the other. Either Rushdie did not appreciate what he was doing, or he did and he simply didn't care. If the answer is the former, he has now lost touch with the ethos into which he was born. If it is the latter, he may just have lost touch with his own soul and humanity.

It is not necessarily incumbent upon the writers of great literature to make us feel good about ourselves, or about each other. The very best literature is often that which deeply challenges and disturbs us. But there is a difference between the kind of writing that provokes a healthy anger in people, such that it ultimately opens their eyes to new thoughts, and hurtful prose that serves only to offend and blind them. Rushdie's book falls into the second category. The ignorance, ridicule, humiliation, and resentment that parts of this book have nourished will neither illumine the human condition nor open the minds and hearts of people on different sides of the great divide between tradition and modernity.

The anger in the Islamic world provoked by Rushdie's book arises from a profound sense of pain caused by calculated and senseless ridicule. The distress and the hurt caused by this work may be powerful forces in making it a best seller, but they are not particularly useful in helping us to better understand either ourselves or the common humanity we need to recognize in each other, especially in the frightening complexity of the contemporary age. In our world, Salman Rushdie has a right to do what he has done. That is an important right, one that we should defend against the ayatollah or anyone else.

But we, as part of a larger collective humanity, also have rights. We have a right to expect more sensitivity from our writers. We have a right to expect our writers to know the power of the written word, and to exercise their right to use the written word in a responsible manner. We have a right to expect them to use their talent to help us understand ourselves and each other. Finally, we have a right to feel disappointed when they let us down.

(*Christian Science Monitor*, 3 March 1989)

In search of the middle ground

JOHN LEO

A few subversive thoughts about the Rushdie case.

Yes, it is monstrous that the Ayatollah Khomeini has put out a hit on author Salman Rushdie, and, no, we are not going to suspend the First Amendment to appease angry demonstrators.

Still, there are problems with the manner in which the debate over the book has unfolded. One of them is that the shocking death threat, like all extremist actions, has cleared out the middle. This is the territory normally occupied by those who wish to make a few distinctions, avoid stereotypes and (gasp!) see the other fellow's point of view.

A spate of articles has solemnly warned us against expressing anything but simple outrage. No complexities, please. We are busy shaking our fists at the Ayatollah. Some of this comes close to being war-fever journalism, which is usually accompanied by sloganeering and a hardening of stereotypes.

This may be why Frances FitzGerald, the author of *Fire in the Lake*, the prize-winning study of Vietnam, leapt into the forbidden middle ground at a rally supporting Rushdie, trying to make a distinction between Iran's leading crazy person and the other 900 million Moslems. "To see the Ayatollah as the representative of Islam," she said, "is to see the Grand Inquisitor as the representative of Christianity."

At the same rally, Leon Wieseltier of the *New Republic* demonstrated the simplicity that often overtakes angry people while they are grasping microphones. "Let us be dogmatic about tolerance," he said. "It was blasphemy that made us free. Two cheers today for blasphemy." This is the voice of a secular intelligentsia that holds nothing much sacred any more, dismissing the concern of backward foreigners who do. The Ugly American redux. Don't we ever learn?

Granted that the terror visited on Rushdie and the threat of censorship must be our primary concerns at the moment. Granted, too, that by American standards Moslems are extremely sensitive about religious slights. In 1962, mobs in Pakistan stoned the American Embassy on the basis of an idle rumor that a U.S.-Italian movie company was about to make a motion picture about the Prophet Mohammed.

Now that we have said that, why can't we admit that something is missing from the black-and-white hero-and-villain discussion of *The Satanic Verses*? How about the fact that our "dogmatic tolerance" calls for a certain amount of deference and self-restraint in discussing other people's religious beliefs?

Salman Rushdie's sendup of Islam is, among other things, a violation of civility, currently overwhelmed by the enormity of the threat against him, but sufficiently large to produce angry protests in half a dozen countries over a period of four months. This sense of grievance is not confined to wild-eyed fanatics. It covers a broad spectrum of opinion, from laborers in Pakistan to Moslem lawyers and accountants in America.

A literary critic, in private conversation, said, "There's no doubt that Rushdie inserted his thumb in the Islamic eye and twisted it around a bit." Galeyn Remington, a negotiation specialist who has worked in Moslem countries, says that Rushdie "manipulated his material in just the way that hurts; he played on Moslem sensibilities in a very knowing way."

Remington's advice is this: Make a clear acknowledgment of what the effect of this book is on Islam. Try to comprehend what Moslems feel and be respectful of it. Say that we are sorry that a clash of cultures exists, but we must hold on to our values and say that we do not ban books. Khomeini is a madman, but we must look past him and ease the polarization, or 10 years from now it will be dangerous for tourists to walk into the wrong Moslem village.

One positive gesture would be for publishers not to push for an Urdu edition of *The Satanic Verses*, which would be seen as another attempt by the West to use its enormous power against Islam.

John Esposito of Holy Cross College, one of the Islamic specialists subjected to nonstop interviews last week, said he knows "of no Western scholar of Islam who would not have predicted that [Rushdie's] kind of statements would be explosive. These are tricky waters that call for self-imposed censorship. The First Amendment right doesn't mean you should automatically say everything you want to."

Luckily enough, self-imposed censorship, also known as deference to the sensibilities of others, is one form of censorship clearly allowed by the Constitution. Many hypothetical examples ripe for such self-squelching have been suggested in recent days: A jokey treatment of Anne Frank, for one, or a musical comedy about the sex lives of Martin Luther or Martin Luther King, Jr. As brilliant as Evelyn Waugh's *Black Mischief* is, many of us would have liked to whisper to the young author; "Don't do it; it's racist." Or to come down a few hundred steps in importance, true friends should have advised Martin Scorsese against stirring up the multitudes with a terrible movie about an excruciatingly bad book, *The Last Temptation of Christ.* Many of us who would have fought to the death for Scorsese's right to embarrass himself in public think he should have just skipped the whole thing.

The estimable columnist Charles Krauthammer wrote at the time: "American pluralism works because of a certain deference that sects accord each other. . . . In a pluralistic society, it is a civic responsibility to take great care when talking publicly about things sacred to millions of fellow citizens."

Shouldn't this apply to Moslem beliefs, too?

(U.S. News & World Report, 6 March 1989)

For scholars of Islam, interpretation need not be advocacy
JOHN O. VOLL

Academic freedom is not the only issue raised by Salman Rushdie's novel, *The Satanic Verses.* The affair illustrates key intellectual and scholarly problems that those of us who are specialists in modern Islamic affairs regularly face. The death sentence imposed by the Ayatollah Ruhollah Khomeini on Mr. Rushdie for slandering Islam in his novel did not create any fundamentally new or different tensions for us, nor would Mr. Rushdie's conversion to fundamentalist Islam cause them to disappear.

The most intractable problems that specialists in Islamic affairs face also face many other kinds of specialists, and I hope that the Rushdie affair can help all in the intellectual community to recognize their significance.

One major issue involves interpreting the interpreter. In the wake of the controversy over *The Satanic Verses,* specialists are often asked, for example, to define Islamic concepts of blasphemy and to explain why Mr. Rushdie's book fits those definitions. Our answers often meet with hostility, however, because the questioners have difficulty distinguishing between an interpreter and an advocate. Scholars attempting to explain why the Ayatollah adopts a particular position are not necessarily themselves advocates of that position, yet we are often treated as if we were.

This problem is not unique to the debate over Mr. Rushdie's book. Rather, it is a continuing problem for specialists who interpret unpopular positions. For example, "the Arabists" in the State Department are often treated by newspaper columnists as though they were advocating Arab causes rather than trying to confront policy-makers with the realities of the Arab world. Scholars explaining the motivations of militant Palestinians or Israeli settlers are sometimes accused of supporting terrorism or violence.

The American intellectual and foreign-policy communities need to be more open to the analyses presented by those who interpret controversial events and groups. In a world of increasing diversity and pluralism, such openness is essential.

At the same time, the specialists themselves, in the heat of the debate, often do become advocates for those whom they are interpreting. There is a real tension between interpretation and advocacy in some of the commentary by scholars on the Khomeini-Rushdie controversy. In the current charged atmosphere, scholars of Islam who are trying to interpret Khomeini's position may end up, for example, supporting the principle of capital punishment even though in their personal lives they oppose it. There is a parallel in the analyses of some literary critics who may have exaggerated the brilliance of the novel in their eagerness to defend its author and attack the Ayatollah.

The scholarly interpreter does have a right to advocate particular causes, but both the scholar and the audience must be clear about when a scholar is interpreting and when he or she is advocating. As humans we have a responsibility and a right to take a stand on the moral dimension of situations like the Rushdie dispute, but we also have additional obligations. We must provide what our colleagues in the academic and intellectual communities need to form intelligent opinions on sensitive, complex issues. This means that we, as specialists, have a special role in explaining people like the Ayatollah Khomeini to people in the West. The specialist is the link between the world being interpreted and the audience being informed.

This linking function is especially complex in the case of Islam and the West because of the long history of frequently hostile relations between Muslim and Western societies. Part of this history involves the development on both sides of traditions of conscious defamation of "the enemy" as a part of the rivalry. Thus, we have to overcome a heritage of misunderstanding and prejudice that is deeply rooted in society.

The "holy-war mentalities" of Crusade and Jihad in this heritage color many of the positions in the debate over *The Satanic Verses*. American commentators speak of the threat to constitutional values in the United States, and Westerners often portray the Ayatollah as engaging in a holy war against the Western values of toleration and freedom of expression. At the same time, many Muslims view Mr. Rushdie's book as being in the Western tradition of defamation of Islam and as a part of the West's Crusade against basic Islamic values of community responsibility and obedience to God. The scholar is caught between these competing positions and has an obligation to interpret one side to the other.

As interpreters, not advocates, we do not have to reconcile the two sides, but we must be fair in presenting one side to the other. This is a challenge to scholars in controversies like the one over Mr. Rushdie's book. Even scholars who personally condemn the actions of the Ayatollah need to be able to present Khomeini's views in such a way that they would at least be recognizable to his followers. Without that dimension, the analysis simply becomes part of the polemic. . . .

The specialist has an obligation to meet the challenges of cross-cultural interpretation constructively. In the Rushdie affair, scholars committed to freedom of expression must oppose what has been called cultural terrorism. At the same time, scholars of Islam, both Muslim and non-Muslim, have a responsibility to explain to non-Muslims why many in the Islamic world responded as they did to Mr. Rushdie's book.

Salman Rushdie has touched a sensitive nerve in us all. When scholars try to explain the Islamic response to his book, they should not be accused of advocating Ayatollah Khomeini's position. The academic community in America not only must defend intellectual freedom for Mr. Rushdie, but also must demonstrate the courage and intellectual openness required to examine and understand why

Ayatollah Khomeini's actions struck such a responsive chord in millions of fellow humans in a globe we all share.

(Chronicle of Higher Education, 22 March 1989)

The value of toleration
MICHAEL IGNATIEFF

Our capacity to get used to anything, no matter how unimaginable, is always amazing. Last week, a German publisher—connected with the publication of *The Satanic Verses*—wrote to me to say that things were at last getting back to normal. Normal? Two imams in Belgium shot dead for daring to suggest that the Ayatollah Khomeini was wrong in calling for the banning of a book and the murder of its author. A writer and his wife still in hiding under police guard after a month and a half, with no prospect of ever resuming ordinary life. Normal?

People say the issue has been talked into the ground. I wonder whether the debate has even begun. The clichés that have rained down have left the entrenched positions on either side virtually untouched. The affair has become a ritual exchange of ancient misunderstandings and venerable condescensions on both sides. I wonder whether either side has learned a thing.

On one side we have fanatical, medieval and intolerant Islam: the whole apparatus of cliché dates back to the Crusades. On the other side, we have the godless, materialist and hypocritical West. Centuries of European condescension mixed with exotic fascination towards Islam were bound to result in a discourse about 'us' as unseeing as our Orientalism has been about 'them'. Both sides are being declared in their indignations.

Yet behind the safe refuge of cliché and public indignation, private uncertainties have grown as the affair has unfolded. Many self-proclaimed defenders of free speech are tying themselves in strange knots. People tell me privately they believe in free speech and then say Rushdie should not have given offence, that he should have 'respected' the sacred beliefs of others, and that he should be willing to withdraw the book from sale in order to show good faith. None of these positions makes clear how a writer is to 'respect' other people's views without putting on the iron mask of self-censorship.

What lies behind these second thoughts, I think, is Western liberal guilt, not simply about imperial injuries to Islam in times past, but essentially about secularism, our supposed lack of deep belief. The shrewdest Muslim voices in the controversy have become expert in playing on that Yeatsian cliché of Western self-doubt, that the best of us lack all conviction, while the worst of us feel passionate intensity.

Many Muslims have been doing well with the line that 'we' can't understand the blasphemy Rushdie has committed because 'we' hold nothing sacred. Liberal rhetoric about free speech, they maintain, is little more than the bombast we deploy to hide our nihilism. In nervous admissions that artistic freedom must respect the sacred, one discerns the guilt of those who envy the Muslims for having noble things called beliefs.

Guilt is never much of a teacher. Contrition never leads to much self-understanding. Europe has always been guilty about its supposed nihilism. Conservative and romantic opponents of the European Enlightenment and the French Revolution first planted this seed of self-doubt, and it flowered among all those, from Schopenhauer to Spengler, who didn't much like liberalism, technological change or the messy clamour of democratic individualism in the nineteenth century.

The image of the godless, nihilist, materialistic West has some authentically reactionary European grandparents—Hitler hated the Weimar Republic, among other reasons, because it was unredeemed by noble collective belief. The fact that Hitler believed this does not make this image of the West false, but neither does it become true simply because it has been taken up by people who have a claim to consider themselves our victims.

In the heated competition to appear full of conviction, some liberals have taken to saying that they hold freedom sacred. This, I think, is a misuse of 'sacred'. If the word means anything it means something which is inviolate to criticism or rational scrutiny. Freedom is not a holy belief, nor even a supreme value. It is a contestable concept. How a free society marks the limits of freedom will change with time. The Muslims are entirely correct to say this society does not believe freedom is unlimited. That is another way of saying it is not sacred. To live in a liberal society is to fight over the meaning of freedom constantly, as we have been doing over the Rushdie affair.

Stripped to its essentials, the debate is not between medieval fanaticism and Western enlightenment, but between incompatible conceptions of freedom, one in which freedom's limit is the sacred, one in which it is not. Behind this disagreement of principle lies another: whether offence can be given to beliefs as such or merely to individuals.

In theocratic States like Iran, the law guarantees the inviolability of certain sacred doctrines. In free societies, the law does not protect doctrines as such; it protects individuals—through the law of libel, or the law against incitement to racial hatred. The blasphemy laws on the statute books of Britain and other countries can be regarded as leftovers from our theocratic past; they are inconsistent with a legal ethos which protects individuals rather than doctrines, and they are incoherent because, as the Muslims point out, they protect some doctrines but not others.

If Muslims and troubled Western liberals want to know what it is that our godless, materialistic societies stand for, they should look back over the religious history of Europe; the struggle has given us a value—toleration—which deserves to be dusted off and redeemed from the pawnshop of the past. It's come to imply lazy relativisms and mutual indifference. It once committed us to something more robust; never to substitute force for persuasion in changing the opinions of human beings, and never to believe that God or reason gives you a monopoly on truth.

There is nothing sacred about toleration—we're not obliged to tolerate those who threaten us because of our opinions. But it does commit us to a habit of mind and a way of life: to listen when we do not want to listen, to endure offence when we would rather retaliate, to struggle to understand when we would rather fight, and to fight, as a last resort, when intolerance will not listen to reason.

(*Observer*, London, 2 April 1989)

Index

Note: *The Satanic Verses* has been abbreviated *SV* throughout the index.

The Rushdie File was composed in 9 on 12
Trump Medieval on a Mergenthaler Lino-
tron 202 by Brevis Press; printed by sheet-
fed offset on 60-pound acid-free Warren
Sebago Eggshell, B05, Smyth-sewn and
bound over binder's boards in Holliston
Roxite Grade A by Princeton University
Press Printers; with dust jackets printed in 3
colors by Princeton University Press Printers;
designed by Kachergis Book Design, Inc.;
and published by Syracuse University Press,
Syracuse, New York 13244-5160.